GREAT BASIN NATIONAL PARK

The view east from Wheeler Peak.

GREAT BASIN NATIONAL PARK

A Guide to the Park and Surrounding Area

Gretchen M. Baker

UTAH STATE UNIVERSITY PRESS
LOGAN, UTAH
2012

Copyright ©2012 Utah State University Press
All rights reserved

Utah State University Press
Logan, Utah 84322-7800
www.USUPress.org

Publication of this book was supported by a subvention from the Charles
Redd Center for Western Studies at Brigham Young University.

Manufactured in China
Printed on recycled, acid-free paper

ISBN: 978-0-87421-840-4 (paper)
ISBN: 978-0-87421-841-1 (e-book)

Library of Congress Cataloging-in-Publication Data

Baker, Gretchen M.
  Great Basin National Park : a guide to the park and surrounding area / Gretchen M. Baker.
    p. cm.
  Includes bibliographical references and index.
  ISBN 978-0-87421-840-4 (pbk.) – ISBN 978-0-87421-841-1 (e-book)
1. Great Basin National Park (Nev.)–Guidebooks. 2. Nevada–Guidebooks. I. Title.
  F847.G73B35 2012
  917.93'1504–dc23
                        2011047549

CONTENTS

ACKNOWLEDGMENTS

This book would not have been possible without the help of many people, including those who allowed me to interview them: Ed Alder, Marilyn Ambrose, Dean Baker, Jerald Bates, Marlene Bates, Reita Berger, Doug Childs, Marjorie Coffman, Bill Dearden, Edith Dearden, Annette Garland, Daisy Gonder, Arlene Hanks, Heber Hanks, Kathy Hill, Ken Hill, Kathy Kaiser-Rountree, RaeJean Layland, Elaine Lewis, Wesley Lewis, Gen Richardson, Bill Rountree, Gene Skinner, Val Taylor, Lorene Wheeler, and Bart Wright. In addition to providing me with interviews, these people deserve special thanks: Tom Sims for venturing into the wilds of Snake Valley with me, Dave Moore for opening up his library and reviewing several chapters, and Patsy Schlabsz for providing additional information.

Many thanks to Wilda Garber for reading and providing edits on the entire manuscript. I am also grateful to Russell Robison, Alana Dimmick, Jay Banta, Steve Taylor, Kristi Fillman, Jenny Hamilton, and Mark Rogers for sharing photographs and maps; Matthew Schenk for designing an illustration; Karla Jageman for assistance with photographs; Denys Koyle for making notes on several chapters; and JoAnn Blalack, Bryan Hamilton, Ben Roberts, and Tod Williams for constructive edits. Conversations with Delaine Spilsbury and Sam Smith provided background information.

Thanks to John Alley and the helpful staff of Utah State University Press for guiding me through the publishing process. I also greatly appreciate the encouragement of my parents, Robert and Germaine Schenk, who made suggestions for the entire book. Finally, this book would not have been possible without the loving support of my husband, Craig Baker, who inspired this project by sharing stories, encouraged me to stay in Snake Valley by marrying me, and explored Snake Valley's many corners with me.

Although I tried to avoid them, any errors or omissions are solely mine. Many more stories about and photos of Snake Valley are out there. If you have any and are willing to share them with me, I will do my best to help preserve history about this special place.

Part 1

The Beginning

This first section of the book sets the stage for exploring Great Basin National Park and the surrounding area. It covers some important safety considerations, gives an overview of the natural history, and provides an outline of the cultural history of the area.

Wheeler Peak rises high above the isolated communities in Snake and Spring Valleys.

INTRODUCTION AND DESCRIPTION

Just the name "Great Basin" evokes images of broad, empty places, barren of vegetation. Although the Great Basin region covers a huge area, including most of Nevada and portions of Utah, California, and Idaho, most people know little about it. In 1986, Congress did something to change that, passing the Great Basin National Park Act, which included the following: "In order to preserve for the benefit and inspiration of the people a representative segment of the Great Basin of the Western United States possessing outstanding resources and significant geological and scenic values, there is hereby established the Great Basin National Park."

Many would say that this national park, located hours from the nearest shopping mall and interstate highway (figure 1-1), preserves not so much representative features but rather superlative features of the Great Basin. Wheeler Peak, at 13,063 feet (3,982 m), is the second-highest peak in Nevada and towers over the surrounding landscape. Ancient bristlecone pines (*Pinus longaeva*), some over three thousand years old, reside in patches near mountaintops and rock glaciers. Subalpine lakes reflect the high peaks around them while preserving records of past climatic conditions in the layers of silt beneath them. Scenic campgrounds allow visitors to enjoy the park with basic amenities, while those who travel into the backcountry

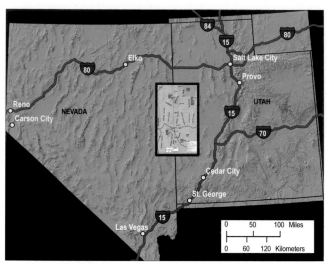

Figure 1-1. The area covered in this book,
straddling the Nevada-Utah border.

find the peace and serenity that some of the early explorers experienced. Those who venture underground into Lehman Caves are surprised to find such a wide array of cave formations packed so closely together. Many who vacation in Great Basin National Park say that it is what a national park should be: unspoiled vistas, abundant wildlife, clean air, and uncrowded attractions.

Those who take the time to visit agree that Great Basin National Park is one of the nation's best-kept secrets. One of the purposes of the park is to provide interpretive information about the entire Great Basin region. Thus, it is fitting for a guidebook to the park to extend beyond the park boundaries.

Beyond the 120 square miles (310 km²) that are protected and encompassed by the park, Snake Valley lies to the east and Spring Valley to the west (figure 1-2). Covering more than 1,500 square miles (3,880 km²), Snake Valley is over 100 miles (160 km) long and contains massive mountains, deep canyons, rolling foothills, flat playas, spectacular caves, and even marshes in the middle of the Great Basin Desert. Today Snake Valley, with about one thousand residents, has about the same population as when white settlers first reached the valley in the 1860s (Warner 1951, 530; Read 1965, 134), although the characteristics of its inhabitants have changed greatly. Very few Shoshone and Goshute Indians inhabit Snake Valley today; now it is a

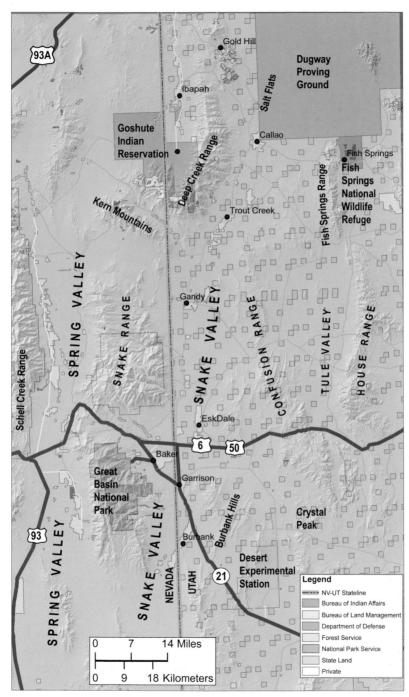

Figure 1-2. Map of Great Basin National Park and the surrounding area.

place of ranchers, miners, government workers, artists, retirees, entrepreneurs, polygamists, communes, and free thinkers. Snake Valley is located in two states, Utah and Nevada. Within the valley and surrounding mountains, one can find a national park, national forest, national wildlife refuge, wilderness areas, and important bird areas. Old-fashioned ranching towns are here, along with ghost towns and some newer communities.

Spring Valley is just as impressive, and so named because of the many springs on the valley floor. Settlers made their homes near some of these springs, which stretch along the length of the valley. No public services are available; thus few people stop to explore. Nevertheless, the valley has its own amazing features, like swamp cedars, or Rocky Mountain junipers (*Juniperus scopulorum*), which normally grow higher on the mountains; a cave providing an important resting spot to over a million migrating bats each year; and numerous old mining areas, some well preserved.

Spring Valley and Snake Valley have long witnessed a variety of travelers. Both valleys are crossed by the Pony Express Trail, the Overland Stage Trail, the Lincoln Highway, the "Loneliest Road in America" (Highway 50), and the American Discovery Trail. Activities abound, including mountain biking, off-highway vehicle riding, hiking, rock climbing, sailing, swimming, canyoneering, and rock hounding. Plants and wildlife are diverse, because the elevations in the area range from 4,300 feet (1,310 m) to 13,063 feet (3,982 m). Animals that make their home here include mountain lions (*Puma concolor*), elk (*Cervus elaphus*), bighorn sheep (*Ovis canadensis*), Bonneville cutthroat trout (*Oncorhynchus clarki utah*), least chub (*Iotichthys phlegethontis*), greater sage-grouse (*Centrocercus urophasianus*), pronghorn (*Antilocapra americana*), and Great Basin rattlesnakes (*Crotalus oreganus lutosus*), to name a few.

After the introductory chapters in part 1, which give an overview of the natural and cultural history of the area, part 2 focuses on the most-visited attraction, Great Basin National Park and its environs. Part 3 describes other places to visit in the area.

The Setting

Several communities are sprinkled throughout Snake Valley. At the north end, tucked away in the mountains, lies Gold Hill, Utah—almost a ghost town, with a few lingering inhabitants. Moving southward,

Callao, Utah, is a collection of ranches centered on the old Lincoln Highway and Pony Express Trail, an oasis of green just before the salt flats that extend north to the Great Salt Lake. Trout Creek, Utah, is in a sea of Russian olive trees (*Elaeagnus angustifolia*), recent invaders of the last forty years, and most of the homes are tucked away out of sight. Partoun, Utah, has scattered homesteads, with the centerpiece of the West Desert High School and its regulation-size gymnasium along the main road. Gandy, Utah, can be missed in the blink of an eye, since there is no gathering of buildings that designate it; rather, it is considered to be a group of ranches that are within a 10-mile (16 km) radius of each other. EskDale, Utah, is a planned community, with the houses arranged in a semicircle around a community center, landscaped flowers, and an outdoor arena. South of US Highway 6/50 is Baker, Nevada—what might be called the most booming part of the valley, with a few restaurants, bars, and gas stations. It is the gateway to Great Basin National Park. Garrison, Utah, is a community centered along the highway, with the green, manicured lawn at the Church of Jesus Christ of Latter-day Saints (LDS) church standing out. Garrison and Baker have the only post offices in either Snake or Spring Valleys at present. Burbank, Utah, consists mostly of abandoned homesteads, but about fifteen people live on scattered ranches within the old boundaries. In total, these communities and the people in Snake Valley have a population density of about two people per square mile. The population density of Spring Valley is even lower.

A few things have changed since the early days. A network of roads now crisscrosses the valleys and extends into the mountain ranges. The federal government now manages over 95 percent of the land, which is administered by a variety of agencies. Among these are the Bureau of Land Management (BLM), the US Forest Service (USFS), the National Park Service (NPS), the US Fish and Wildlife Service (USFWS), and the Department of Defense. Contact information for these agencies is in appendix A. Private land is scattered throughout the valley floors, generally where water is available. Many of the early settlers are commemorated by places named after them (appendix B). Along with names, fortunately some other things have stayed the same over the centuries, including clean air, beautiful night skies, and lots of quiet places.

Climate

The Great Basin National Park area is a place of extremes. Years with virtually no moisture may follow each other—as they did from 1896 to 1898, or more recently, from 2001 to 2004—and then be followed by years of abundant rain and snow. The valley floors generally receive the least precipitation, with about 9.6 inches (24 cm) on average at Shoshone in Spring Valley, about 6 inches (15 cm) on average near EskDale, and less than 6 inches (15 cm) on average in Callao (table 1-1), while the high peaks in the Snake and Deep Creek Ranges can be buried by 20 to 30 feet (6 to 9 m) of total snow over the winter. Temperatures also vary greatly. During the summer, daytime temperatures can exceed 100°F (38°C) on the valley floors, although the mountains are usually substantially cooler. At night, the temperature often drops 20 to 40°F (10 to 20°C) due to the low humidity. Temperature swings in the winter are also common, with the coldest temperatures reaching -40°F (-40°C). The low humidity also makes the air exceptionally clear, allowing one to see distant mountain ranges, and at night, distant galaxies.

The average year-round temperature is about 52–58°F (11–14°C) for elevations at 4,300–6,500 feet (1,310–1,980 m). This, by the way, is also the temperature of the many caves at these elevations, because caves reflect the average annual temperature of an area. Caves above 10,000 feet (3,048 m) are generally about 34°F (1°C).

The prevailing weather patterns come from the southwest and west. In winter, Pacific storms can bring in moisture unless a large high-pressure system sits in the middle of the Great Basin, which commonly happens for weeks at a time. In early spring, the Tonopah Low pushes the high-pressure system away; this is the period of greatest precipitation. In July and August, monsoons can develop. Monsoon moisture is generally pushed up from Arizona and circulates in a large clockwise motion over several southwestern states. The day can start out sunny, but clouds build up quickly, and by early afternoon thunderheads may produce lightning over the mountains. Sometimes precipitation falls, but often the rain evaporates before reaching the ground, a phenomenon called virga. Without the rain, the dry lightning from the storms can easily ignite wildfires. As the afternoon progresses, some of the clouds may drift into the valleys. The first winter snow is unpredictable, sometimes coming as early as mid-September and sometimes as late as late November.

Table 1-1. Climate summary at locations in and near Snake Valley

Station	Period of Record	Average Annual Maximum Temp (°F)	Average Annual Minimum Temp (°F)	Average Annual Precipitation (in)	Average Annual Snowfall (in)
Callao, UT	11/1/1902–12/31/2010	64.8	34.7	5.7	8.4
Desert Experimental Range, UT	1/1/1950–9/30/1984	65.7	32.4	6.2	10.2
EskDale, UT	3/27/1966–12/31/2010	66.9	34.8	6.3	13.6
Fish Springs, UT	6/1/1960–12/31/2010	66.3	39.8	7.9	13.1
Garrison, UT	1/1/1903–7/31/1990	65.9	34.6	7.4	26.8
Gold Hill, UT	5/1/1966–7/31/1990	63.4	39.8	11.1	38.5
Great Basin National Park, NV	7/1/1948–12/31/2010	60.7	35.7	13.4	72.9
Partoun, UT	2/1/1905–12/31/2010	66.4	33.8	6.8	11.0
Shoshone, NV	10/1/1988–5/31/2007	64.4	31.3	9.6	15.5

Source: Western Regional Climate Center, Desert Research Institute

Safety

The Great Basin National Park area is generally far from what is considered unsafe in urban areas. The greatest dangers to people visiting the area include falling asleep while driving (which has caused many fatalities), running out of gas out in the middle of nowhere, running into a cow or wildlife on the highway, and suffering from heat stroke or dehydration.

There are a few potentially dangerous animals. The Great Basin rattlesnake makes its home here, although if you spot one you can count yourself lucky, because few people see them. Like other rattlesnakes, it would rather avoid people and generally rattles its tail if you are within its comfort zone. Always give the rattlesnake plenty of room and you will avoid getting bitten. If you do happen to get bitten by a rattlesnake (which most often happens when a person unwisely picks one up), go to the hospital emergency room in Delta, Utah; Wendover, Utah; or Ely, Nevada, as soon as possible to get the anti-venom. Do not panic—Great Basin rattlesnakes often fail to inject venom when biting, and their venom, even if injected, is the least toxic of the American rattlesnake venoms. However, you will still need medical attention. Mountain lions are also in the area, although they are rarely seen. If you happen to encounter one, look big, make a lot of noise, and it will most likely leave. If you have small children with you, pick them up. No mountain lion attacks on humans have been recorded in the area. There is very little pressure from human developments in Snake and Spring Valleys, so the mountain lions have plenty of space.

The peaks in the area reach elevations of up to 13,063 feet (3,982 m), so some people are affected by altitude sickness. This generally takes the form of a bad headache, sometimes accompanied by nausea and fatigue. Drink plenty of water, eat a little food, and if you do not feel better, go to a lower elevation to recover. If you are trying to climb one of the higher peaks, give yourself a couple of days to acclimate before your attempt, especially if you are coming from sea level. Even experienced mountaineers can be caught off guard. In the 1990s, one gentleman who had summited Mount Everest died on the shoulder of Wheeler Peak.

Both hyperthermia (getting too hot) and hypothermia (getting too cold) can be problems. In the summer be sure to drink plenty of water, at least a gallon (4 L) a day for regular activities, and more if you are exercising. Along with that water, you will need some salt to keep your electrolytes in balance. A sports drink or salty snacks are good to consume regularly. In the winter, dress in layers and avoid cotton next to your skin because it increases the risk of hypothermia if it gets wet. Above all, use common sense.

Other Necessary Information

Gas is often a long way off. The two gas stations in the area are at the Border Inn on Highway 6/50 and the Sinclair station in Baker on Nevada Highway 487. Outside Snake Valley, gas is available 90 miles (145 km) north of Baker in Wendover; 85 miles (137 km) to the east

Figure 1-3. Some roads in Snake Valley are extremely remote.

in Hinckley, Utah; 82 miles (132 km) to the south in Milford, Utah; and 65 miles (105 km) to the west in Ely, Nevada. Always be sure to fill up when you can.

Many of the areas described in this book are remote (figure 1-3). Always travel with the thought that you could break down and not be found for days—or in the winter, for weeks. Tell someone where you are going and take enough food, water, and warm clothes to spend a night or two away. Remember that although cell phones work in many places in Spring Valley, they often do not work in Snake Valley. If you cannot get cell phone service, climb to a high peak and you will probably get reception. Help is a long way off in most cases.

Ambulance and fire services are provided in many communities but are run by volunteers who sometimes must travel long distances, so be prepared to wait. You can obtain these services by dialing 911.

Ecology and Natural History

The Great Basin National Park area is located in the Great Basin Desert, one of four deserts in North America. The Great Basin Desert is higher and cooler than the Mojave, Chihuahuan, and Sonoran Deserts. Because of its climate, the Great Basin Desert can be defined by the vegetation it supports, which consists of large amounts of sagebrush (*Artemesia* spp.), rabbitbrush (*Chrysothamnus* spp.), greasewood (*Sarcobatus vermiculatus*), Mormon tea (*Ephedra viridis*), and shadscale (*Atriplex confertifolia*), with very few cacti.

The term "Great Basin" was coined by one of the first explorers to see the area, John C. Frémont. Frémont crossed the basin in 1843–44 and again in 1845 on his government-funded expeditions. He realized that all the water is contained in the basin; none of it flows out to the oceans. The Great Basin consists not of one basin but of 90 basins, separated by 160 mountain ranges, most of them trending north–south. The undulating topography is another characteristic of the Basin and range geologic province. The boundaries of this geologic province are larger than the boundaries of the hydrologic Great Basin, extending far down into Mexico. Early geographer C. E. Dutton described the mountain ranges on a map of the Great Basin as an "army of caterpillars crawling toward Mexico" (R. Elliott 1987, 3).

Table 2-1. Geologic time scale during the Phanerozoic eon

Era	Period	Notes	Rock Layers in Snake Valley
Cenozoic	Quaternary	Age of Man	Lake Bonneville, alluvial, & eolian deposits
65 mya to present	Tertiary	Age of Mammals	Tunnel Spring Tuff, Needles Range Group
Mesozoic	Cretaceous	Age of Reptiles	Thaynes Formation in Northern Confusion Range (but most ranges have no rock layers from this era)
	Jurassic	(Dinosaurs)	
248 to 65 mya	Triassic		
Paleozoic	Permian	Age of Amphibians	Gerster Limestone, Plympton Formation, Kaibab Limestone, Arcturus Formation
	Pennsylvanian	Coal beds formed	Ely Limestone
540 to 248 mya	Mississipian	First winged insects	Chainman Formation, Joana Limestone
	Devonian	Age of Fishes	Pilot Shale, Guilmette Formation, Simonson and Sevy Dolomite
	Silurian	First land plants	Laketown Dolomite
	Ordovician	Diverse marine invertebrates	Ely Springs and Crystal Peak Dolomite, Eureka and Watson Ranch Quartzite, Pogonip Group
	Cambrian	Age of Trilobites	Notch Peak Formation, Pole Canyon Limestone, Prospect Mountain Quartzite

*Modified from Hintze and Davis 2003. *mya = million years ago*

Geologic Overview

The complex geology of the area is best addressed in Frank DeCourten's excellent book *The Broken Land: Adventures in Great Basin Geology* (2003) and in John McPhee's *Basin and Range* (1982). Following is a much simplified version (tables 2-1 and 2-2).

Most of the rocks that make up what is now Great Basin National Park and the surrounding area formed when a large inland sea covered the area, fluctuating in depth over millions of years during the Paleozoic era, creating many layers. The sea dried up during the Mesozoic era, and massive windstorms deposited enormous coastal eolian (windblown) sand dunes that covered most of Utah. Navajo

Table 2-2. Detailed geologic time scale during the Cenozoic era

Era	Period	Epoch	Age	Notes
Cenozoic	Quaternary	Holocene	11,000 years ago to present	Human impacts
		Pleistocene	0.01-1.8 mya	Glaciers come and go; Lake Bonneville
	Tertiary	Pliocene	1.8-5.3 mya	Savannahs and grasslands
		Miocene	5.3-24 mya	Basin and range topography begins
		Oligocene	24-34.5 mya	Grasslands expand
		Eocene	34.5-58 mya	Modern mammals
		Paleocene	58-65 mya	Forests

mya = million years ago

Sandstone, prominent in Zion National Park, was eroded from Snake and Spring Valleys during later uplifting. Granite intrusions during the Cretaceous and Jurassic periods occurred in several places in Snake Valley, including the band in the foothills of the South Snake Range west of Baker, Nevada, and the prominent outcroppings in the Kern Mountains and Deep Creek Range.

The basin and range topography that is such an important part of the Great Basin came about during the Miocene epoch, about 17 million years ago, when the crust stretched and the Sierra Nevada mountain range began to rise—but only to about 1,000 feet (305 m). The mountains continued to get higher and the basins dropped, and a regional uplift brought the area to an average elevation of about 5,000 feet (1,524 m). The climate became drier in the Pliocene epoch, and the forests changed to savannas and grasslands, supporting grazing and browsing mammals such as camels, bison, horses, mastodons, rhinos, and a dozen species of pronghorn. The camels, horses, and pronghorn evolved in North America, while others crossed the Bering land bridge, along with plants like sagebrush, saltbush, and Mormon tea (Trimble 1989, 45).

The Pleistocene epoch, beginning 1.8 million years ago, alternated between cool, wet glacial periods and warm, dry interglacial periods. In the last eight hundred thousand years, at least fifteen major periods of warming and cooling have occurred. Although the vast Pleistocene ice sheets crept down out of present-day Canada four times, they never reached Snake or Spring Valleys or the Great Basin; instead, glaciers were found only in the mountains (Trimble 1989, 47), extending down to about 8,000 feet (2,440 m; Osborn and Bevis 2001).

During the latter part of the glacial period, the main event for Snake Valley was the appearance and disappearance of Lake Bonneville (figure 2-1). The lake began forming about twenty-five thousand years ago as the temperatures cooled, evaporation rates decreased, and precipitation increased slightly. The lake continued growing for about nine thousand years and eventually filled the bottom of Snake Valley almost as far

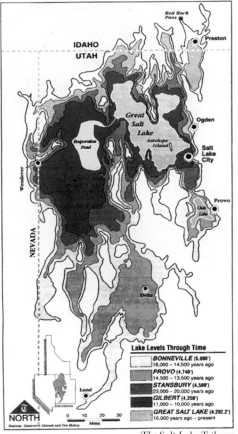

Lake Levels Through Time

BONNEVILLE (5,090') 16,000 – 14,500 years ago
PROVO (4,740') 14,500 – 13,500 years ago
STANSBURY (4,500') 23,000 – 20,000 years ago
GILBERT (4,250') 11,000 – 10,000 years ago
GREAT SALT LAKE (4,202.2') 10,000 years ago - present

The Salt Lake Tribune

Figure 2-1. Map of Lake Bonneville shorelines at different water levels.

south as the present town of Garrison. The lake was comparable in size to Lake Michigan. About fifteen thousand years ago, a natural dam at Red Rock Pass in southern Idaho gave way, and the lake level dropped about 325 feet (100 m), retreating in Snake Valley to the vicinity of present-day Gandy. The lake fluctuated but remained at certain levels long enough to leave large terraces. One of these is known as the Provo terrace, which is evident on the mountains to the east and northwest of Callao. By about eleven thousand years ago, Lake Bonneville had shrunk to about the level of today's Great Salt Lake, approximately 1,000 feet (305 m) lower than the maximum depth. The Great Salt Lake and Utah Lake are remnants of Lake Bonneville, as is Sevier Lake to the east of Snake Valley. All of these lakes continue to fluctuate depending on wet and dry cycles (Trimble 1989,

83). Lake Bonneville did not extend into Spring Valley. However, a lake was present in Spring Valley in early Wisconsin time, and as Lake Bonneville receded, this Spring Valley lake also receded, eventually forming two smaller lakes, both north and south of today's Highway 6/50 (Waite 1974, 132–33).

Starting about 10,500 years ago, the warming accelerated, causing subalpine conifers to disappear and be replaced by sagebrush. At the same time, the Lake Bonneville lake bed dried and shadscale grew out of it. A new tree arrived, the pinyon pine (*Pinus monophylla*), which benefited when the temperature increased suddenly, from 7,500 to 4,500 years ago. This period is named the Hypsithermal ("high temperature") and was a worldwide event, with the mean annual temperature 4.5 to 9°F (2.5 to 5°C) above today's average. Lakes shrank and different plants moved in (Trimble 1989, 49). By about 2,500 years ago, the vegetation looked quite similar to what we see today.

Wildlife Diversity

The dramatic variation in elevation caused by the basin and range topography in the area, coupled with a high diversity of microclimates, promotes great biological diversity. Of the fifty states, Utah ranks tenth in overall biological diversity and Nevada ranks eleventh, each with over 3,800 species of plants and vertebrate animals (Stein 2002).

Mammals

Mammals in Snake Valley vary from the extremely small, such as the vagrant shrew (*Sorex vagrans*), to the exceedingly large, like elk, which weigh more than one thousand pounds. Many people are more interested in the larger common animals, such as mule deer (*Odocoileus hemionus*), pronghorn, bighorn sheep, wild horses (*Equus caballus*), and mountain lions. Over sixty species are present in the area, including shrews (Order Insectivora); bats (Chiroptera); a variety of mice, squirrels, and other rodents (Rodentia); rabbits and hares (Lagomorpha); numerous carnivores (Carnivora); and four native ungulates in the order Artiodactyla, the even-toed mammals (NDOW 2005, 47). A complete list is found in appendix C.

Reptiles and Amphibians

The area is home to approximately eight snake species and eight lizard species, including the Sonoran mountain kingsnake

(*Lampropeltis pyromelana*), striped whipsnake (*Coluber taeniatus*), and the Great Basin collared lizard (*Crotaphytus bicinctores*; appendix D). Amphibians are scarce in this water-limited area but include the Columbia spotted frog (*Rana luteiventris*), northern leopard frog (*Rana pipiens*), Great Basin spadefoot toad (*Spea intermontana*), Woodhouse's toad (*Bufo woodhousei*), and the introduced bullfrog (*Rana catesbeiana*).

Fish, Gastropods, and Crustaceans

Within Snake Valley, seven fish species are native: Bonneville cutthroat trout (*Oncorhynchus clarki utah*), least chub (*Iotichthys phlegethontis*), Utah chub (*Gila atraria*), Utah sucker (*Catostomus ardens*), mottled sculpin (*Cottus bairdi*), speckled dace (*Rhinichthys osculus*), and redside shiner (*Richardsonius balteatus*). Restoration projects are active for some species (Baker et al. 2008). At least eleven nonnative species are found (appendix D). Spring Valley was originally fishless but is now a refuge for Pahrump poolfish (*Empetrichthys latos*) and relict dace (*Relictus solitarius*) at Shoshone Ponds in the southern part of the valley (see chapter 18). Relict dace and Utah chub are found in some other springs, while trout have been introduced to many mountain streams.

The Bonneville cutthroat trout is the only trout native to Snake Valley (figure 2-2). It originated in Lake Bonneville and was one of several species of fish inhabiting the Snake Valley arm of the lake. As the lake started drying up nearly ten thousand years ago, the Bonneville cutthroat took refuge in some of the creeks that flowed from the mountain ranges. Here the trout lived for millennia until early settlers and miners arrived and introduced their favorite fish into the creeks. These fish, including brown trout (*Salmo trutta*), brook trout (*Salvelinus fontinalis*), and rainbow trout (*Oncorhynchus mykiss*), soon outcompeted and/or hybridized with the Bonneville cutthroat trout, nearly causing the native fish to disappear. In the 1950s, Bonneville cutthroat trout were thought to be extinct from the area. In the 1990s, state and federal agencies came up with a plan to restore the native trout, and over a period of about ten years, they put the Bonneville cutthroat back into over 40 percent of its native habitat, using source populations that had persisted in places such as Hendrys Creek and Mill Creek (Baker et al. 2008; figure 2-3).

The California floater (*Anodonta californiensis*) is a freshwater mussel found in Snake Valley, in Pruess Lake and north of Callao. In

Photo courtesy Great Basin National Park

Figure 2-2. Native Bonneville cutthroat trout can vary in coloration. Note the pink color under the mouth—a distinguishing mark in cutthroat trout.

addition, fingernail clams, pea clams, and several species of snails are found in many springs and some streams. The largest genus of springsnails, *Pyrgulopsis,* occurs in the Great Basin region, with four different species inhabiting Snake Valley, including two that are endemic (*P. saxatilis* and *P. anguina*).

Thirty crustacean species are found in Nevada, including the exceptionally disruptive introduced crayfish (NDOW 2005), which has been seen in Lake Creek and other streams in the south part of the valley.

Birds

Great Basin National Park and the surrounding area are great spots for birding, and four Important Bird Areas have been recognized by the Audubon Society: Fish Springs National Wildlife Refuge, David E. Moore Wildlife Sanctuary, the North Snake Range, and Great Basin National Park. Over three hundred species of birds have been spotted in Snake and Spring Valleys (see appendix E),

Photo courtesy *Great Basin National Park*

Figure 2-3. Many people have helped restore native fish, including
Trout Unlimited and a biology class from nearby EskDale High School.

and the combination of playas, mountain streams, wetlands, and
sagebrush can make for an interesting bird-watching experience.
Part of the Pacific Flyway is over the area, and raptor migration
can be an impressive sight. In addition, this area is a good place to
see gray-crowned rosy-finches (*Leucosticte tephrocotis*) and black rosy-
finches (*Leucosticte atrata*) at higher elevations, American three-toed
woodpeckers (*Picoides dorsalis*) in recently burned and beetle-killed
forests, long-billed curlews (*Numenius americanus*) near agricultural
areas, and American white pelicans (*Pelecanus erythrorhynchos*) at
Fish Springs.

Annual breeding bird surveys are conducted in parts of the area
in cooperation with the Great Basin Bird Observatory, which operates a statewide program in Nevada and analyzes the data to see how
bird populations are fluctuating in different habitat types. Their
reports are available on the Internet at http://www.gbbo.org. Annual
Christmas Bird Counts are held around Baker and Fish Springs
National Wildlife Refuge.

Figure 2-4. The strange looking Jerusalem cricket is one of many insects that inhabit Snake Valley.

Insects and Other Invertebrates

Thousands of insect species also make the area their home, although little is known about most of them (figure 2-4). Over one hundred butterflies and moths have been identified in the Snake Valley area. An excellent source for learning more about these small and colorful creatures is http://www.butterfliesandmoths.org, where you can find out which species live in which county and learn about their life history. In addition, at least thirty ant species (Cole 1942; Wheeler and Wheeler 1986) and two hundred bee species (Griswold 2006) have been found in Snake Valley. Caves in Snake Valley, with their high humidity and nearly constant temperature, provide a specialized habitat for insects, as well as other unique arthropods. Recent surveys in Great Basin National Park have found several species new to science that are endemic to the Snake Range, including two species of cave millipedes, a springtail, and several flies (S. J. Taylor et al. 2008).

Plant Diversity and Habitats

The elevation changes in Snake Valley allow for a wide diversity of plants. The most common are listed in appendix F. Some can

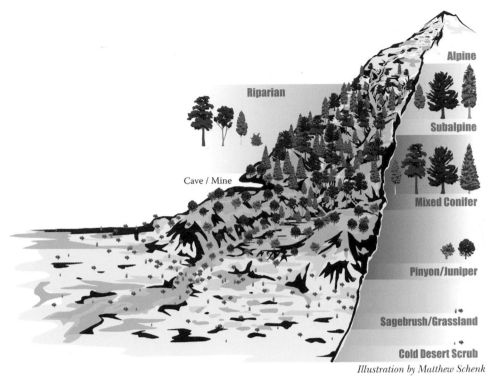

Riparian

Cave / Mine

Alpine

Subalpine

Mixed Conifer

Pinyon/Juniper

Sagebrush/Grassland

Cold Desert Scrub

Illustration by Matthew Schenk

Figure 2-5. Overview of habitats by elevation.

tolerate extremely hot temperatures and alkaline soils, while others thrive in extremely cold and windy areas. An excellent display of these habitats can be found at the Great Basin Visitor Center in Baker, Nevada. A brief description of different habitat types, beginning with the valley floors and ascending to the mountain peaks, is provided above (figure 2-5).

Intermountain Cold Desert Scrub

Covering most of the valley floor is the Intermountain Cold Desert Scrub habitat (figure 2-6), which happens to be the most extensive habitat type in Nevada and Utah. The predominant plants are from the goosefoot family and include shadscale, greasewood, and winterfat (*Krascheninnikovia lanata*). Also present are Virginia glasswort (pickleweed; *Salicornia virginica*), quailbush (*Atriplex lentiformis*), Indian ricegrass (*Achnatherum hymenoides*), and needle-and-thread grass (*Hesperostipa comata*). Some of the animals typically found in this habitat include the kit fox (*Vulpes macrotis*), dark kangaroo

Figure 2-6. Desert shrub habitat in the middle of Snake Valley.

mouse (*Microdipodops megacephalus*), loggerhead shrike (*Lanius ludovicianus*), long-nosed leopard lizard (*Gambelia wislizenii*), and pallid bat (*Antrozous pallidus*). The invasion of exotic plants has been a problem, and cheatgrass (*Bromus tectorum*), saltlover (halogeton; *Halogeton glomeratus*), and Russian thistle (*Salsola kali*) are common (NDOW 2005).

Sometimes there are large gaps in the vegetation on the valley floor and it appears as if vast expanses are void of any life (figure 2-7). Upon closer inspection, you might be able to detect small, bumpy, variously colored growths on the soil. These are biological soil crusts, a combination of photosynthetic bacteria (cyanobacteria), other bacteria, green algae, lichens, mosses, and microfungi that colonize soil when nothing else can. The cyanobacterial and microfungal filaments infiltrate the top few millimeters of soil and essentially glue it together, providing soil stabilization and also reducing erosion, retaining soil moisture, discouraging annual weed growth, and fixing atmospheric nitrogen. Biological soil crusts can take decades to form (Belnap et al. 2001).

Figure 2-7. Biological soil crusts help stabilize the soil.

Sagebrush/Grassland

The sagebrush habitat is often found in a mosaic with other habitat types. It occurs from 4,500 to 10,000 feet (1,400 to 3,000 m) and receives more precipitation than the Intermountain Cold Desert Scrub habitat, with 8–30 inches (20–76 cm) annually. Sagebrush is more complicated than it might appear at first: there are twenty-seven recognized species and distinct subspecies just in Nevada. The most common are basin big sagebrush (*Artemisia tridentata tridentata*), mountain big sagebrush (*Artemisia tridentata vaseyana*), Wyoming big sagebrush (*Artemisia tridentata wyomingensis*), low sagebrush (*Artemisia arbuscula*), and black sagebrush (*Artemisia nova*). Healthy sagebrush areas have a lush undergrowth of bunchgrasses and forbs. Eight animal species are dependent on sagebrush for most of their life cycle: pygmy rabbit (*Brachylagus idahoensis*), Great Basin pocket mouse (*Perognathus parvus*), sagebrush vole (*Lemmiscus curtatus*), sagebrush lizard (*Sceloporus graciosus*), greater sage-grouse, sage thrasher (*Oreoscoptes montanus*), Brewer's sparrow (*Spizella breweri*), and sage sparrow (*Amphispiza belli*).

Much of the sagebrush steppe habitat is out of balance. Shrub cover is increasing, crowding out grasses and forbs that are used by many animals. In addition, nonnative cheatgrass and medusa head (*Taeniatherum caput-medusae*) also use up valuable space. At the upper elevation limit, pinyon and juniper are invading the sagebrush, causing it to die and leave behind its dead branches, called skeletons (NDOW 2005). Some efforts are underway to restore the sagebrush steppe.

Pinyon/Juniper Woodlands

Singleleaf pinyon pine and Utah juniper (*Juniperus osteosperma*) dominate the lower woodlands between 6,000 and 8,000 feet (1,800–2,400 m), and they make up the most extensive forest in the area. The pinyon/juniper woodland (commonly called PJ) used to occur at higher elevations, but it has been gradually invading lower-elevation sites due to climate change and fire suppression. Pinyon/juniper communities support wildlife such as pinyon jays (*Gymnorhinus cyanocephalus*) and cliff chipmunks (*Tamias dorsalis*). Curl-leaf mountain-mahogany (*Cercocarpus ledifolius*), a drought-resistant evergreen, occurs in scattered pockets, including old-growth stands more than 700 years old, with some individuals up to 1,350 years old (Schultz et al. 1990). Mountain-mahogany stands appear to be stable in size.

The pinyon nut crops are extremely important to a variety of animals, including the pinyon jay. These nuts are not produced every year, so Indians who depended on the pine nuts as a major food source had to travel to different mountain ranges to find the best nuts in a given year. A surplus crop is produced every three to seven years (Trimble 1989, 144).

Mixed Conifer and Subalpine Forest

The mixed conifer forest includes Douglas-fir (*Pseudotsuga menziesii*), white fir (*Abies concolor*), ponderosa pine (*Pinus ponderosa*), quaking aspen (*Populus tremuloides*), greenleaf manzanita (*Arctostaphylos patula*), mountain snowberry (*Symphoricarpos oreophilus*), mountain-mahogany, creeping barberry (*Mahonia repens*), mountain big sagebrush, and common juniper (*Juniperus communis*). It is often found from 8,000 to 11,800 feet (2,400–3,600 m). Snags and dying trees are important habitat for the American three-toed woodpecker. Other animals living here are dusky grouse (*Dendragapus obscurus*), northern goshawk (*Accipiter gentilis*), Inyo shrew (*Sorex tenellus*), and vagrant shrew (*Sorex vagrans*; NDOW 2005).

Ponderosa pines are especially dependent on fire to survive and reproduce. In the past, fires occurred throughout the Great Basin and the entire West at a regular frequency. Native Americans recognized that fire helped rejuvenate vegetation and they would often set fires. Early settlers, though, were afraid of fire and started putting fires out as soon as possible. This fire suppression, along with heavy logging in early settlement days, has made it difficult for ponderosa pines to survive. Instead of a forest that is easy to walk through, a closed canopy exists, filled with white firs. The white firs provide a fire ladder, or a vegetative means for fire to quickly get into the crowns of ponderosa pines. Previously, fires stayed near the ground around ponderosa pines, the heat opening up the seeds and allowing new ones to germinate. With the fire ladders, the whole tree can burn, incinerating the seed source. In addition, shade from dense stands of firs also inhibits germination and growth of young ponderosa pines.

The subalpine habitat includes Engelmann spruce (*Picea engelmannii*), limber pine (*Pinus flexilis*), and Great Basin bristlecone pine. Clark's nutcrackers (*Nucifraga columbiana*) are a common inhabitant, as are golden-mantled ground squirrels (*Spermophilus lateralis*). Understory components include common juniper, currant (*Ribes* spp.), Ross's sedge (*Carex rossii*) and Fendler's meadow-rue (*Thalictrum fendleri*; NDOW 2005).

Alpine

Alpine habitat is found above tree line, from 10,500 to 13,063 feet (3,200–3,982 m). One of its characteristics is cryptogamic crusts of lichens, mosses, cyanobacteria, and fungi. Animals specializing in this habitat include the black rosy-finch and gray-crowned rosy-finch (NDOW 2005). Rock wrens (*Salpinctes obsoletus*), Piute ground squirrel (*Spermophilus mollis*), and bighorn sheep are occasionally seen.

Riparian

Streams and springs make up a small percentage of the habitat in the area, but they and their associated riparian areas are the most biologically diverse habitats. Both Snake and Spring Valleys have over a dozen streams flowing from the mountains toward the valley floors, and thousands of springs at all elevations. Vegetation ranges from Woods' rose (*Rosa woodsii*) and narrowleaf cottonwood (*Populus angustifolia*) at lower elevations to water birch (*Betula occidentalis*), redosier dogwood (*Cornus sericea*), and willow (*Salix* spp.) at middle elevations, and quaking aspen and a variety of herbs at higher elevations. Animals found near water include wandering garter snakes (*Thamnophis elegans vagrans*; sometimes called water snakes), water shrews (*Sorex palustris*), MacGillivray's warblers (*Oporornis tolmiei*), American pipits (*Anthus rubescens*), and more.

Threats to riparian areas include dewatering, channelization, invasion of exotic plants like tamarisk, or saltcedar (*Tamarix ramosissima*), Russian olive, common reed (*Phragmites australis*), and tall whitetop (*Lepidium latifolium*). In places, erosion can be a problem, as can heavy use by wild horses, burros, elk, and livestock (NDOW 2005).

Caves and Mines

Both caves and mines are common in the area. Caves are created by natural processes, usually including water, while mines are made by humans. Both provide access to the earth's interior, and some animal species are found only here. Several endemic species have been found in the caves of Great Basin National Park (S. J. Taylor et al. 2008), and as cave biota surveys expand to other caves in the area, it is likely that more will be found. Some species of millipedes, springtails, and pseudoscorpions live their entire life cycles in caves, while many others, such as cave crickets and beetles, use the underground environment for just part of their life cycle. Caves and mines are also home to up to nineteen bat species (NDOW 2005).

Island Biogeography

The Great Basin mountain ranges separated by valleys can be compared to islands in the ocean. Instead of water reaching to the horizon, sagebrush waves in the wind. Like islands in the ocean, the mountain ranges in the Great Basin can have distinct flora and fauna due to difficulties in moving from island to island. The distance of an island from a source population, in addition to the size of the island, determines how many species can colonize it and survive. Jim Brown noted in his pioneering work on island biogeography in the Great Basin that mammalian diversity in more isolated boreal habitats was apparently reduced by local extinctions. In contrast, birds had superior dispersal capabilities and thus had balanced rates of colonization and extinction (1978).

One example that can be explained by island biogeography in the Great Basin is the absence of black bears. Although black bears are found in the Wasatch Range to the east and the Sierra Nevada to the west, they are not found in or around Great Basin National Park. Most likely the "oceans" of valley floors, with their hot climates and sparse vegetation, acted as barriers to the bears. Because the Snake and Deep Creek Ranges are not that far from the Wasatch Range of Utah, they contain more species than ranges that are farther away from the "mainland."

During the Pleistocene epoch, when glaciers formed in the mountains and Lake Bonneville flooded some areas and restricted animal movement, the mountain ranges were also isolated. So in some cases, mountain ranges really were islands.

Climate Change

Climate change is a natural process, and Snake Valley has undergone some significant changes. During the Ice Age (25,000 to 17,000 years ago), temperatures were substantially cooler and more precipitation fell than today, while during the Hypsithermal, temperatures were warmer than they are today. Plants and animals have had to adapt to these changes or vanish. Many of the species that used to be in the area, like pikas (*Ochotona princeps*), dire wolves (*Canis dirus*), and bison (*Bison bison*), were not able to adapt to the changes and disappeared.

One of the largest impacts of climate change is the shifts it induces in vegetation. Scientists throughout the Great Basin region are studying how pinyon pine and juniper forests are growing in what used to be sagebrush and grasslands. Over 16,000 acres (6,500 hectares [ha]) in Great Basin National Park alone has changed in about the last 150 years (Neal Darby, personal communication, 2007). This overtaking of one plant community by another is called encroachment. The changing plant communities lead to alterations in wildlife communities. Greater sage-grouse, sage sparrow, and Brewer's sparrow are sagebrush obligate species: they depend on sagebrush habitat, and if it is not present, neither are they. Some mammal, reptile, and insect species are also obligates to one habitat type or another. If too much of that specific habitat disappears, so does the animal species.

Ecologists today are concerned that the climate is changing faster than normal, and this rapid change is due to the impact of humans living on the earth and putting contaminants in the atmosphere. It is still under debate how much climate change is due to humans and how much is natural, but it is evident that the temperature has been warming especially quickly since about 1970 (IPCC 2007).

Other plant communities that are changing due to encroachment are aspen stands and ponderosa pine stands, which are being invaded by white firs; and subalpine areas, where bighorn sheep habitat is being reduced because of the invasion of Engelmann spruce and Douglas-fir. This encroachment is most likely due to a combination of climate change and fire suppression.

Other Changes

Many habitats depend on natural disturbances, such as floods, fires, and avalanches. Cottonwood communities along riparian areas depend on periodic floods to remove old trees and provide space for new trees. Aspen groves are naturally fire resistant, so fires in close proximity remove conifers and allow the aspen to expand. In addition, fire helps to reestablish sagebrush and grassland habitats (figure 2-8). Subalpine and alpine grasses and forbs are rejuvenated after avalanches remove taller vegetation.

Some of the changes in the area are not due to natural disturbances but rather to human-induced change. This is illustrated by the diversion of water for irrigation, which has dried up some water sources. Additional applications for water use are likely to have even more widespread effects.

An example of wildlife change involves mule deer. Today mule deer are a common sight in and around the area, but that has not always been the case. Few mule deer bones have been found at the Baker and Garrison archaeological sites, indicating that there were fewer before Euro-American settlement. Deer populations are known to be cyclical, with populations building to huge numbers before crashing due to disease outbreaks. State wildlife agencies attempt to regulate these cycles to some degree by changing the number of hunting permits issued from year to year. The reason that mule deer have gone from rare to abundant has to do with more than just population cycles, however.

Deer prefer to browse on shrubs, and historically much of what today is shrubland consisted of many more grasses. When Euro-American settlers arrived in the area, many brought livestock with

Figure 2-8. Fire is an important process in Snake Valley that renews plant communities.

them, and the grazing of annual grasses promoted the increase of shrubs. Fire suppression allowed these shrubs to get bigger, and annual grasses decreased further. At the same time, the federal government was aggressively removing predators, and the deer population continued to rise until it reached its peak in the mid to late 1950s. In 1958 the deer population fell dramatically in sync with a widespread drought. Populations gradually rebounded, but in the winter of 1992–93, another catastrophic deer die-off occurred due to extremely deep snow. The wildlife agencies continue to monitor deer closely, and despite lower numbers than the peak in the 1950s, more deer still make their home in the region today than they did before 1850 (Wasley 2004). Deer and other wildlife are especially abundant in agricultural areas.

Plants in particular have changed greatly due to humans. Before 1900, some exotic plants, or plants introduced by humans either intentionally or unintentionally, had made it to the Great Basin, including Russian thistle (tumbleweed), redstem stork's bill (*Erodium cicutarium*), cheatgrass, and several mustards. Many of these become a fire hazard because they dry out so quickly and are more likely to burn during lightning strikes from the summer monsoons. Tamarisk arrived in the Great Basin in 1926 at Utah Lake and soon spread throughout the area. Russian olives arrived in about the 1960s in Snake Valley and have expanded rapaciously, especially in the northern valley. The expansion and proliferation of these new species, which would not be so prevalent in the Great Basin without the influence of humans, is likely to cause the greatest changes in Snake Valley for at least the next one hundred years.

Night Skies

Snake Valley has some of the darkest night skies in the entire country. With Salt Lake City at least three hours away and Las Vegas over four hours away, major urban light pollution can be seen only from the tallest peaks. More attention is being paid to dark skies as biologists realize that some animals take their cues from lights for migration and breeding. Some of the local communities are trying to reduce the small amount of light they produce by shielding lights and carefully considering their placement. Great Basin National Park is seeking designation as a dark-sky national park. Under the Bortle Dark-Sky Scale, with one the darkest and nine the lightest, Great Basin National Park scores a three (NPS 2005).

Special night sky programs are held periodically during the summer at Great Basin National Park. Often astronomers come from Salt Lake City and Las Vegas and sometimes even farther away to share their knowledge of the night sky. On moonless nights, the Milky Way galaxy dominates the night sky, and the dark abyss is speckled with seemingly countless stars.

HUMAN HISTORY

Humans have been coming to the Great Basin National Park area for thousands of years for many different reasons, including hunting, gathering, exploring, mining, ranching, sightseeing, and isolation. This chapter presents an overview of the human history of the area. More detailed historical events are found in the chapters about specific places.

Early Cultures

Archaeological surveys have found artifacts that indicate people were in the area as early as twelve thousand years ago (Bryan 1977). The first humans in the area, called the Paleo-Indians, lived when Lake Bonneville filled Snake Valley, white firs grew down to the shoreline, and fantastically different animals inhabited the area. The Paleo-Indians hunted the Pleistocene megafauna, such as mastodons and bison, using stone implements (Wilde and Soper 1993, 3; P. Wilson 1999, 14).

The Desert Archaic Culture either evolved from or displaced the Paleo-Indians about nine thousand years ago. They preferred living in flat areas like Fish Springs and developed the atlatl (spear-thrower). They also used grinding stones called manos and metates and made fur robes and baskets. They hunted about forty different species of animals and had to be generalists due to a drastically changing

Figure 3-1. Rock art by some of the earliest inhabitants of Snake Valley, the Fremont.

climate. The Indians of the Desert Archaic Culture remained in the area until about AD 500 (P. Wilson 1999, 15).

The Fremonts arrived about AD 500 and during the next two hundred to four hundred years were a much more sedentary culture, developing horticulture and having time to make ceramic jugs and pots (Wilde and Soper 1993, 3; Wells 1993, 3; P. Wilson 1999, 16–17). They lived in small communities, and two have so far been excavated in Snake Valley: the Garrison Site, near the town of Garrison, and the Baker Village Site, north of the town of Baker. These excavations have revealed many additional details about Fremont life, such as what crops they planted and where they went to trade. A distinctive rock art style was also present (figure 3-1), as well as a grayware pottery pattern (Wells 1993, 4).

The next cultural groups to live in the area were the Shoshones and Goshutes. These groups were hunters and gatherers who did not build permanent structures as the Fremonts did. Instead, they lived in caves, under overhangs, and in brush huts (P. Wilson 1999, 24). Their lives were changed forever by the arrival of Euro-American settlers. Eventually the Goshutes signed a treaty that established the Deep Creek Goshute Indian Reservation in 1914, and they agreed to ranch and farm. More details can be found in chapter 12.

The Explorers

The Great Basin area is said to have been the last part of the continental United States to be explored and mapped. Fur trader Jedediah Smith may have been the first white person in Snake Valley, exploring the northern portion. He noted in his journal that he saw many antelope near present-day Gandy on June 22, 1827, but could not catch any. He continued northward, camping along the east slope of the Deep Creek Range. The description he gave of this arid landscape discouraged others from exploring the area.

Mormon Missions

The first permanent Euro-American settlers in the Great Basin region were Mormon pioneers, who arrived in the Great Salt Lake Valley on July 24, 1847. Within a decade, they had made an additional forty settlements in the relatively wet and fertile areas along the Wasatch Range.

In 1855, a mission was organized to explore an area with a strange white mountain that the Indians had mentioned. The expedition members arrived in "Grease Wood Valley" (Snake Valley), camped near a creek, and then traveled to the base of what the Indians called Pe-up Mountain (Wheeler Peak), Pe-up signifying "big mountain." Some of the group made it to the summit and renamed the peak Williams Peak, after the first white man on the summit (Unrau 1990, 25–27).

After descending, the group traveled southeast to the site of present-day Garrison and were impressed by the fertile soil and plentiful springs. They also traveled farther south to Meadow Creek (Lake Creek), with meadows 10 miles (16 km) in length and averaging 2 miles (3 km) in width (Burbank Meadows); they also noted a small lake (Pruess Lake). Soon the group reached the foot of White Mountain (Crystal Peak). Ezra Williams reported to Mormon leaders that they marveled at the "white sandstone rock, interspersed with bastard diamonds" (as quoted in Unrau 1990, 28).

In 1858, the White Mountain Expedition returned to Snake Valley and the present site of Garrison, Utah. Forty-five men were left to clear land and plant crops, while the rest of the expedition continued exploring. Those that stayed at the so-called Snake Creek Farm cleared about 50 acres (20 ha) by the end of May. They dug ditches and planted grain. In late July, water from Snake Creek dried up and the expedition members returned to Fillmore, Utah (Unrau 1990, 29–34).

Miners and Nevada Statehood

Many miners traveled through Nevada in 1848 on their way to California, but it was not until 1859 that western Nevada had its own mining boom, with silver found at the Comstock Lode. Some of the miners who had been in California came across the mountains to search other parts of the basin and range country to strike it rich. As minerals were found, instant communities formed. Some of these were tent cities that disappeared in a few months, while others had banks, schools, saloons, and other businesses that continued even after the mining boom ended.

In 1861, President James Buchanan declared the Territory of Nevada. The Civil War increased demand for ore and agricultural products, and the Territory of Nevada helped provide these. The Union wanted another state on its side and helped champion the cause of statehood, even though the total population was too small for such status. Finally, on October 31, 1864, President Abraham Lincoln accepted Nevada as a state.

The same year, a mining town became established relatively close to Snake and Spring Valleys, at Pioche, Nevada. A year later, ore was found at Hamilton, Nevada, southwest of present-day Ely, where a town of ten thousand people emerged. Other mining districts were soon formed, with many of them producing silver. Osceola in the Snake Range was an exception; it was the site of placer gold mining and had one of the longest runs of any in the state. See chapter 18 for more details.

Transportation and Communication Routes

When gold was discovered in California in 1848, a need for transportation and communication routes to the promised land emerged.

Photo courtesy Fish Springs National Wildlife Refuge

Figure 3-2. The Pony Express route was one of the first communication routes across the country. Every June the route is celebrated by re-riding it from California to Missouri.

A route to the north of Snake and Spring Valleys, following the Humboldt River for a considerable distance, was called the Overland or Humboldt Trail, and eventually the railroads used it. A route south of Snake and Spring Valleys was called the Old Spanish Trail. And the central route, sometimes called the Egan-Simpson Trail, included part of Snake and Spring Valleys (Unrau 1990, 35). This central route was eventually used to transport mail in the exciting Pony Express days of 1860–61 (figure 3-2). More details can be found in chapter 13.

Additional Exploration

In 1869, the US Army Corps of Engineers began scientific exploration and military reconnaissance of the area under First Lieutenant George M. Wheeler. This systematic study provided some of the first written reports of the conditions found in Snake Valley. When the expedition crossed the pass into Snake Valley, it encountered about two hundred Snake Indians. The expedition noted that the Indians could not depend solely on wild game for their diet due to its scarcity but had to supplement it with numerous, protein-rich pinyon pine nuts (Unrau 1990, 54, 56).

Accompanying Wheeler was geologist Grove Karl Gilbert. He visited northern Snake Valley and reported on the geology of the area and recognized that an enormous lake had once occupied the valley bottom. He spent the next twenty years studying Lake Bonneville (Bluth 1978, 135–36).

Wheeler recorded that the soon-to-be-renamed Wheeler Peak was 13,063 feet high, based on careful barometric pressure readings (Unrau 1990, 57). That is still the elevation recognized today. After finishing in Snake Valley, Wheeler continued on his way, surveying much of the West over the next ten years. The information that he and his survey gathered helped to open up the West and encouraged more people to come.

Utah Statehood

Just two years after the Mormons crossed the Wasatch Range and settled, they attempted to have their Territory of Deseret designated a state. Their request was denied, as were several more attempts. It was not until 1896, after the prohibition of polygamy, a public relations campaign, intensive lobbying, the disbanding of the Mormon People's party, and the enlistment of some high-level friends that the state of Utah became official (Lyman 2007). Utah became the forty-fifth state in the union on January 4, 1896.

Permanent Settlements

Euro-Americans settled in Snake and Spring Valleys beginning in the 1860s, most of them making their living by agriculture. Many Shoshones worked on ranches, the men as cowboys and hay cutters, the women as household servants. Most employers allowed the Indian workers to leave in September to harvest pine nuts (Crum 1994, 31). Some ranches produced enough to supply food to the miners and visiting sheepmen. Before long, small communities were organized, including Burbank, Garrison, Baker, Trout Creek, Callao, and Gandy.

Humboldt National Forest and Lehman Caves National Monument

In 1906, L. von Wernstedt of the Forest Service made a trip through Snake Valley. Based on his recommendations, national forest land was designated as early as 1909, including a large part of the South Snake Range and some of the North Snake Range. In 1912, boundaries were expanded to include most of the North Snake Range. In 1957, the Nevada National Forest became part of the Humboldt National Forest. In the 1990s, it was expanded to become the Humboldt-Toiyabe National Forest, encompassing 6.3 million acres (2.5 million ha), the largest national forest outside of Alaska.

Although the Deep Creek Range is not much farther north than the Snake Range, it was not marked for designation within the national forest system. Today it is administered by the Bureau of Land Management.

In 1922, President Warren G. Harding declared Lehman Caves National Monument within a 1-square-mile (3 km²) area surrounded by the Nevada National Forest (figure 3-3). The Forest Service managed the monument until 1933, when the National Park Service took over. More information can be found in chapter 4.

Civilian Conservation Corps

In March 1933, President Franklin Roosevelt introduced a bill to establish the Civilian Conservation Corps (CCC), a work program for young men to help better the economy and the country's morale, both of which had taken a nosedive in the Depression. Within ten days, it passed both houses of Congress. The program extended to Snake Valley, where a CCC camp was established south of Callao and operated from 1938 to 1941, and a spur camp with fewer men was set up near Burbank. In Spring Valley, a camp was set up near Shoshone Ponds, one of which the CCC constructed. Other projects included building roads, reservoirs, and stock trails. In return for their work, the men received food, clothing, shelter, and thirty dollars a month, twenty-five of which they had to send to their families. With the US entry into World War II in 1941, the CCC program ended.

Figure 3-3. Dedication of Lehman Caves National Monument, August 6, 1922.

World War II

With the onset of World War II, many of the United States' normal trade routes were closed. The cotton crop was particularly affected. Grown in the South, the crop needed to be treated with arsenic to keep insects from decimating it. Because overseas supplies were unavailable, Snake Valley became an important supplier of arsenic, with increased mining of arsenic in Gold Hill. Another important product from the area was molybdenum, which is used in steel production. In 1942, Dugway Proving Ground, at the north end of Snake Valley, was established to provide testing of biological and chemical defense systems. Many young men from the area went off to serve their country, while others stayed behind to help raise the cattle and sheep used to feed the country.

Following the war, the search was on for black gold. Oil companies have visited Snake Valley since 1952, drilling wells at various locations (table 3-1), with the deepest in the Confusion Range at a depth of 16,058 feet (4,894 m; Hintze and Davis 2003). To date, no one is producing any oil in Snake Valley, although oil companies have resumed their searching in recent years.

Newer Settlements: Partoun, EskDale, Home Farm

In 1949, Dr. Maurice Glendenning established Partoun, one of the newer communities in Snake Valley, south of Trout Creek. He and his followers thought this was the perfect place to practice their religion, but after a few years it was clear that not enough water was available. Many moved south about 30 miles (48 km) and started the community of EskDale in order to live a communal life (Denton 1999). More details are found in chapters 13 and 15.

About 1957, another community, called the School of the Natural Order, was established in Snake Valley on the Home Farm, west of the town of Baker. This commune had moved from California to find a peaceful place where members could concentrate on their leader's teachings. Additional information is in chapter 9.

Fish Springs National Wildlife Refuge

In 1959, the US Department of the Interior purchased some private ranches to the northeast of Snake Valley, where a series of

Table 3-1. Selected oil wells in Snake Valley

Name	Location	Date	Company	Depth (ft)
Burbank	East of Garrison	1952	Standard Oil of California	6,955
Desolation Anticline	Northeast of Gandy Salt Marsh	1952	Standard Oil of California	6,200
Bishop Springs	Northeast of Gandy Salt Marsh	1952; 1980	Gulf Oil; Tiger Oil Company	9,058; 16,058
Baker Creek	East of Border Inn	1956	Shell Oil	4,218
Amerada Hess	Near Beck Place	1979	Amerada Hess	7,782
Ensign	Near Mormon Gap	1980	Commodore Resources Corporation	12,238
Outlaw	Near Needle Point Springs	1982	Commodore Resources Corporation	13,000
Cobra Well	Northeast of Gandy	1995	Balcron Division- Equitable Energy	3,765
Mamba	South of Gandy	1996	Equitable Resources	3,265
Hamlin Wash No. 19-1	8N 70E S19 SE/4 NE/4	1996	Falcon Energy LLC	6,980
Outlaw #1 Federal	10N 70E S1 NE/4	1983	Commodore Resources Corporation	13,000
Baker Creek No. 12-1	13N 70E S12 SE/4 NE/4 NW/4	1993	J.R. Bacon Drilling, Inc.	4,787

Source: Hintze and Davis 2003.

ponds supported a great deal of waterfowl, migratory birds, and other wildlife. Some additional land was transferred from the BLM to create Fish Springs National Wildlife Refuge. See chapter 14 for more details.

Modern Amenities

Snake and Spring Valleys were one of the last areas of the country to get centralized electricity, as detailed in Jeanette Griggs's book *Let There Be Light* (1974). Efforts began in 1949 to bring electricity to the valley. These and subsequent actions did not find electricity at a sufficiently low price. By 1967, the Rural Electrification Association (REA) had helped supply electricity to 98 percent of rural areas in the country. Nevada was the last state with large areas that were still unconnected. A loan was applied for, and in September 1969, the REA approved a $15.1 million loan that would form the 999th cooperative. It would serve 16,000 square miles (41,440 km²), the largest area of any electric cooperative in the United States. Work soon began on a 230-kilovolt line, the first heavy power line across Nevada. During the winter of 1970, power lines reached Baker and Garrison. Soon twinkling lights lit up patches of the desert floor. Many residents commented that once Mt. Wheeler Power came, the valley sounded quieter, since the diesel generators no longer had to run (Griggs 1974).

The first telephone in Snake Valley came in the early 1920s, when Baker was known as "Basque Town" because Basque rancher Guy Saval operated the largest ranch. He wanted telephone service and paid to have telephone lines installed from Ely. Anyone wanting to make a call had to go to the Baker Ranch, hand crank the telephone to get the operator and Ely, and then request a number (Quate 1993, 176). A telephone system was also developed in the early years between Burbank and Garrison for ranch communications (Dearden 2007). Eventually, a telephone system reached the majority of the valley, arriving in 1957 with the help of Art Brothers of Beehive Telephone. This was a party-line system, with different rings signifying whom the call was for. That was eventually phased out with a single-line system in the 1990s. At the time of this writing, no cell towers are present in Snake Valley, so cell phone service is sporadic, found principally along Highway 6/50 and on mountaintops. Spring Valley has more coverage, due to a tower in the Schell Creek Range, above Cave Lake.

MX Missile Crisis

In 1979, President Jimmy Carter proposed an audacious plan to protect the United States during the Cold War. He wanted to establish a system of railroads and missile silos in the almost deserted areas of western Utah and eastern Nevada. With this system, missiles could be kept moving so that the Russians would never know exactly where to target their warheads. See chapter 15 for more details.

Great Basin National Park

President Ronald Reagan signed a bill in 1986 to create Great Basin National Park in eastern Nevada. A national park had been proposed since the 1920s, with the idea waxing and waning over the decades. See chapter 4 for more details. Senator Harry Reid helped to get the bill signed, with the compromise that the park boundaries would exclude private mining claims and private land and that grazing would continue to be allowed within the national park. Although many locals were opposed to the park, it did bring additional recognition to the area, provided extra jobs, and increased visitation slightly.

Mount Moriah Wilderness and Wilderness Study Areas

Another federal designation came three years later, in 1989, when the US Congress designated Mount Moriah Wilderness in the North Snake Range, which now covers over 89,000 acres (36,000 ha). In 2006, numerous other areas close to Great Basin National Park were designated as wilderness areas as part of the White Pine County legislation (table 3-2, figure 3-4).

Parts of the Deep Creek Range have been considered for wilderness designation, and until a decision is made, this area is considered a Wilderness Study Area, bound by the same laws as a wilderness area, with mechanized travel prohibited. Other Wilderness Study Areas in Snake Valley are in the Confusion Range, near Crystal Peak, and in the Fish Springs Range.

Southern Nevada Water Authority Pipeline Project

Many residents of Snake and Spring Valleys like how things almost never seem to change there. This way of life was interrupted in 1989,

Table 3-2. Wilderness areas near Great Basin National Park

Name	Range	Size (acres)	Date Designated
Mount Moriah	North Snake	89,000	1989
Highland Ridge	South Snake	68,622	2006
High Schells	North Schell	121,497	2006
Mt Grafton	South Schell	78,754	2006
Becky Peak	North Schell	18,119	2006
Fortification Range	Fortification	30,539	2004
Government Peak	North Snake	6,313	2006

when the Las Vegas Valley Water District applied for groundwater rights in many rural areas in Nevada, including Snake and Spring Valleys. Interested parties had a thirty-day period to protest, and an extensive campaign generated hundreds of protests. Then nothing happened until 2004, when the Southern Nevada Water Authority (SNWA), which now included the Las Vegas Valley Water District, applied to the BLM for a right-of-way to build a pipeline from the valleys where it had applied for water.

Residents on both the Nevada and Utah sides of Snake Valley quickly came together to explore options to deal with what was seen as a foreign invader eager to suck over 50,000 acre-feet (60 million m³) of water a year from Snake Valley and about 100,000 acre-feet (120 million m³) of water a year from Spring Valley. A group called the Great Basin Water Network formed to get information about the amount of water available, to contact legislators, to inform the media, to maintain a website (http://www.greatbasinwater.net), and to provide information to others interested in this far-reaching project (figure 3-5). Since the project must get the approval of both the Nevada State Engineer and the BLM, it is not clear at the present what the outcome will be. In April 2007, the State Engineer ruled that the SNWA would be allowed to take 60,000 acre-feet (74 million m³) a year from Spring Valley in a staged withdrawal, beginning with 40,000 acre-feet (49 million m³) per year for the first ten years. Litigation has made the Nevada State Engineer reexamine

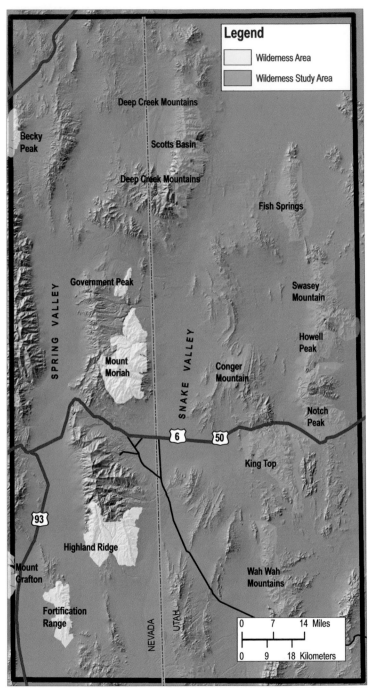

Figure 3-4. Map of wilderness areas near Great Basin
National Park.

Figure 3-5. The water bucket has become a symbol for those who want to protect Snake and Spring Valleys' water from exportation.

this ruling, and it is likely that the water battles will continue long into the future.

Great Basin National Heritage Area

In 2006, Snake and Spring Valleys received an additional designation as part of the Great Basin National Heritage Area. A national heritage area is a place designated by the US Congress where natural, cultural, historic, and recreational resources combine to form a cohesive, nationally distinctive landscape arising from patterns of human activity shaped by geography. These areas tell nationally important stories about our nation and are representative of the national experience through both the physical features that remain and the traditions that have evolved within them.

The Great Basin National Heritage Area includes both Millard County, Utah, and White Pine County, Nevada, and seeks to preserve the history and way of life of these areas. A bill passed Congress in July 2006 and was signed by the president in October, enabling the heritage area to receive federal funds.

Timeline

12,000 years ago	Paleo-Indians in Snake Valley
9,000 years ago	Desert Archaic Culture
AD 500	Fremont Culture begins in Snake Valley
AD 1000	Shoshones arrive
1827	Jedediah Smith explores the Great Basin area
1852	Major Howard Egan develops mail route across northern Snake Valley
1855	Mormon mission camps near Snake Creek
1859	Simpson Expedition, some of the first scientific writings about Snake Valley area; Callao (Willow Springs) established
1860–61	Pony Express in operation
1864	Nevada statehood
1869	Burbank established; Wheeler Expedition visits the area
1870	Garrison settled
1873	Baker established
1896	Utah statehood
1922	Lehman Caves National Monument established by President Warren J. Harding; *Covered Wagon Days* filmed
1929	Great Depression starts
1933	CCC camps started
1934	Taylor Grazing Act reforms grazing; launches precursor to Bureau of Land Management (BLM)
1942	Dugway Proving Ground created for biological and chemical testing
1949	Partoun founded
1952	Last section of US Highway 6/50 paved between Delta and Ely
1955	EskDale founded
1957	School of the Natural Order moved into Snake Valley; party-line telephones in most of Snake Valley
1959	Fish Springs National Wildlife Refuge established
1970	Electricity in Snake Valley
1979	MX missile proposal
1986	Great Basin National Park established
1989	Mount Moriah Wilderness created
2004	Southern Nevada Water Authority pipeline proposal
2006	Great Basin National Heritage Area declared by Congress; additional wilderness areas added

Bristlecone needles and cones.

Part 2

Great Basin National Park

Most visitors to the area come to visit Great Basin National Park, one of the least visited national parks in the United States. This section focuses on the park, its gateway community, and other nearby points of interest.

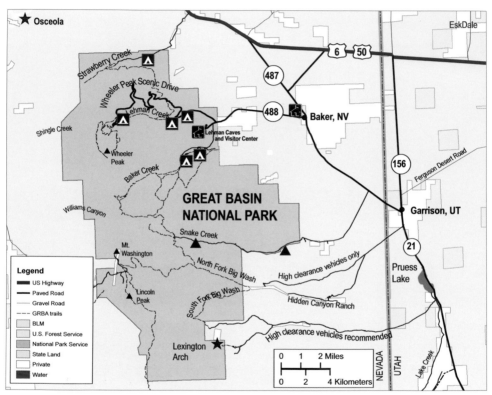

Figure 4-1. Map of Great Basin National Park.

LEHMAN CAVES AND GREAT BASIN NATIONAL PARK OVERVIEW

Great Basin National Park (figure 4-1) appears on the map as just a small spot in the enormous Great Basin Desert. It is 234 miles (377 km) from Salt Lake City, reachable by driving south on I-15 to Nephi, then heading west through Delta. From Delta, Utah, the park is about 100 miles (160 km) away. From US Highway 6/50, turn south on Nevada Highway 487 and travel 5 miles (8 km) to Baker, Nevada, home to the new Great Basin Visitor Center. To reach the park headquarters, turn west on Highway 488 and travel 6 miles (10 km) to the park headquarters. From Cedar City, Utah, the park is 142 miles (229 km). Travel on Utah Highway 130 through Minersville, then turn west (left) onto Utah Highway 21 through Milford (be sure to turn left in town and stay on Highway 21; otherwise you will be making a detour to Delta). The mile markers count down to the state boundary, and then the highway becomes Nevada 487. Continue into Baker, Nevada. From Las Vegas, Nevada, the park is 286 miles (460 km). To get there, head east on I-15 for about 26 miles (41 km) to the junction with Highway 93. Stay on the highway for 224 miles (379 km), through Alamo, Ash Springs, Caliente, and Pioche. When the highway meets Highway 6/50, head east for about 30 miles (50 km) to Baker. From Reno, Nevada, the park is 385 miles (620 km). Simply head west on Highway 6/50 until the junction with Nevada Highway 487, and follow the signs from there.

Upon arriving, the approximately ninety thousand visitors a year find a gem. They can visit the fascinating Lehman Caves, enjoy the vistas along the Wheeler Peak Scenic Drive, go for a solitary back-packing trip on an uncrowded trail, hike to bristlecone pines thou-sands of years old, or enjoy the Milky Way under some of the dark-est night skies in the country. Great Basin National Park is relatively new, created in 1986 by Congress and signed into law by President Ronald Reagan. It preserves the second-highest peak in Nevada, Wheeler Peak, at 13,063 feet (3,982 m), along with a large portion of the South Snake Range. Despite being the only national park entirely within the state of Nevada (a part of Death Valley National Park is also in Nevada), Great Basin National Park remains relatively undis-covered, and that is part of its appeal. The campgrounds rarely fill up, there are no traffic jams, and it is easy to find a quiet place near a mountain stream to relax.

In this chapter, you can learn about the main attraction in the park, Lehman Caves, as well as get a feel for the rest of the 77,180 acres (31,230 ha) that make up the park. These are explored in more detail in subsequent chapters.

How to Spend Your Time at Lehman Caves

Lehman Caves garnered national and international attention for Snake Valley beginning in the late 1800s. It should be noted that although Lehman Caves is just one cave, the original name was plural, and that is the official name of the cave. The cave is located just behind the Lehman Caves Visitor Center, 6 miles (10 km) west of Baker.

The first thing to do upon arriving is visit the Lehman Caves Visitor Center. You can buy tickets for a cave tour, get information about the area, watch a video, explore the exhibits, and browse the offerings of the Western National Parks Association bookstore. Cave tours are offered at least four times a day year-round. The ninety-minute tour is the longest tour, visiting more passageways than the other tours, so if you have the time and interest, this is the best tour. The sixty-minute tour is good if you have limited time or very small children. A thirty-minute option is offered for handicapped visitors; ask at the front desk.

If you have some time before your tour, you have a number of options. Next door to the visitor center is the Lehman Caves Café and Gift Shop, serving breakfast, lunch, and ice cream from mid-April to early October. If you brought your lunch, the nearby picnic area will provide a bit of quiet away from the hubbub of the visitor center. If you have only a half hour or so, a short nature trail behind the visitor center, which includes a peek into one of the historic cabins, is a great option. If you have more than two hours, you might like to go for a drive up the Wheeler Peak Scenic Drive, although you will need more time if you want to hike any of the trails.

The Finding of Lehman Caves

Absalom "Ab" Lehman is often given credit for finding the cave, although an abundance of Indian artifacts in the cave shows otherwise. In addition, over forty stories persist about others who discovered the cave first and how they found it, ranging from prospectors to Ab Lehman's brother Ben Lehman, US land surveyors, and other early settlers. Nevertheless, it is certain that Ab Lehman did much of the early development of the cave, making it more accessible. Some of his techniques would no longer be permissible by today's standards. An example of the early caving ethic (or lack of one) is evident in this excerpt from the *White Pine Reflex*, published at Taylor, Nevada, on April 15, 1885:

> Ab Lehman of Snake Valley reports that he and others have struck a cave of wondrous beauty on his ranch near Jeff Davis Peak. Stalactites of extraordinary size hang from its roof, and stalagmites equally large rear their heads from the floor. A stalactite weighing six hundred pounds has been taken from the cave and planted beside the monument erected by Ivers to mark the spot where he observed the last transit of Venus on Lehman's ranch (Governmental Survey of 1882). The cave was explored for about 200 feet when the points of stalactites and stalagmites came so close together as to offer a bar to further progress. They will again explore the cave armed with sledgehammers and break their way into what appears to be another chamber. (Read, 1965, 137)

Figure 4-2. Lehman Cave Ranch, also known as Cave Ranche. This photo was taken before the dedication in 1922, as the barn is missing from that photo. Note the field next to the barn.

Early Development of the Cave

Ab Lehman recognized early on that Lehman Caves was unique, and he thought that others would like to come and see it. He spent a good deal of time making it easier for others to enter and explore the cave. One of the first groups into the cave included Nettie Baker, the first white woman to venture inside it. Apparently she explored until she heard word that her baby was crying and would not be comforted, and then she quickly went to the surface, where she was teased that although the unknown terrors of the cave could not make her flee, her crying baby could (Quate 1993, 97).

When Lehman died in 1891 at the age of sixty-four, his hired hand George D. Coburn took over guiding cave tours and caring for the animals and orchards at Cave Ranche (figure 4-2). Coburn developed kidney problems, possibly because he frequently drank from the limy cave pools, and passed away in 1895. He was buried over the first hill south of the cave in an unmarked grave. W. N. McGill,

Photo by R. D. Adams from Great Basin National Park files

Figure 4-3. Visitors to Lehman Caves in 1921, in the Grand Palace. Note the lady on the right and her light-colored dress, the men up by the Parachute Shield, and the candles.

administrator of Lehman's estate, sold Cave Ranche to Charles W. Rowland, who had earlier bought Lehman's previous ranch, about 1.5 miles (2.4 km) east. Mrs. Rowland guided cave tours from 1886 into the early 1900s (Lambert 1991, 51).

In 1911, Phillip "Doc" Baker bought Cave Ranche from the Rowlands and hired Ernest C. Adams as caretaker. Adams was the first person to obtain a legal title to the 47 acres (19 ha), which had previously been claimed under squatter's rights. About 1920, Clarice T. and Beatrice Rhodes bought the ranch after selling their café in Milford, Utah (Lambert 1991, 74). The Rhodeses took care of the cave for the next ten years, making many improvements (figure 4-3).

National Forest Land

While Lehman Caves was continually being promoted, the land around it was also being noticed. In 1909, the majority of the South Snake Range and part of the North Snake Range was withdrawn from the public domain to become part of the Nevada National Forest. In 1912, the boundaries changed, doubling the size of the Mount Moriah area and adding a large area to the east side of the forest's Snake Division. The boundaries now also included Lehman Caves and the private inholding adjacent to it.

The Snake and Moriah Divisions of the Nevada National Forest were administered by one ranger in Baker until 1957, when they were combined with the Ely District. The Forest Service buildings, now administered by the National Park Service, are still intact on the north edge of Baker and are listed on the National Register of Historic Places.

Establishment and Development of a National Monument

Many thought that Lehman Caves was extraordinary enough to receive special status, and the government was petitioned to make it into a national monument. On January 24, 1922, President Warren G. Harding made a presidential proclamation declaring Lehman Caves National Monument. The Forest Service administered the cave, with Mr. and Mrs. Rhodes as the caretakers. Some important improvements were made in the 1920s. In order to bypass the tight Fat Man's Misery, a narrow tunnel called the Panama Canal was dug next to the cave passage and lined with rocks and broken cave formations. In addition, carbide lanterns replaced the unreliable candles that had been used to that point (Trexler 1966, 25–27).

The rest of the decade was full of memorable events. The cave area was designated as a state recreation ground and game refuge in April 1923. Not to be outdone, White Pine County proclaimed the entire Wheeler Peak area as a county wildlife preserve. Starting the same year, pack trips or day rides to Wheeler Peak were offered, and the first wedding ceremony was held in the "Wedding Chapel" in the cave. In 1924, a bill was introduced into Congress to make Lehman Caves National Park, but it did not pass. At the cave, the Rhodeses developed the Lodge Room into a group meeting space,

Figure 4-4. The National Park Service took over running Lehman Caves from the US Forest Service in 1933. In this 1934 photo, visitors are standing at the Lehman Caves Headquarters with caretaker Otto Neilson.

and community groups came out from Ely to make use of it. Outside the cave, a ballroom was completed in 1925, which the community used frequently for square dancing and other events. A heater for the swim tank was installed, adding to the comfort. The big event of the year was Flag Day, when one thousand people came. In 1928, fifteen new cabins were built to serve overnight guests, and a log lodge became the monument headquarters until 1961 (Trexler 1966, 25–29).

In 1933, the National Park Service (NPS) took over the administration of Lehman Caves from the Forest Service (figure 4-4). Some people grumbled a bit at this, because the Forest Service had worked on a number of improvements and the NPS was a bit slow in showing progress. In addition, the Rhodeses had left, selling the inholding to the county, which later transferred it to the federal government. With the Great Depression putting people out of work, a number of federal work programs were established. The Civil Works Administration (CWA) had fifty-six workers at the national monument from December 1933 to March 1934. The CWA workers repaired the water line, which at that time was getting water from Lehman Creek; improved the cave trail; and cleaned or removed surface buildings. During the summer of 1934, crews from the Transient Relief Camp stationed on Lehman Creek cleaned more of the surface area of the monument, which had accumulated a lot of building materials and trash. In the fall of 1934, a Civilian Conservation Corps (CCC) spur camp was set up at the monument to work on campgrounds and the parking area, to construct a new culinary water line, and to do some work in the caves. This continued through the winter. After a two-year hiatus, the Works Progress Administration entered the monument with a work proposal that promised many things: to construct new cabins, a lodge hall, a comfort station, grounds cleanup, and more. Plans were cut back due to bureaucracy and it is uncertain exactly what got completed (Trexler 1966, 32–38).

The Lehman Caves tour route had a major change in the 1930s. Although the tour route was continually being improved to make it safer and more spacious, the entrance into the cave still required climbing a steep set of stairs. It was decided that an entrance tunnel into the cave would make access safer, and an exploratory shaft was drilled in 1937. It turned out that the entrance tunnel was not as simple as was first thought; a lot of loose rock fell, and a number of Indian bones were found. Once these obstacles were dealt with, the tunnel was drilled from May 1938 to October 1939 (Trexler 1966, 49). It was during this decade that the cave began to receive more scientific scrutiny. In 1936, monument custodian H. Donald Curry wrote the paper "The Geology of Lehman Caves." In the next years, the new monument custodian, T. O. Thatcher, examined the invertebrates of the cave, sending some of them to specialists. One of his finds, a pseudoscorpion, was not specifically identified until 1962, when it was classified as a new species, endemic to the cave. An archaeological survey of the Indian bones began in August 1938, and further work was done in September 1963. Finally, a weather station that is still used today was established outside the headquarters building in September 1937 (Trexler 1966, 54–55).

Another remarkable change in the cave was the installation and completion of the first electrical system in 1941. Some thought that the cave looked much smaller with the electric lights, but others enjoyed seeing some of the recesses and high ceilings. Visitor numbers increased due to a number of roads being paved. The state road from Baker to the national monument boundary was paved in 1947 and from the boundary to the visitor center in 1948. Highway 6/50 was paved from Ely to Baker in 1947. This was a reason to celebrate, and on September 5, 1948, the Ely Chamber of Commerce and Mines celebrated the paved highway with free cave tours, a free barbeque that served over six hundred pounds of beef, and two orchestras that entertained the two thousand attendees. This successful event may have helped spawn the next one a year later, when "Lehman Caves-Beaver County Day" was held at the cave to acquaint the governor of Utah with the need to construct Utah highways to meet paved roads in Nevada, and another two thousand people attended. It must have worked, since Highway 6/50 was paved from Baker to Delta in 1952, and the state highway from Milford in 1955 (Trexler 1966, 43–44, 49, 51, 58).

With more visitors coming, the first official concession business, which consisted of a restaurant and gift shop, opened in 1948. It was difficult to find someone to run the concession, and eventually the superintendent's wife, Mrs. Marcella Wainright, opened the Wheeler Lodge. She operated it until 1951. A new operator could not be found, so the next superintendent's wife, Mrs. Olive Broom, took over in February 1952. Due to the appalling conditions, including having no refrigerator in the lodge and having to boil all the drinking water, she decided one year was enough. No one ran the concession in 1953 or 1954, but then in 1955 Mrs. Blanche Yersin took over for two years, and then Mrs. Thelma Gregory Bullock ran the café for over a decade (Trexler 1966, 45–46).

In 1950, part of the cave trail was paved with blacktop, although much of it was still covered with gravel and sand until 1955 to 1958. In contrast to the "civilizing" of the cave tour route, Tom Sims and John Fielding, who both spent some time working at the national monument, found an unexpected new passage in 1947. They named it the Lost River Passage for its resemblance to a stream with convoluted twists and turns. Just a few years later, in 1952, the Gypsum Annex was found, a stunning white gypsum area of the cave off the Talus Room. With these finds, it was realized that an accurate survey of the cave was needed. In 1958, the Salt Lake Grotto (caving club) completed a survey and map of the cave under the lead of Dale Green. The grotto recommended that the tour route be extended by 900 feet (274 m) to go through the large Talus Room and decorated West Room, and by 1961 this extension was completed, adding to the total tour length by nearly one-third (Trexler 1966, 52–54).

During the 1960s, some major changes occurred in the infrastructure of Lehman Caves National Monument. The National Park

Service instituted what it called Mission 66, a program to have services and buildings upgraded by 1966. In 1962, four residences were constructed, along with a new visitor center, a power plant and utility building, a twenty-five-unit picnic area, and some new roads. The dedication of the new visitor center in June 1963 was a considerable event, with school bands from several towns, extra chairs brought in from Delta, a barbeque prepared by service clubs, and a square dance hoedown. An estimated fifteen hundred people attended (Trexler 1966, 64–65).

Staffing also increased, from three permanent and two seasonal employees to five permanent and eight seasonal employees. The Lehman Caves Natural History Association was established and incorporated in early 1963 to provide educational materials about the cave. In 1965, a portion of the movie *The Wizard of Mars* was shot in the cave (figure 4-5)—although the movie is so terrible that it is not recommended. In that same year, a three-hour Spelunker Tour was offered in passageways above the Gothic Palace. Evening campfire programs were held, and work on an exit tunnel to reduce congestion in the cave during tours was begun and completed a year later. It should also be mentioned that Bell Telephone service reached the national monument in 1965 (Trexler 1966, 40, 60, 62, 64, 109).

Improvements in the 1970s included resurfacing the cave trails with concrete in 1974 to make them safer. Also, a dump station was constructed, and in 1973 the monument created sewage lagoons in the old borrow pits, which were pits where earth was "borrowed" to make roads. To celebrate the country's bicentennial in 1976, the Baker grade school helped plant twenty fruit trees in the islands between the parking lots. And finally, in 1977, the cave was rewired and lighting fixture outlet boxes were replaced with nonmetallic ones (Trexler 1966, 110–12, 116).

The major event of the 1980s was the expansion of Lehman Caves National Monument into Great Basin National Park in 1986. Leading up to this event, many meetings were held and tours of the area conducted. With the expansion from 1 square mile (3 km²) to 120 square miles (320 km²), less attention was focused on the cave and more on the rest of the park. A variety of ideas on how to best manage the park emerged, and a general management plan was written to guide the park for the next twenty years. In 1998, the human remains found below the natural entrance were repatriated back into the cave.

Figure 4-5. Filming of *The Wizard of Mars* in Lehman Caves in 1965.

Since 2000, Lehman Caves has reentered an age of more study. Cave biologists are examining what lives in the cave to better understand how the underground ecosystem functions. Cave lights have been switched from energy-intensive incandescent and halogen lights to more energy-efficient light emitting diodes (LEDs), which use a fraction of the power and emit much less heat. The green moss and algae formerly seen around many of the lights is greatly reduced with this new lighting system. Sections of old cave trail and lighting systems have been removed to restore the cave to a more natural state.

Cave Geology

Why is Lehman Caves where it is? It is situated in a layer of Pole Canyon Limestone, which was made about 550 million years ago when a shallow sea covered the entire area. As the small organisms that lived in it died, they sank to the bottom, eventually making an oozy mass that over time was compacted into rock. It is estimated that this process continued for millions of years. This limestone covered the entire region, but about five million years ago, block faulting brought up the older, underlying Prospect Mountain Quartzite. The softer limestone and other rocks weathered off the tall mountains like Wheeler Peak, leaving just the harder quartzite. Lower on the mountain, patches of the limestone still remain (Orndorff et al. 2001, 217, 223).

It is within this limestone that Lehman Caves developed. The limestone experienced high heat and pressure, turning it into a low-grade marble during the process of metamorphism. Starting about two million years ago and continuing to about ten thousand years ago, the cave formed by the process of dissolution. Water and carbon dioxide mixed as they entered cracks in the ground, forming carbonic acid. This is a weak acid—in fact, it is found in soda pop—but the rock is rather soft and it dissolved away, particle by particle. We can tell that the cave dissolved after the faulting that uplifted the mountains because the rock layers are tilted; but the cave is mostly on the same level, the level where the water table used to be. If the cave were even older, it would be at a tilt just like the surrounding rocks (Orndorff et al. 2001, 230–33).

Eventually the water table dropped, and the dissolution process stopped. Water still seeped into cracks and entered the cave, picking up carbon dioxide as it passed through organic material; but when the carbonic acid reached the air in the cave, the process reversed and carbon dioxide was released into the air. The water, infused with a little bit of the limestone it had dissolved on the way down, deposited that limestone in the form of calcium carbonate.

The way that the calcium carbonate is deposited differentiates the types of speleothems, or cave formations (figure 4-6). One of the most common formations is a soda straw, when the calcium carbonate–laden water drops straight down. The calcium carbonate is deposited on the outside in a ring, and the water drops through the middle, creating over time a rock straw. Sometimes the straw can get plugged, and then the water flows over the outside, creating a stalactite, which resembles an icicle. If the water drops to the floor and still holds calcium carbonate, an upside-down stalactite, called a stalagmite, forms. An easy way to remember the difference between these two similar words is that stalactites hang on "tight" to the ceiling, while stalagmites "might" grow up to the ceiling someday. If a stalactite and a stalagmite grow together, the resulting formation is called a column.

Figure 4-6. The soda straw is spouting water after a period of heavy precipitation. This is a rare event.

Other common formations in the cave are flowstone, when the calcium carbonate forms over a sloping surface and looks like a frozen waterfall, and draperies or curtains, which can have tendrils coming off a bulge or look like cave bacon. Some formations, such as helictites, do not follow gravity. It is thought that these odd formations, which can twist and turn at unusual angles, are formed when hydrostatic pressure pushes the water out of a tiny hole. You may see interesting ripples on the floor, called rimstone dams, formed when the water rises to a certain level and the calcium carbonate makes a rock dam. Other times the calcium carbonate may make a shelf on top of the water. Cave popcorn or coral looks just like its name and decorates several passages in the cave. It is often formed in passages with strong airflow.

Two special formations found in Lehman Caves are bulbous stalactites and cave shields. Bulbous stalactites look like turnips, with a wide, rounded upper section that narrows into a point at the bottom. One possible explanation for these oddly shaped speleothems is that air bubbles form on the soda straw or regular stalactite, causing the calcium carbonate to be deposited in a wider-than-normal circle. Cave shields also have a bit of mystery about them. They consist of two rounded plates with a narrow crack between them, similar to an Oreo cookie. It is possible that water is forced through the crack and then for some reason makes the disk on either side. Most are situated at an angle, with some emerging from the floor, some from the ceiling, and some from the walls. They range in extent from the size of your hand to over 8 feet (2 m) in diameter. Some are solely the shield, while others have formations hanging from them. Lehman Caves contains one of the greatest concentrations of cave shields in the world, with over three hundred.

Lehman Caves is not renowned for its length, which is about 1.5 miles (2.4 km), or the size of the rooms, although one football field could fit into the Talus Room. It is known for being a highly decorated cave. Around each corner there is something new to see. Certainly much more remains to be learned about the cave.

Cave Ecology

While caves are usually celebrated for their fantastic formations and meandering passageways, an important part of the cave is the life that inhabits it. Most of this life is exceedingly small and difficult to see, in addition to being quite rare. Lehman Caves has had more biological studies in it than any of the other forty-plus caves in the park. The first close look at cave biota was by cave custodian T. O. Thatcher and resulted in the discovery of a new species of pseudoscorpion, *Microcreagris grandis* (figure 4-7), although it was not identified until the 1960s by pseudoscorpion specialist Dr. William Muchmore (Muchmore 1962). It is quite common for some preserved specimens to wait in their vials until a suitable specialist is found. The name *pseudoscorpion* refers to a "false" scorpion, and indeed this tiny creature is not a scorpion, since it does not have a stinger on its tail. Pseudoscorpions in Lehman Caves are about 0.5 inch (1.3 cm) wide and long, are dark red, and have little pincers. The females are lighter in color than the males. They move quickly and can use their pincers to grab their prey. Since they have an exoskeleton, they molt as they grow, leaving behind the old shell. They may molt up to a dozen times during their lifetime (Steve Taylor, personal communication, 2006).

The next major examinations of cave life were in the late 1960s and early 1970s, when the Desert Research Institute initiated a series of cave life studies. The institute examined how the lighting system

Figure 4-7. The pseudoscorpion *Microcreagris grandis* was first found in Lehman Caves. It has since been found in several other caves in Great Basin National Park.

was changing the native cave fauna and identified some of the micro-organisms in the cave. Virtually no biological studies were done during the next three decades, until 2006, when the park hired cave biologists to do a biological inventory of the cave and train park staff to continue monitoring (Taylor et al. 2008). Since then, a millipede new to science, *Nevadesmus ophimontis*, has been discovered in Lehman Caves as well as in several other caves in the park (Shear et al. 2009).

The basic ecology of Lehman Caves is based on guano (scat). The nutrients that support cave life come primarily from animals that periodically enter the cave. These visitors deposit guano, food from the outside, eggs, and sometimes their carcasses. One example is a montane vole that found its way into the cave and died. Within a day, it was covered with tiny springtails, invertebrates that look like crawling dandruff. Within about four months, no part of its body was left except a small portion of its tail.

Tiny springtails, flies, and beetles are eaten by spiders and pseudoscorpions. These in turn may be consumed by small rodents that accidentally come into the cave. Much remains to be learned about the life cycles of many of these creatures because they do not usually survive outside the cave environment and thus cannot be studied in a laboratory. In addition, they are small in size and number and are therefore difficult to find. If you happen to see cave life during your cave tour, you can consider yourself extremely lucky.

Bats play an important part in the ecosystem of some caves but are rarely seen because they most frequently move at night. Although Lehman Caves seldom houses bats due to unsuitable microhabitats (they are, for example, too drafty or too warm or cool), several other park caves are important winter or summer (maternity) colonies. Seven species of bats have been identified in the park, with most belonging to the genus *Myotis*. These bats are all insectivores, eating up to one-third of their weight every evening in insects. The best place to see bats is on a summer evening near a light, where they will chase the insects that are circling the light.

Other Caves

Although Lehman Caves is the best-known cave in Snake Valley, many more exist, with over forty in Great Basin National Park. The variety of cave types is impressive. Some are horizontal, while others are vertical and require ropes to enter. Numerous caves are dry and dusty, while a few are muddy and even fill with water at certain times of year. Many have tight passageways that necessitate crawling or even slithering on one's belly, but a small number of caves have large passages where it is difficult to see to the other side of the room. Several caves have extensive cave decorations, while others are barren of speleothems. Caves at lower elevations are rather warm, over 50°F (10°C), while those near the tree line are below freezing and are often filled with ice. The park contains the highest-elevation cave in Nevada, at over 11,000 feet (3,350 m); the deepest, at over 400 feet (120 m) deep; and Lehman Caves is the longest, at 1.5 miles (2.4 km). Some consider the Baker Creek Cave system, at over 2 miles (3.2 km), to be the longest, but this cave system has thus far been connected only hydrologically; no person has been able to squeeze through the holes connecting one part of the system to another.

Biological inventories have recently been completed in some of the caves (Krejca and Taylor 2003; Taylor et al. 2008). Of note are several species new to science that have been found only in or near the park. These include the Great Basin millipede (*Idagona lehmanensis*; Shear 2007), the Shoshone springtail (*Pygmarrhopalites shoshoneiensis*;

66

Zeppelini et al. 2009), and the White Pine amphipod (*Stygobromus albapinus*; Taylor and Holsinger 2011). All three of these have specific habitat requirements. For example, the amphipod is found only in water of certain temperatures. Any changes to the caves or water that helps form them could put these sensitive species in danger.

Most of the caves in Snake Valley are on public land. The three major land management agencies, the BLM, the Forest Service, and the National Park Service, have different policies regarding entry into these caves. Some caves are gated and require a permit for entry. General requirements for obtaining a permit are having between three and six people in a group, including an experienced leader; possessing the proper cave gear, including a helmet, three sources of light, rugged clothing, and vertical gear if it is a vertical cave; and embodying a good cave ethic to leave no trace of the visit. For more information, contact the agencies (appendix A) and ask for the cave specialist.

The Making of a National Park

Although Lehman Caves was the area that most people focused on and visited over the last century, some people wanted to expand the national monument into a national park and include some of the spectacular features nearby. This was easier said than done. It took several decades and many attempts before a national park was created. In the 1920s, Senator Key Pittman supported the establishment of a national park, but after hearing many negative comments from several parties, he decided not to pursue the idea. The next attempt to make a national park came in the 1930s. Congressman James Scrugham asked for a study to determine which sites in Nevada would be good for a potential national park. While several ideas were proposed, nothing came to pass.

The next big effort came in the 1950s. Darwin Lambert was the president of the Ely Chamber of Commerce and he spent many weekends camping in the South Snake Range. He promoted the idea of a national park, and when he was elected a Nevada assemblyman, he took the idea with him to the assembly (Lambert 1991, 79–80, 85, 93). The idea attracted national attention, with Senate and House bills introduced in September 1959, and things looked favorable. The glacier in the Wheeler Peak cirque was "rediscovered," although the Forest Service did not acknowledge it as a true glacier. In fact, it appeared that those who recognized the glacier wanted a national park, while those who did not favored Forest Service administration. The Forest Service furthered its cause by creating the Wheeler Peak Scenic Area on March 13, 1959. This area covered 28,000 acres (11,300 ha) and included not only Wheeler Peak but also the largest known mountain-mahogany tree in Nevada, bristlecone pines, lakes, natural arches, and a wide variety of flora and fauna. The discovery of beryllium under Mount Washington, on the west side of the proposed national park, put a twist in things, but additional bills were submitted to Congress with that area excluded, for a total national park size of 124,500 acres (50,400 ha). The bills did not pass, and the idea faded into the background (Lambert 1991, 96–126).

Sporadic efforts to make a national park continued during the next couple of decades, but it was not until the 1980s that things seemed to speed up. Those who opposed the park due to concerns about potential negative economic impacts from a loss of hunting, mining, and grazing remarked that the actions they had used previously to discourage the park did not seem to make a difference this time. The majority of people in Nevada supported having a national park, and the idea finally came to fruition in 1986, when President Ronald Reagan signed the bill that Congress had passed to form Great Basin National Park, encompassing over 77,000 acres (31,000 ha). Lehman Caves National Monument, which was 1 square mile ($3 \ km^2$), was suddenly a small part of the new 120-square-mile ($320 \ km^2$) national park.

What Else to See

Besides Lehman Caves, there is much to see at Great Basin National Park. If you have a half day, head up the Wheeler Peak Scenic Drive and take a trail or two to visit the historic Osceola Ditch, the beautiful subalpine lakes, ancient bristlecone pines (figure 4-8), or a rock glacier (chapter 4). If you have more time, you can explore the network of trails of varying lengths in the Baker Creek watershed or try to find elk up Strawberry Creek (chapter 5). Other good options are a hike to Lexington Arch or a ramble up Snake Creek Road (chapter 6). Over 50 miles (80 km) of trails are available for hiking (table 4-1). Other activities include fishing, bird-watching, mountain biking on developed roads, pack trips, attending campfire programs with park rangers, stargazing, and relaxing.

Figure 4-8. The Bristlecone Trail is a favorite destination in summer and fall.

Table 4-1. Hiking trails in Great Basin National Park

Name (Chapter trail description found in)	Distance (miles) (one way)	Elevation change (feet)	Notes
Mountain View Nature Trail (4)	0.3 (round trip)	6,825-6,905	A guide is available from the Lehman Caves Visitor Center.
Grey Cliffs-Baker Creek Campground Trail (6)	0.5	7,200–7,500	Gradual elevation change. Good for kids.
Lehman Campground Trail (5)	1	7,350–7,700	Connects Upper and Lower Lehman Campgrounds.
Strawberry Loop (6)	1 (round trip)	7,640–8,160	Trailhead at end of Strawberry Creek road.
Bristlecone / Glacier Trail (5)	1.4 / 2.3	9,800–10,400 / 10,900	The trail to the rock glacier extends beyond the bristlecone trail.
Dead Lake (7)	1.6	8,240–9,560	Trail not marked; begins on old road.
Lexington Arch (7)	1.7	7,440–8,160	Trail leads to six-story limestone arch. Dogs on leash are permitted.
Pole Canyon Trail (6)	2	7,000-7,600	Begins at Pole Canyon Picnic Area. Possible to loop to Timber Creek trail.
Snake to North Fork Big Wash (7)	2.2	8,240–8,900	Trail infrequently used; goes up and over pass.
Alpine Lakes Loop Trail (5)	2.7 (round trip)	9,800–10,400	Beautiful views.
South Fork Baker/ Baker Creek Loop (6)	3.1 (round trip)	8,000–8,954	Good for families. The connecting trail begins in a scenic meadow.
Johnson Lake from Snake Creek (7)	3.2	8,320–10,740	Very steep trail.
Lehman Creek Trail (5)	3.4	7,750–9,800	Connects Upper Lehman and Wheeler Peak Campgrounds.
Highland Ridge	4	8,600–11,597	This is a route, not a trail, which means you absolutely need a good map. The route starts north of Lincoln Peak and goes to Decathon Canyon.
Wheeler Peak Trail (5)	4.1	10,160–13,063	Start early to avoid afternoon thunderstorms.
South Fork Big Wash (7)	4.2	6,760-8,030	Remote trail; may be longer hike due to road washouts

Name (Chapter trail description found in)	Distance (miles) (one way)	Elevation change (feet)	Notes
Osceola Ditch Trail (5)	4.5	8,565–8,120	Follows the old Osceola Ditch to Strawberry Creek. Mostly level trail.
Baker Lake (6)	6	8,000–10,620	Elevation gained gradually.
Timber/Pole Canyon Loop	7 (round trip)	7,000–8,460	This is also a good winter trail for snow-shoeing or cross-country skiing.
South Fork/Timber Loop (6)	7 (round trip)	8,000–9,680	Timber Creek trail is very steep.
Baker Lake/Johnson Lake Loop (6)	13.1 (round trip)	8,000–11,290	Great backpacking option.

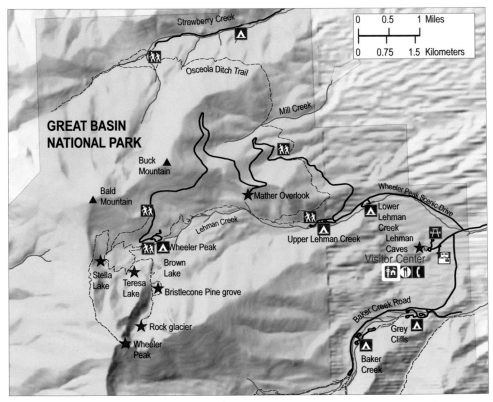

Figure 5-1. Map of Wheeler Peak Scenic Drive and the northern part of
Great Basin National Park.

WHEELER PEAK SCENIC DRIVE

After Lehman Caves, the most popular destination in Great Basin National Park is Wheeler Peak Scenic Drive (figure 5-1). This road ascends about 3,500 feet (1,100 m) from near the park boundary to the subalpine area below Wheeler Peak. Along the way are excellent hiking trails and campgrounds. During the winter, the lower section of the road is open to at least Upper Lehman Campground, and sometimes farther depending on snow conditions. Beyond that, the road is open for snowshoeing and cross-country skiing for those with backcountry equipment and expertise. The Natural Resources Conservation Service installed a SNOTEL site in 2010 at the end of Wheeler Peak Scenic Drive that records temperature and precipitation. Hourly data is available online, and the site is most easily found by searching the Internet for "Wheeler Peak Snotel."

Traveling this 12-mile (19 km) long road is a lesson in life zones, the equivalent of driving over 2500 miles (4000 km) to the Yukon. You begin with sagebrush stands near the park boundary and then traverse five other ecosystems as you gain elevation: pinyon pine/ juniper, mountain-mahogany, aspen, mixed conifer, and subalpine. The transitions between some of these ecosystems along the scenic drive can be abrupt, but also confusing, because of large differences between north- and south-facing slopes. One example is near Mather

Overlook, where mountain-mahogany is dominant on the south-facing slope, while mixed conifers (white fir and Douglas-fir) are dominant on the cooler, moister, north-facing slope.

During this drive you will have the opportunity to marvel at the towering mountains. They are made primarily of Prospect Mountain Quartzite, a metamorphic rock common in the northern part of the South Snake Range. This hard rock keeps more water at the surface, and thus most of the perennial streams within the park are found here.

Lehman Campgrounds

Wheeler Peak Scenic Drive begins just inside the park boundary, at a marked turnoff from the main road. The first 3 miles (5 km) are relatively straight but steep and lead to two campgrounds, Upper and Lower Lehman. About 150 years ago, nearly everything at this elevation was sagebrush steppe, but due to a warmer climate and fire suppression, juniper trees and, later, pinyon pines moved in and now dominate most of the landscape. Along this stretch, you will be able to locate Lehman Creek by noticing the stately ponderosa pines that grace its banks. This is one of the lowest elevations in the park where you can find ponderosa pines, which are scarce in the park due to limited habitat and heavy logging around the turn of the century.

Lower Lehman Campground is about 2 miles (3 km) up the road and is the only campground in the park open year-round. It is small, with only eleven sites, but several of these are pull-throughs, making it popular with motor homes.

Another mile (1.6 km) up the road is Upper Lehman Campground and a trailhead. The campground is very appealing, with over twenty large campsites near the creek. This campground is the oldest in the park, established in the 1920s and called the Governor's Camp. In the 1930s, a Transient Relief Camp was established by the state of Nevada, and workers helped improve and enlarge camping facilities as well as start developing a road up to Stella Lake (Unrau 1990, 275–76).

Before the creation of the national park, the upper campground served as the meeting place for the annual Snake Valley Reunion over Labor Day weekend. This event was inaugurated in 1960 to give former residents an excuse to come back and visit. A cow was roasted in a large pit surrounded by coals, and many locals swear that there was nothing to compare to that taste. A dance was held in Baker at night, with a picnic the following day (Waite 1974, 572). Today the reunion, called Snake Valley Days, is still held, with the barbecue in the town of Baker and a dance at the Border Inn. Old-timers and new visitors alike are invited.

At the west end of the campground is the trailhead for a 3.4-mile (5.5 km) trail that connects to Wheeler Peak Campground. The steep, scenic trail passes through a variety of habitats.. The campground is a favorite place of mule deer, and some can become quite tame by the end of summer. Mule deer move up and down the mountains during the year in response to the amount of snow. As more feed is uncovered, the deer move higher in elevation, although it is possible to see some deer near agricultural fields in the valley bottoms year-round.

The Nevada Conservation Corps constructed a 1-mile (1.6 km) trail between Upper and Lower Lehman Campgrounds in 2007. It is a pleasant hike in the woods near the creek.

Ascending Higher

Upper Lehman Campground is at about 7,700 feet (2,350 m), and the road beyond ascends to 10,000 feet (3,050 m) in 9 miles (14.5 km). The road is narrow and curving, so vehicles over 24 feet (7 m) in length are not recommended past Upper Lehman Campground. Completed by the Forest Service in 1966, Wheeler Peak Scenic Drive was constructed partly as a protest to the proposed Great Basin National Park, which in its plan had Strawberry Creek as the grand entrance.

During the summer, the narrow paved road is accessible to vehicles and bicycles, and in winter to skiing and snowshoeing. The scenic drive makes a series of turns as it winds its way up the mountain. The next signed turnoff above Upper Lehman Campground is the Osceola Ditch trailhead. A sign next to the turnoff gives a brief overview of the Osceola Ditch, which was built from Lehman Creek around the mountain to the mining town of Osceola (chapter 18) in 1889–90 to provide water for gold mining. This 18-mile (29 km) ditch was the second such ditch for these purposes; the first was constructed along the west side of the Snake Range but did not carry enough water to meet mining needs. Alas, the east-side water diversion also proved to have its problems. Leaky flumes, drought years, and decreasing gold veins combined to put the ditch out of commission by 1899. Nevertheless, the ditch remains in some areas, and if you follow the trail about 0.5 miles (1 km), you will reach the ditch itself. It has been cleared to the west, and following it 4.5 miles (7.2 km) will lead you to Strawberry Creek. This is the most level trail in the park, although it is a bit rocky at the beginning. Much of the ditch has been obscured by an old abandoned road, which makes walking quite a bit easier.

There are many ponderosa pines near the Osceola Ditch turn-off, and you may also notice other vegetation that differs from the lower-elevation pinyon/juniper habitat. East-facing slopes are often covered with dense thickets of mountain-mahogany. Occasional ponderosa pines are found on north-facing slopes, along with the more abundant white fir. White fir is common; it is one of the tree species in the park that is expanding because it is able to tolerate a variety of habitats and soil conditions. As you ascend, Douglas-fir is mixed in with the white fir. Not a true fir, the Douglas-fir produces small cones with appendages that look like mouse tails sticking out from between the scales.

The mixed conifer habitat may be the first place where you notice that some of the trees are dead. This is largely due to native bark beetles. The bark beetles are spreading rapidly throughout many forests in western North America, attacking trees that are stressed and therefore more prone to infestation. The trees are often stressed as a result of drought and unhealthy forest conditions, such as overcrowding due to lack of wildfires. One of the most common beetles in Great Basin National Park is the white fir engraver beetle, which attacks white fir trees, first killing the crowns and then working down the entire tree. Mountain pine beetles attack limber pine, Great Basin bristlecone pine, and ponderosa pine. Spruce beetles attack Engelmann spruce, while turpentine beetles and pinyon ips attack pinyon pine. What is remarkable is how fast the beetles spread. In 2001, only isolated trees were noted to have bark beetles. By 2009, large patches of the park had been infested. Because bark beetles are native, and because such large areas have been affected, natural processes are allowed to take place in most of the park. However, in areas close to trails and campgrounds and in other high-use visitor areas where safety is an issue, some hazardous trees are removed, and pheromone pouches are used to help protect healthy trees. More information about forest health is available at the visitor centers.

The next opportunity to stop along the scenic drive is a turnout with good views of the North Snake Range and Mount Moriah. The large turnout is on a curve and it is safer to stop here on the way up. Snake Valley spreads out below you, with views of canyons, foothills, and the valley floor dotted by green fields marking ranches.

Above 9,000 feet (2,740 m) is a signed road leading to the south that goes to Mather Overlook. This viewpoint is a good spot to see Jeff Davis Peak and Wheeler Peak. Mather Overlook is named for Stephen T. Mather, who helped convince the Department of the Interior to create the National Park Service in 1916 and then served as its first director, from 1917 to 1929.

A few switchbacks later, you reach the marked Wheeler Peak Overlook. From here you have some of the best views of the remnant glacier as it creeps down the dramatic cirque between the steep walls of Jeff Davis and Wheeler Peaks. Occasionally people try to climb these precipices from the cirque, but the loose Prospect Mountain Quartzite falls daily onto the rock glacier below. Attempting such a climb is not recommended.

Wheeler Peak Trail

About 1 mile (1.6 km) down the road is the parking lot for the Wheeler Peak trailhead. It is 4.2 miles (6.8 km) to the summit of Wheeler Peak, with an elevation gain of nearly 3,000 feet (900 m). It generally takes three to five hours to summit and two to three hours to return. Be especially careful climbing during monsoon season, usually July and August, when afternoon storms are common and little shelter exists above tree line. Many people start their hikes at sunrise to avoid the afternoon bad weather, but sometimes bad weather occurs in the morning, too, so use common sense to stay safe.

The hike can be started at the Wheeler Peak trailhead or at the Stella Lake trailhead, located close to the campground. The Wheeler Peak trailhead is 0.2 miles (0.4 km) longer but requires slightly less elevation gain. Nevertheless, you are starting at nearly 2 miles (3.2 km) above sea level. If you develop a headache while hiking, stop, drink some water, and eat some food. If you do not feel better, you might be experiencing altitude sickness, which can be extremely dangerous. Descend immediately if you do not feel well, because you will not feel any better if you continue, and you could be putting your life in danger.

The trail is fairly gradual as you hike up and above the tree line onto a long ridge, which is the halfway point. At this elevation, though, you may have to stop frequently to catch your breath. The views are spectacular, looking west toward Spring Valley and the Schell Creek Range and to the east along the Lehman Creek drainage and into Snake Valley. Bald Mountain is to the north and can be reached by following the ridge. The second half of the hike is much steeper and requires a slower pace. The trail nearly disappears as you climb from rock to rock up the steep northwest ridge. Patches of snow often linger into July. The views from the summit are dramatic; on a clear day you can see over 100 miles (160 km) to the Wasatch Front in Utah and several mountain ranges to the west in Nevada. Immediately to the south is the cirque of the North Fork of Baker Creek, with Baker Peak looming as the first peak to the south and a ridge extending south toward Pyramid Peak and Mount Washington (figure 5-2). To the north, three little lakes appear as puddles 3,000 feet (900 m) below you. In the fall, yellow and red aspen leaves make a resplendent scene.

On the summit ridge of Wheeler Peak are several round stone shelters. One of these was made as far back as 1881, when H. J. Davis of the US Coast and Geodetic Survey went on a reconnaissance mission to determine how suitable the summit was for the geodetic survey. This survey would help determine the size and shape of the earth and was planned along the thirty-ninth parallel. During his five-month investigation, from August to December, Dr. Davis stayed in the round rock structure, topped with a canvas roof (Waite 1974, 576). The site was determined to be viable, and in 1882, William Eimbeck was directed to lead the geodetic survey in Nevada. He and his sizable crew arrived at the Lehman Ranch in late September. Although the scientific part of the study could be accomplished by three officers and a recorder, they also needed packers, drivers, and cooks, so the whole party often consisted of twelve or thirteen people. Typically, about 10,000 pounds (4500 kg) of gear and provisions had to be transported to the upper camp, which usually took two weeks' labor. Before they could even use pack mules to carry loads, they had to establish a trail to the top of the range. They also created two camps along the way. Upon reaching the summit, their goal was to determine the horizontal directions to five other peaks. This was done using a theodolite, a 200-pound (90 kg), high-precision transit, to run a series of triangulations during the study. In addition to the triangulations, it was also possible to communicate from each peak with a heliograph station using a mirror to flash messages during daylight hours. The so-called heliogram could be transmitted from the Sierra Nevada to the southern Rocky

Figure 5-2. Looking south from Wheeler Peak. Note the rock glacier in the North Fork of Baker Creek watershed.

Mountains in a short time. The working conditions were not always favorable. Eimbeck noted one storm that left snowdrifts 10–12 feet (3–4 m) deep and temperatures dipping to -20°F (-29°C). The deep snow actually served as insulation and kept him and his crew from freezing to death. In order to continue their work, they had to cut trenches in the snow to be able to use their instruments (Unrau 1990, 61–72). Despite these adverse conditions, a crew returned in 1883 for further work, arriving "after a tedious and toilsome journey through two hundred miles of a desolate country" (USC&GS 1885). They had established their camp at the summit by July 26, but bad weather kept them from completing the necessary three days' worth of observations. Mr. Eimbeck remarked that

> the trials of the ten days' life of the party among the clouds were more severe and dangerous than had been experienced for several years. The violence of the electric discharges, the thunder-claps, and the energy of the piping sound of the escaping electricity was not infrequently so alarming that the party had

> to seek safety behind and under ledges of rock some distance below the summit of the peak, which was often struck by lightning. The tent occupied by the men was also struck, but fortunately at a time when no one was in it. (USC&GS 1885, 78–79)

When they were unable to work on the mountain, they did some state boundary surveys, and in 1883 Eimbeck provided the first detailed description of the "glacieret" below Wheeler Peak. By 1895, the US Coast and Geodetic Survey had completed a 2,500-mile (4,000 km) arc of triangulation along the thirty-ninth parallel (Unrau 1990, 69).

The winds on Wheeler Peak can be significant. It is fairly common for gusts to blow more than 30 mph (48 kmph), and in the winter, streams of snow are seen blowing off the mountaintop. High winds are blamed for a helicopter crash on Wheeler Peak in 1959. A Forest Service helicopter was transporting personnel to make an aerial inspection of the Lehman Creek area to determine where to put the new road. As the helicopter started to land on the peak, it was caught in a sudden downdraft that slammed it against the boulders and tipped it on its side. Fortunately, the three crewmen suffered only minor injuries and were able to hike 9 miles (14.5 km) to Lehman Creek Campground. The helicopter was later disassembled and packed out on mules and horses (Waite 1974, 705–7).

This peak had several names before Wheeler Peak. The Indians called the summit Pe-up, meaning "big mountain." In 1854, Colonel Steptoe called it Jefferson Davis Peak in honor of the US secretary of war at that time. The next year it was renamed Williams Peak for the first white man to summit it, Ezra Williams of the Mormon White Mountain Mission. The earlier name was more favored and shortened to Jeff Davis Peak. In 1859, Captain James H. Simpson crossed Sacramento Pass and had an outstanding view of the mountain. Due to its connected form, he named it Union Peak. In 1869, Lieutenant Wheeler and his party climbed the peak from the west, and it was eventually christened for him. The name Jeff Davis was applied to the slightly lower peak to the east (Waite 1974, 542–44).

Subalpine Trails

Continuing on Wheeler Peak Scenic Drive past the Wheeler Peak trailhead, you will descend about 200 feet (60 m) and arrive at the entrance to Wheeler Peak Campground (figure 5-3) and a parking

Figure 5-3. Wheeler Peak campground in the fall.

lot for the Alpine Lakes, Nature, and Bristlecone Trails. All three are worth your time.

Alpine Lakes Loop Trail

The Alpine Lakes Trail is a 2.7-mile (4.3 km) loop that visits Stella and Teresa Lakes, with an elevation change of 600 feet (180 m; figure 5-4). Both the lakes are rather shallow, about 12 feet (4 m) deep when the water is high and about 5 feet (2 m) deep by the end of the summer when much of the water has evaporated. Although the lakes freeze solid in the winter, fish were stocked in them for several years (Waite 1974, 437). A dam on the northeast side of Stella

Figure 5-4. Teresa Lake is located in a small
cirque, a reminder of when several glaciers
emanated from the higher peaks in Snake Valley.

Lake was constructed to make the lake deeper so that it would store
more water to help keep Lehman Creek flowing down the Osceola
Ditch and also to provide better fish habitat. It doesn't appear that
the dam helped much because its base is often above the water level.
Researchers from Ohio State University have recently been taking
sediment core samples from Stella Lake and installing temperature
data loggers both in and out of the lakes to learn more about current and past climate history. From the sediment cores, they study

tiny flies called midges. Based on what species they find, they can infer what the climatic conditions were at different times. So far they have been able to analyze a seven-thousand-year-old sample and have found significant climate cycle changes, including the current warming trend (Reinemann et al. 2009). The elevation gain on this trail is rather minimal, so it is a good one to take for beautiful views and to help get acclimated. Allow two hours for a leisurely walk.

Nature Trail

Beginning at the same trailhead is a 0.3-mile (0.5 km) nature trail that is handicapped accessible. This is also an excellent trail for children or those who want to take a short stroll to explore the Engelmann spruce and limber pine forest. Squirrels abound, including golden-mantled ground squirrels, which are found only at high elevations. You may notice that quite a few trees have lightning strike scars, results of the numerous storms at this elevation. In addition, the forest floor is quite open, an outcome of a short growing season due to abundant snow and plenty of shade from the trees overhead.

Bristlecone/Glacier Trail

The Bristlecone Trail gains 600 feet (180 m) of elevation in 1.4 miles (2.3 km; one-way) to reach ancient Great Basin bristlecone pines, some over three thousand years old (figure 5-5). During the early summer, part of the trail is often covered in snow. Ranger-led hikes may take place in July and August; check at one of the visitor centers for details. The bristlecones are fascinating, so do not make this a rushed trip. Take your time exploring the grove, examining how some of the trees are barely alive. This is one of their survival strategies, because a smaller live section requires less water, nutrients, and food. Needles can function on the tree for forty years, but the trees form new phloem tissue annually to transport sugar and hormones. Bristlecones can grow excruciatingly slowly. Some forty-year-old seedlings are less than an inch (2.5 cm) tall, and Great Basin bristlecones in the Wheeler Peak area in the South Snake Range are estimated to grow at the rate of one inch (2.5 cm) in diameter per century. Bristlecones can grow quickly at lower elevations in good conditions. These faster-growing trees are also more susceptible to challenges such as root rot decay, pine beetle infestations, white pine blister rust, soil erosion, and localized fire (Howard 2004).

The Wheeler Peak grove is on quartzite, which is a bit unusual

Photo courtesy Alana Dimmick
Figure 5-5. A bristlecone pine tree reaches towards the sky.

since most groves are found on limestone. It is hard to say how long the Great Basin bristlecones have been growing in this particular spot, because it is a glacial moraine, and about ten thousand years ago there was probably ice covering this same spot.

The oldest living Great Basin bristlecone, named Prometheus by a group of naturalists in about 1960, was found in this grove. Because bristlecones live for such a long time, scientists have used them to get clues about past climates. To do this, they generally screw a special instrument, an increment borer, into the tree to remove a 1-inch (2.5 cm) or smaller cross section. In this way, the age of the tree can be determined without cutting it down to count the rings. Large spaces between rings indicate good growing years. Dendrochronologists can date further back than the age of the oldest trees by dating pieces of dead bristlecone pines. In the 1950s, Dr. Edward Schulman was leading the search for the oldest living tree. In 1957, he dated 4,700-year-old Methuselah in the White Mountains of California. In 1964, a graduate student named Donald Currey was searching the Wheeler Peak bristlecone grove for an older tree. Several stories exist for what happened next. One is that he used his increment borer to core a tree he called WPN-114, the 114th tree in his study, and his borer got stuck. He was not able to remove it and requested and received permission from the Forest Service to cut down the tree. After cutting it, over 4,900 annual rings were counted, making it the oldest—but now dead—bristlecone in the world (Waite 1974).

It is possible that older bristlecone trees exist but have not been dated. The Wheeler Peak grove is just one of several in the park, but it is the easiest one to access. Bristlecone groves are also located in the North Snake Range, the Deep Creek Range, and the Mountain Home Range.

Rock Glacier

The fascinating sights do not stop at the bristlecone grove. If you would like to see a rock glacier (figure 5-6) along with some snow and ice, continue farther south about a mile (1.6 km) on the trail (follow the sign). A true glacier is a mass of ice moving slowly over land, formed by snow in an area where snow accumulation is greater than melting or sublimation. Although some glaciologists have set a minimum size for a glacier, the latest peer-reviewed article about the Wheeler Peak glacial ice states that "the exposed ice at the base of the cirque headwall is perennial and deforms under its own weight, and hence can be considered to be a glacier, but it is rapidly disappearing as a result of a strongly negative mass balance" (Osborn and Bevis 2001). This ice can sometimes be seen in the autumn at the extreme back of the rock glacier, with one large crevasse about 50 feet (15 m) up the wall. Fortunately, the rock glacier is much easier to see, even from a distance, with its rounded front and hummocky surface. An insulating rock layer covers the glacial ice, slowing its melt. The rock continually falls from the ragged walls above, so walking around parts of the glacier can be

Figure 5-6. The Wheeler cirque rock glacier extends from the north cliff face nearly to the bristlecone pine grove.

treacherous. Use common sense and caution.

Snow is generally in the cirque year-round, and during the spring and summer you may notice that some of it is pink. This is due to snow algae, *Chlamydomonas nivalis*, sometimes called watermelon or strawberry algae. These unicellular organisms are members of the diverse group of green algae and contain a bright red carotenoid pigment in addition to chlorophyll. They thrive in the cold, and *nivalis* is Latin for snow. As the sunlight increases in May and June, an algal bloom can turn most of a snowbank pink. As with yellow snow, it is not wise to eat pink snow, as it may cause intestinal problems. Many other species of snow algae exist, but this pink variation is one of the most common. During the winter, it is likely that the algae lie dormant, and then in the spring, meltwater and nutrients stimulate germination so that smaller swimming cells are released by the resting cells and swim their way to the surface. The snow algae use detrital matter from rocks and windblown fragments to sustain themselves. In turn, they form the basis of a high-elevation food chain. Tiny herbivores like snow worms and snow fleas eat the snow algae. They are in turn eaten by minuscule carnivores like insects and mites, who are then consumed by birds like rosy-finches, rock wrens, and juncos (Armstrong 2007).

In 2003, a visiting geologist found that this rock glacier is not the only one present in the park. There is also one (or a remnant of one) near Stella Lake and another in the North Fork of Baker Creek, visible from the top of Wheeler Peak (John Van Hoesen, personal communication, 2004). Further studies are needed to determine the status of these rock glaciers.

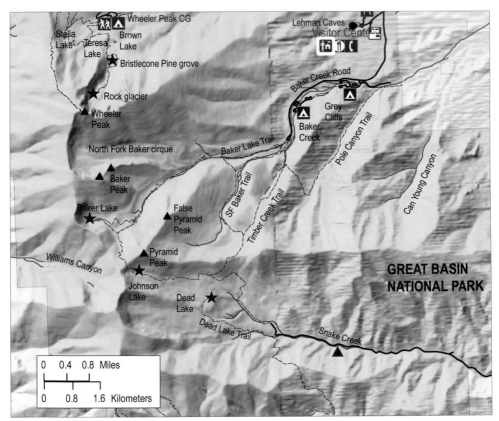

Figure 6-1. Map of South Snake Range—central part. See page 72 for map of Strawberry Creek.

NORTHERN AREA
BAKER AND STRAWBERRY CREEKS

The northern part of the South Snake Range includes Baker Creek north to Mill, Strawberry, and Weaver Creeks and the Sacramento Pass area (figure 6-1). This chapter focuses on the Baker and Strawberry Creek areas. These are both easily accessible during the warmer months and have many options for visitors. They also are good places for backcountry skiing or snowshoeing.

Baker Creek Road

After Lehman Caves and the sights along Wheeler Peak Scenic Drive, the next-most-visited area in the park is the Baker Creek watershed, with its excellent hiking trails, less-crowded campgrounds, picnic area, and interesting sights, including pictographs. The Baker Creek Road begins a quarter of a mile inside the park. At about 1.5 miles (2.4 km), a sign marks the Grey Cliffs turnoff. These noteworthy limestone cliffs house the longest cave system (hydrologically connected) in Nevada, parts of which may be accessible to experienced cavers with cave permits from the park. Baker Creek runs near the base of some of these cliffs, cutting a canyon in a section called the Narrows. Before the creek cut the canyon, the stream flowed into caves and traveled underground. Over time, the upper galleries of the caves collapsed and allowed the creek to flow aboveground (Lange 1958). Cave passages extend underneath the creek in places, and some of the caves in this area flood during spring runoff.

It is in these narrows that a large number of pictographs grace the walls. If you decide to take a look at the pictographs, do so with respect. They are fading due to sunlight and weathering, although new photographic techniques are making it possible to capture the older images in amazing detail. These pictographs were done with red pigment, possibly extracted from hematite, which is a dull rust color. The pigment was mixed with a binder like eggs or plant resins, and also with a medium such as water or animal oils. The pictographs show a variety of characters, including kachinas, or humanlike figures. It is believed that the Fremont Culture made these pictographs sometime between AD 1000 and 1300. They had a hunting camp nearby (Wells et al. 1993).

Pictographs are considered a form of rock art. Another form, called petroglyphs, was made by scratching the rock with an object to leave an etching. Petroglyph and pictograph sites are located throughout the area, but due to a few careless people who destroy them, archaeologists keep location information on a need-to-know basis. If you happen to find any during your travels, observe and enjoy them, but be careful not to touch them since oil on your fingers can hasten their demise.

Visitor amenities in the vicinity include Grey Cliffs Group Campground (advance reservations required) and Pole Canyon Picnic Area, about 0.5 miles (0.8 km) to the east. The picnic area is also the trailhead for Pole Canyon, a long canyon that you usually have to yourself for a scenic hike. The 3-mile (5 km) primitive trail begins with a footbridge over Baker Creek. The streamflow in Baker Creek is at its lowest in February, with an average discharge of 1.3 cubic feet per second (cfs; 0.4 m^3/s), and at its highest in June, with an average of 39 cfs (1.1 m^3/s), but it can peak for a few days during spring runoff in May or June at 150 cfs (4.2 m^3/s) or even more (USGS data). This huge fluctuation is common in many Great Basin streams. Baker Creek is the largest stream in the park and in Snake Valley. Continuing across the bridge, the trail follows an old road up the narrow canyon. Often the lower part of Pole Canyon Creek is dry due to the underlying porous limestone rocks. A cave passage goes under Pole Canyon. The limestone canyon walls near the beginning of the Pole Canyon Trail are pocked with small openings, although none have been found to go far. Eventually you reach an area where water flows perennially, and it is a pleasant walk through a narrow riparian zone. The trail crosses Pole Canyon Creek twice and then ascends into a meadow with beautiful Basin wildrye (*Leymus cinereus*), a grass that can grow to several feet high. This sagebrush-grassland meadow gives way to patches of aspen trees interspersed with white fir. The surrounding hillsides have been hit hard by the white fir engraver beetle in recent years. A trail from Timber Creek intersects at about mile two (km three) and is described later in this chapter. The rest of the Pole Canyon Trail continues farther up the canyon, eventually petering out. There is no final destination in this canyon, so simply turn around whenever you have had your fill of the beautiful scenery and solitude. This lower-elevation trail is a great choice in spring or fall, when higher-elevation trails are still snow covered. It is also a good cross-country ski option in winter. Summer hikes can be quite hot.

It is possible to drive east beyond Pole Canyon Picnic Area. The road eventually leads into Baker after a stream crossing and four-wheel drive sections made even rougher by the 2005 floods. This was at one time one of the main roads from Baker to the caves. There are also many roads that branch off this one into Can Young Canyon and Kious and Young Basins, so take a good map if you go. Some fun mountain bike routes exist on the old, overgrown two-tracks that wind their way up and down among the granite intrusions and sagebrush- and pinyon-covered hills.

Continuing west on the Baker Creek Road past Grey Cliffs, you have excellent views of Jeff Davis Peak, which blocks the view of taller Wheeler Peak from this vantage point. The pinyon pines along this road are a favorite place for many to gather pine nuts in the fall.

Yellow-bellied marmots (*Marmota flaviventris*) frequent Baker Creek Road below and near Baker Creek Campground, and marmot-crossing signs remind you to watch your speed (figure 6-2). Nearly every year a marmot is hit and killed by a vehicle, and with a small population, every marmot counts. Marmots are found in open habitats, and the Baker Creek population considers the road to be an open habitat and the road base an excellent place to make their burrows. Marmots may hibernate longer than any other animal. They generally emerge from their burrows in late April and browse the emerging spring vegetation until about mid-July. Then they climb back into their burrows, and except for a few that might come out for a week or two in September, hibernate until the following April

Photo courtesy Jenny Hamilton

Figure 6-2. Yellow-bellied marmots are often only seen from April to early July, as they spend most of the rest of the year hibernating.

(Ballenger 2002). Marmots are scarce in Snake Valley. Several other populations besides the one in Baker Creek exist, but all are small.

Baker Creek Trails

Baker Creek Campground is often a good place for quiet camping, with over thirty campsites at about 7,500 feet (2,290 m) elevation. Some of the sites are next to Baker Creek, which flows through the campground. At the eastern end of the campground is a 0.5-mile (0.8 km) trail that connects to loop C of Grey Cliffs Campground. This is a fun shorter hike in summer. In the winter, it is possible to do a 3-mile (5 km) cross-country ski loop from the road closure up through Grey Cliffs, along the trail, through Baker Creek Campground, and then back via the snow-covered road to your parked vehicle.

The end of Baker Creek Road is the trailhead for Baker Lake, 6 miles (9 km) each way, and four loops, each of different lengths. The South Fork-Baker Creek loop is 3.1 miles (5 km) and takes about two hours; the South Fork-Timber Creek loop is 7 miles (11 km) and takes about four to five hours; the Baker-Johnson Lake loop is 13 miles (21 km) and takes about ten hours with a day pack or makes a good backpacking route; and the Timber Creek-Pole Canyon loop is about 7 miles (11 km) and takes four to five hours.

South Fork-Baker Creek Loop

The South Fork-Baker Creek loop gains and loses 870 feet (270 m) of elevation over 3.1 miles (5 km). This is the shortest of the loop trails. Begin at the trailhead for South Fork Baker Creek. The trail crosses a couple of meadows where deer are frequently seen, passes some currant and raspberry bushes, then crosses the South Fork of Baker Creek and ascends steeply. When the trail starts leveling off again, you emerge into a large, picturesque meadow(figure 6-3). Bonneville cutthroat trout have been reintroduced into the stream here and farther above. You will reach a junction, where the trail then heads into the trees, across a ridge, across the main stream of Baker Creek, and back to the parking area.

South Fork-Timber Creek Loop

If you would like a longer hike, try the South Fork-Timber Creek loop, which is about 7 miles (11.3 km) long and gains roughly 1,200 feet (370 m). Begin as above, but at the meadow junction, continue up the South Fork Baker Creek Trail through the coniferous forest for another 2 miles (3.2 km), until you reach another big meadow. Over halfway through the meadow, you will reach a trail junction; head east toward Timber Creek. The Timber Creek Trail is not maintained, so it may have additional trees across it. It is extremely steep in places, although the Nevada Conservation Corps recently made improvements.

Baker Lake-Johnson Lake Loop

The longest loop, to Baker and Johnson Lakes, is 13.1 miles (21.1 km) round-trip, with an elevation gain of 3,290 feet (1,000 m). It can be done as a long day hike or a backpacking trip. Begin at the Baker Creek trailhead (the one on the right), and continue 6 miles (9.7 km) up the trail to get to Baker Lake. It takes about three to four hours with a medium-weight pack. The trail has many switchbacks, so the elevation gain is gradual, and the upper sections often have snow patches into late June.

Photo courtesy National Park Service

Figure 6-3. The large meadow along South Fork Baker Creek contains a trail junction. A crew is looking for fish in the small stream using electrofishing equipment.

Baker Lake is hidden back in a cirque. It is the only subalpine lake in the park to contain fish, introduced Lahontan cutthroat trout (*Oncorhynchus clarki henshawi*) and brook trout (figure 6-4). The latter are native to most of the rest of Nevada, but not to this area, where the Bonneville cutthroat trout is the native subspecies. Baker Lake is one lake during the early summer, but by late summer enough water has evaporated that it forms three lobes. The two main parts of the lake are deep enough for the trout to overwinter. Researchers from Ohio State University are doing studies on this lake to learn about the climate history. There is good camping on the north side of the lake at the obvious campsite. At this high elevation, vegetation grows slowly, so it is imperative to use leave-no-trace methods to minimize impact. Also, campfires are not allowed in Great Basin National Park above 10,000 feet (3,050 m), so if you want to cook, be sure to bring a stove.

Photo by Keith Trexler, Courtesy of Great Basin National Park
Figure 6-4. Planting fish via airplane at Baker Lake, July 1963.
Fish were no longer stocked in streams and lakes once Great
Basin National Park was established in 1986, but most fish
populations continued to reproduce well. Lahontan cutthroat
trout and brook trout are found in Baker Lake.

From here, you can retrace your steps 6 miles (10 km) back to the
same trailhead. Or you can add 1 mile (1.6 km) and an additional
600 feet (180 m) of elevation gain and go back via Johnson Lake. The
trail to the ridge between the lakes can be very faint but is usually dis-
cernible. The views are outstanding, even if the air seems thin. Look
for the rock cairn that marks where the trail goes over the edge to
Johnson Lake on the other side. This is an extremely steep section,

but the Nevada Conservation Corps improved it in 2008. Johnson Lake is covered in more detail in the next chapter. Head down the trail, past the mill site, to the marked trail junction. You will have to go up for about 0.8 miles (1.2 km) to cross over to the South Fork Baker Creek drainage, and then just follow the trail back to the parking lot.

Timber Creek-Pole Canyon Loop

A less-used, lower-elevation loop option is to head up the Timber Creek Trail about 0.5 miles (0.8 km) and take the Pole Canyon turnoff. Hike up and over the ridge through pretty manzanita and mahogany patches into Pole Canyon, then 2 miles (3.2 km) down the canyon. You will come out at the picnic area; then walk up the road to loop C of Grey Cliffs Campground, take the connecting trail to Baker Creek Campground, and then the trail to the Baker Creek trailhead. This is the lowest-elevation option, best hiked in the spring and fall. It is also a viable option for a backcountry ski loop.

Strawberry Creek Road

If the main part of the park in the Lehman Creek and Baker Creek areas seems too busy and developed for your taste, one option is Strawberry Creek. This large canyon on the north end of the park offers beautiful scenery, free camping at designated campsites, a wide array of birds, Bonneville cutthroat trout, bugling elk, dendroglyphs (tree carvings), and more. To get to Strawberry Creek, go north from Baker and then head west on Highway 6/50. The Strawberry Creek turnoff is near mile marker 92, where a paved road heads south to a white highway maintenance shed at the end. A sign in front of the shed directs you to the road to Strawberry Creek canyon. By following the main road, you reach the national park boundary in about 3 miles (5 km), marked by a sign. The road continues on the west side of the creek through aspen patches, pinyon/juniper, and occasionally water birch. The main camping area is about 1 mile (1.6 km) from the park boundary, and the road ends at a trailhead about 1 mile (1.6 km) farther up the canyon. Fishing throughout this area is good for native Bonneville cutthroat trout, which were reintroduced to the creek in 2004; catch-and-release techniques are recommended to allow the population to expand. In 2006, three other native fishes were reintroduced to Strawberry Creek that used to coexist with

Figure 6-5. Strawberry Creek meanders through an aspen stand.

Bonneville cutthroat trout: mottled sculpin, speckled dace, and red-side shiner.

The road crosses a bridge, exits the aspen, and turns into a sage-brush meadow (figure 6-5). About 0.5 miles (0.8 km) from the bridge, a faint road leads into an aspen stand and the old Robison corral. The Robison family had grazing rights in the area for decades and frequently camped here. Aspens are also part of human history, because early sheepherders carved them to show they had been in the area, to communicate with other sheepherders, and to pass free time. Many of these early sheepherders were Basque, and those who came later were from Peru. The carvings on these trees are called dendroglyphs, and studies throughout the Great Basin are record-ing them for posterity because aspens generally live only 100 to 150 years. Carving trees today is not permitted and is considered graffiti, but it is fun to search for the historic carvings.

After the turnoff to the historic corral, the road goes through some trees, followed by another meadow. Then the maintained road ends at a creek, which contains the combined waters of Strawberry Creek and Blue Canyon. Blue Canyon extends far up into the watershed toward the northeast side of Bald Mountain. Logging has occurred in this area, and there was a road up to about 9,600 feet (2,900 m) elevation that has since been reclaimed.

Cross the footbridge to access a hiking trail through a large sagebrush steppe area. This is one of the best places in the park to see elk. Reintroduced outside the park in the 1980s, the herd has gradually increased, and now sixty to eighty animals regularly use the Strawberry Creek area. Several of the cow elk have radio telemetry collars, enabling biologists from the park and the Nevada Department of Wildlife to track them. Listening to them bugle in the fall is an eerie experience. Check at the visitor centers for the latest information.

An unnatural-looking line crosses the top part of the meadow; this is a remnant of the Osceola Ditch. The ditch crosses Strawberry Creek at about 8,000 feet (2,400 m) elevation and then crosses the meadow. At this point, the ditch builders faced a large obstacle: a pass several hundred feet higher than the ditch. Because water will not flow uphill, the ditch had to extend around the mountain—or did it? The builders chose another option: tunneling through the pass and sending the water through the mountain. The tunnel was about 600 feet (180 m) long. It has since collapsed, but it is possible to see remnants of this amazing feat.

The trail crosses the creek at the top of the meadow. You can follow the trail made in 2010 on the other side of the creek back to your vehicle (a 1-mile (1.6 km) loop) or continue up the trail improved by the Nevada Conservation Corps in recent years. The trail leads up toward Bald Mountain via the Willard Creek pass and follows an old road that crossed over into Willard Creek, with spurs for logging. This was one of the original routes for climbing Wheeler Peak, because for decades, Strawberry Creek Road ascended higher than the one in the Lehman Creek drainage. At about 8,600 feet (2,600 m), an old road leads to the west to Windy Canyon, where a marmot colony was discovered in 2003. This is also an excellent place for birding in a higher-elevation sagebrush stand.

When the idea of creating a national park in this area was first being considered, the Strawberry Creek area was proposed as the park entrance, providing dramatic views of Wheeler Peak. The development of Wheeler Peak Scenic Drive by the Forest Service changed this plan. Another proposal for this area was to develop a ski area on Bald Mountain. This came about during the winter of 1958 and 1959, when ski clubs combed the Ely area looking for the best place to build a new ski resort. They determined that of the 5,000 square miles (12,950 km²) of mountain terrain surveyed, the best place was Bald Mountain. The plans called for an access road up Strawberry Canyon; a ski lodge complete with dining room, overnight accommodations, and ski shop; and seven runs ranging from 1,500 to 7,800 feet (460–2,400 m) in length, with two combined runs lasting 12,100 feet (3,690 m). Several lifts would take skiers up the runs, including up to near the summit of Bald Mountain at 11,562 feet (3,524 m). A 2.3-mile (3.6 km) rope tow or ski lift would be constructed from Bald Mountain to the summit of Wheeler Peak at 13,063 feet (3,982 m). Financial backers could not be found for this remote location, and the ski area remains a dream on paper (Waite 1974, 708–16).

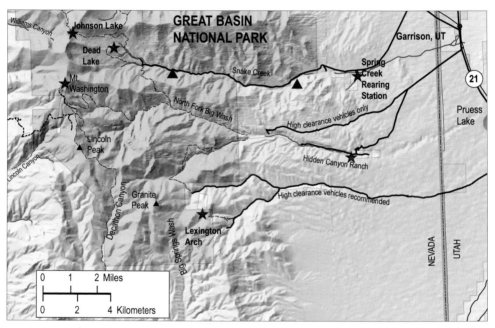

Figure 7-1. Map of South Snake Range—southern part

7

SOUTHERN AREA

SNAKE CREEK, BIG WASH, AND LEXINGTON ARCH

The main attractions in the southern part of the South Snake Range (figure 7-1) include Snake Creek, a scenic canyon with camping and hiking trails, and the enormous Lexington Arch, made of limestone. For those wanting a luxurious getaway, Hidden Canyon is an option and is also a good starting place for exploring the rugged North Fork and South Fork of Big Wash. The Mount Washington area provides a high-elevation getaway for those who like their beauty in difficult-to-reach locales. The southern part of the range has fewer streams due to the more prevalent limestones and dolomites, permeable rocks that allow more of the water to sink underground. This allows for some slightly different vegetation, making it worth a visit.

Snake Creek

Snake Creek, like Strawberry Creek, is a good alternative for those who want to visit a quieter part of Great Basin National Park but still travel on good roads. Camping is free at designated campsites, and the gravel road follows a scenic stream bordered by cottonwoods and aspens. Sights near the road include a fish rearing station and old mines. Trails depart from the end of the road. To get to Snake Creek, head south from Baker on Nevada Highway 487. At mile marker 1, a mailbox for the Spring Creek Rearing Station and a National Park Service sign for Snake Creek mark the turnoff. Snake Creek reportedly got its name because when pioneers traveled to the sawmill for lumber they had to follow a serpentine road that included ten bridges and four stream crossings (Quate 1993, 121). Reset your trip odometer to 0 at the turnoff to help locate some of the features on Snake Creek Road.

Spring Creek Rearing Station

Spring Creek Rearing Station, run by the Nevada Department of Wildlife (NDOW), is located at mile 3.6 (figure 7-2). It was created in 1949 and in the early days was called "the hatchery" by locals. A rearing station differs from a hatchery in that it raises fish from fry (young fish) to adults, while hatcheries raise fish from hatched eggs. The rearing station has several concrete-lined runways. At present it raises rainbow trout for release in various reservoirs in eastern Nevada for sport fishing. The main water supply for the rearing station is Spring Creek, a steady stream of water with a springhead located inside the NDOW property. The water stays at a steady temperature and supports springsnails along with a variety of macroinvertebrates. At times the rearing station also uses Snake Creek water for its operations. The rearing station is open to visitors, so if you would like to see the fish, follow the driveway into the parking area and observe the posted rules (no throwing items into the water, no walking on catwalks, etc.). This is also an excellent place for bird-watching; look for great blue herons (*Ardea herodias*), wrens, ducks, and belted kingfishers (*Megaceryle alcyon*).

One-half mile (0.8 km) beyond the rearing station you cross a cattle guard that used to mark the beginning of the Humboldt-Toiyabe National Forest, before management switched to the BLM in 2006. An inholding to the south contains private property with meadows and wetlands. Northern harriers (*Circus cyaneus*), once called marsh hawks, frequent this wetter spot looking for prey.

Continuing into Snake Creek Canyon

At about mile 4.8 is a road to the north, nicknamed the Repeater Road, which switchbacks up to the television and radio repeater, installed in 1974. The park boundary is at mile 5.2. No off-highway vehicles are permitted past this point unless they are street legal; all vehicles must stay on designated roads. The canyon walls get a little

Figure 7-2. Spring Creek Rearing Station raises tens of thousands of
rainbow trout every year in the raceways.

closer, cottonwoods line the flowing creek, and during the fall this is
one of the most beautiful areas of the South Snake Range. Camping
along Snake Creek is primitive but free.

The road passes more campsites and interesting rock formations
as you head farther into the canyon. At mile 7.6 you see the end of
a 3-mile (5 km) pipeline, constructed by area ranchers and the US
Department of Agriculture in the 1960s to get more water to the
farms. Without the pipeline, most, if not all, of the water sinks into
a karst section of the stream and is believed to be channeled toward
the Big Springs area to the south (Elliott et al. 2006).

At mile 8.1, Horse Heaven Creek may cross the road during wet
years. Most years, though, you will not even know that water could
cross the road, because no riparian vegetation is present. Horse
Heaven is a high-elevation sagebrush area, visible from the highway and many areas of the valley. It is distinctive because it forms
a large light-colored patch high on the mountainside, surrounded
by darker trees and rocks. Marmots and other small mammals make
their home there. Although no trail leads to Horse Heaven, it can be

reached from all sides, depending on how steep and long a route you would like to follow.

Tilford Mine

At mile 8.7 is a turnout on the south side of the road, with some old mining equipment in the vicinity. Silver ore was discovered nearby in 1869. However, the silver ore was less important than the tungsten ore scheelite, which was discovered in 1912 by John Dixon Tilford. The Tilford or Bonita Mine was developed, with miners staying in nearby Camp Bonita. The area was christened the Bonita District, and scheelite was successfully mined in 1913. A two-stamp mill with concentrating tables was installed along Snake Creek that could process two tons every twenty-four hours. As the price of tungsten rose during World War I, increased mining took place in 1915 and 1916. A San Francisco firm erected a twenty-ton mill, but the company soon went bankrupt and left (Unrau 1990, 85–86).

The mining camp remains are located to the northwest. It was here that John Tilford built a house and stone cellar for his wife, Sarah Overson, and their five children, born between 1909 and 1917, including one they named Bonita. A small house for the Chinese cook, Toy Fong, was built next to the stone cellar, and a large bunkhouse and other assorted buildings were also constructed to accommodate the forty-man crew of the Bonita Mine. As World War I ended, the demand for tungsten diminished and the mine was closed and machinery removed. The family home was sold and moved from Snake Creek to Ely. The Forest Service used the cook's house and stone cellar as survival shelters, but eventually the cook's house was destroyed by fire, and the Forest Service bulldozed the ruins and covered them (Charleston and Pascuzzo 1992). The foundation stones of the house are still present, as is the cellar. Mining activity resumed with the onset of World War II, with exploration for placer scheelite, resulting in forty-four pits and shafts. The building remains are now called the old Tilford site. The miners got most of their water from Tilford Spring. There is also a nearby spring that emerges from a cave during high water. During low water, the water table drops to lower levels of the cave.

Upper Snake Creek

A cattle guard at mile 10.7 marks where the pipeline begins. Above this section, native Bonneville cutthroat trout were restored to the

stream in 2005, with more added in 2008. They appear to be repro-
ducing well. Here at the cattle guard is an interesting mix of vegetation. Since entering the park, you have been mostly in the pinyon
pine/juniper habitat. Here you can spot both of these species, and
also white fir, limber pine, and ponderosa pine. The coniferous forest continues as you drive upstream, interspersed with aspen.

At mile 11.3, a dip in the road with lots of water birches on both
sides designates the location of the rarely flowing Granite Creek. The
area to the north of the road is called Granite Basin, one of the few
locations in the South Snake Range containing granite. The granite
borders limestone that rises up to the 10,840-foot (3,304 m) Eagle
Peak. The extensive limestone cliffs are topped with a grove of bristlecone pines.

At mile 12.1, two creeks merge: the South Fork and the North
Fork of Snake Creek. Here the road enters an aspen grove, makes a
ninety-degree turn to the north, and arrives at a junction. The road to
the southwest follows the South Fork of Snake Creek before becoming impassable. A couple of campsites are available (although they
are slated to be removed), as are an old, unmaintained trail to Dead
Lake and the seldom-maintained Shoshone Trail, which leads to the
North Fork of Big Wash. Both are peaceful hikes with great promise
for solitude. Near the junction are the remains of the first cabin that
John Tilford built in 1909; he also built a sawmill nearby (figure 7-3).

The main road continues just 0.2 miles (0.3 km) farther and ends
at the Shoshone Campsite. It is also the trailhead to Johnson Lake, a
deceptive 3.2 miles (5.1 km) away but over 1,500 feet (460 m) higher
in elevation. It generally takes two to four hours to hike to the lake.
This high, subalpine lake was naturally fishless, although like many
water bodies in the West it was stocked by early miners and the state.
The park removed all the brook trout from the lake in 2004 to better
protect the Bonneville cutthroat trout population in the stream below.

The Johnson Lake Trail begins in the forest, passing some beautiful granite rocks. It passes through some meadows, crosses a small
spring, and then winds into the sagebrush. After reentering the trees,
it leads to a marked cutoff that heads over to the Baker Creek drainage and is part of the Baker-Johnson Lake loop trail. This part of the
trail was reportedly built by the CCC back in the 1930s. The main
Johnson Lake Trail gets steeper as it goes through an area of trees
blown over by a severe windstorm. The vegetation gets sparser as you
climb higher and arrive at a large wooden structure that served as

Photo courtesy Russ Robison

Figure 7-3. Logging up Snake Creek. Note the oxen used to pull the logs
and the horses, boiler, and ladies in dresses off to the side.

a stamp mill for refining ore mined near Johnson Lake, about 0.8
miles (1.2 km) farther up the trail (figure 7-4).

About 1909, Alfred Johnson, a Swede, found tungsten high up in
Snake Creek and applied for a water rights permit for mining and
power purposes. He eventually developed a tungsten mine and mined
ore worth about $1,000 a year, enough to buy food. He and other
miners built several cabins that can be seen along the trail near the
lake and have been designated a National Historic District. National
Park Service specialists have worked to stabilize the buildings.

Johnson was called "Timberline Johnson" by the locals, and the
little lake near his mines was named Johnson Lake. A cableway still
exists today and goes from near the lake up to the mine on the side
of a cliff. A cabin used to be located near the mine entrance but
was mostly demolished in subsequent avalanches. The majority of
mining ceased about 1920, although some ore was shipped in 1935
(Unrau 1990, 87–88).

Figure 7-4. Johnson Lake is a scenic high elevation lake in Great Basin National Park.

Johnson Lake is a scenic, 2.5-acre (1.0 ha) lake. It is deepest at the west end near some granite outcroppings. A small spring on the south side serves as an inlet. The miners built a dam on the east end to increase the lake volume and ensure a better water supply for the mill. Many old mining remnants have been found on the lake bottom. A 2005 avalanche deposited many trees into the lake. You can camp near the lake, but be aware that high winds and frequent summer thunderstorms make it advisable to pitch a tent in the trees for a little more protection. This lake is at almost 10,800 feet (3,300 m) elevation, so campfires are not allowed.

Big Wash Road and Hidden Canyon

Just south of the town of Garrison is a road leading to the west marked with a sign for Hidden Canyon Ranch. It is nestled in Big Wash, a remote area with rugged terrain and solitary hiking trails. The road ascends the foothills. Going around a curve and up into some trees,

Figure 7-5. Hidden Canyon Ranch is located in Big Wash, a narrow, scenic canyon.

you reach the pass and then start descending into Hidden Canyon (figure 7-5). From this perspective, it is easy to see how the area got its name. The canyon is spectacular, with sandstone cliffs lining a green oasis. Off in the distance are mountain peaks of many different shapes and sizes.

Elias M. (Bob) Smith drove the first team and wagon into Big Wash in the 1880s and said that the greasewood was so high and thick he had to stand on the spring seat of his wagon to see over it. He and his family owned all the lower part of Big Wash and half the upper streams, with W. T. Fowler purchasing the other half. A public school district was organized, and teachers came and boarded with the families. Both families made their living farming; in addition, Bob Smith used his carpentry skills to build houses. He was also the official coffin maker for the valley (Quate 1993, 161). Although pioneer life was difficult, Big Wash and Snake Valley had more resources than some of the nearby valleys, such as Wah Wah Valley. Mr. Paul, Smith's father-in-law, became lost there, and Smith's diary records part of the search:

Figure 7-6. The Hidden Canyon lodge has spectacular views of Castle Butte, the rock formation separating the North and South Forks of Big Wash; and of Mt. Washington, the gray-colored slanted mountain at the head of the North Fork.

July 26, 1901—started from Snake Creek, going to hunt for Mr. Paul who is my wife's father. He was lost on the Wa Wa Desert about two months ago and perished for water, there being no water for miles in the country in which he perished. Found the first traces of Mr. Paul, a bloody rag and some pieces of cotton. His dead dog was found. My dog gave out and I divided my water with him, but he could not follow and died. (Read 1965, 148)

Ron and Robin Crouch bought the lower section of Big Wash in the 1990s, and later the upper section, and have developed it into the upscale Hidden Canyon Bed and Breakfast (figure 7-6), open year round (http://www.greatbasinpark.com/hiddencanyon.htm).

The Big Wash scenery is outstanding due to spectacular rock formations. The softer conglomerate of Big Wash has been eroded away, leaving tall cliff faces bare of vegetation so that the rock is easily seen. Cottonwoods line the creek, which has cut deeply into the soft soils during flash floods and high-water years. Bonneville cutthroat trout have been reintroduced into the creek. Looking to the west it is possible to see a distinctive limestone crag called Castle Butte, which separates the North Fork and South Fork of Big Wash.

North Fork of Big Wash

The North Fork of Big Wash is one of the biggest watersheds in the area, beginning on the eastern slopes of Mount Washington. This mountain is easy to identify by its light gray limestone rock and its gentle, slanting peak. At one time you could literally drive to the top of it via a jeep road that began on the other side of the mountain and then went across and down the North Fork of Big Wash side. The road on the west side of the mountain still takes you most of the way to the top (see later section for details), but the road on the east side was washed out by a flash flood in 1983. Although the watershed is large, it contains few springs because of the karst geology. Nevertheless, sudden downpours or quick snowmelts can cause canyon-changing floods. A trail is shown on maps from the lower watershed up to Mount Washington, but expect some bushwhacking through recent avalanche areas.

The steep slopes and cliff faces are the scene of many avalanches, making this one of the most rugged areas of the range. Some logging was conducted in this watershed, but the main reason people ventured into this canyon was to look for ore. With tungsten prices high in 1915, miners were combing the area looking for it. W. L. Chapman and A. D. Taylor found scheelite in a 2-foot (0.6 m) vein. They packed the high-grade ore off the mountain with burros. The next year they found "the best and highest scheelite prospect in the county" at "the head of Big Wash, under Mt. Washington, at an elevation of 9500 ft" (2,900 m). As prices dropped late in 1916, the Chapman-Taylor mine was abandoned, although its location is still marked on some signs and maps of the area (Unrau 1990, 152–53).

In addition to the trail that begins at Big Wash and ends at Mount Washington, another trail exists that connects the lower part of the North Fork of Big Wash to Snake Creek. This is part of the old Shoshone Trail that the Forest Service developed for livestock movement. Today this is a scenic and seldom-used trail.

South Fork of Big Wash

The South Fork of Big Wash is the southernmost stream that descends from the east side of the South Snake Range. Because the area has so much karst terrain, the stream emerges and disappears several times throughout the canyon. The head of the canyon is incredibly steep, eventually emerging from the wooded area into a small meadow, where there are remnants of a stamp mill that was used to process the ore from nearby mines. At one time a road entered from the south side (North Lexington Canyon), with a pack trail running along the north side to the forks of Big Wash; today this is a hiking trail that connects to the lower section near Hidden Canyon Ranch. Near where the trail crosses the upper creek channel is the old Stoddard sawmill. Several pieces of equipment still remain, including a large firebox boiler. The mill was built and operated by Joe Stoddard (Waite 1974, 618). The ruins of a cabin are located on the other side of the streambed. The creek is dry here except for spring runoff and floods.

A wildfire near this area burned over 600 acres (240 ha) in 2001. Vegetation quickly recovered, and due to stabilization efforts, the steep slopes for the most part did not erode much into the stream, which contains a restored Bonneville cutthroat trout population. Downstream, the creek enters a slot canyon, with limestone walls full of intriguing holes.

Lexington Arch

Hidden in the mountains of the South Snake Range is a massive limestone arch (figure 7-7). With a span of 125 feet (38 m) and an opening 75 feet (23 m) high, the arch could contain a seven-story building. Possibly once part of a cave, the arch could have formed by water eroding the surrounding rock and leaving only the part we now see.

To reach the arch, take Lexington Road, starting on the south end of Pruess Lake. The road crosses Lake Creek, which meanders into Pruess Lake. Between the road and the lake is a small bit of private land, marked by old cottonwood trees. This is the Ackinson Place, homesteaded by Billie and Rosie Ackinson (Quate 1993). They used water from Lexington Creek to irrigate their fields. Lexington Creek rarely runs to the lake anymore, possibly because of the extensive expansion of pinyon and juniper trees farther up the watershed. Big sagebrush and greasewood in the area indicate good soil with groundwater close by.

Reset your odometer at the turnoff from the pavement. At mile 0.4 a road takes off to the south. This road follows the west side of Burbank Meadows and at one time was the main road for southern Snake Valley. The vegetation consists of low sagebrush and rabbitbrush, and on the north side of the road you may be able to spot a

Figure 7-7. Lexington Arch spans 125 feet and is 75 feet tall.

ravine that holds Lexington Creek when it is running. The ravine turns into a wash as you drive farther west, and juniper trees start appearing sporadically over the landscape. The mountains to the west provide spectacular scenery.

You cross the state line at mile 3.0, and at mile 4.4 a road heads to the northeast, connecting to the north side of Pruess Lake. A road leads to the south at mile 5.7, connecting to Big Springs Ranch and providing access to Black and Chokecherry Canyons. This road is rarely traveled, so if you take it, be prepared for backcountry travel. The main road descends into the wash, with some pinyon pine dotting the countryside. Down in the wash you will be able to spot more riparian vegetation—willows, rose, and cottonwood. If the stream is not flowing, it seems unlikely that these plants can survive, but even when the stream is dry, the water is usually not too far underground. When the stream is flowing, it goes under the road through a culvert at mile 7.5. Just beyond are the remains of an old cabin, built in the "Lincoln-log" style, with chinks of wood between the big logs. This was the home of the Woodward family, who inhabited the cabin year-round for a few years in the 1890s. They had originally come to Snake Valley to settle land that the Pruess Lake and Irrigation Company had said was available, but then they found it was a speculative project (chapter 17). They worked on various ranches and at the sawmill in Lexington Canyon before deciding it was time to move to greener pastures (Neal Woodward diary in Quate 1993, 286–97).

You cross a cattle guard at mile 9.3 and the road forks. Just to the south are the remnants of an old livestock-watering trough, slowly being swallowed by the sagebrush. The north fork leads to the old Ponderosa Mine area, where silver was found in April of 1870. Several mines opened within weeks, including American Eagle, Sunset, Pine Nut, Bald Hornet, Mountain Chief, Blue Cloud, and White Man. The ore produced up to $16,000 per ton, but the deposits were small and within two years most of the mines were abandoned. In 1917 mining resumed, this time for tungsten. A small mill was built, and the Bonanza Mine was developed, producing $20,000 in scheelite before closing a year later. In 1941 the Bonanza Mine was reopened and a fifty-ton concentrating plant was constructed. Within a year, the mine produced $80,000 worth of ore, and then it closed (Hall 1994, 159–60). A couple of cabins still remain there, along with a pond. The road washed out in 2005 about 1 mile (1.6 km) from the fork but was partially repaired in 2006. This is the way to access the upper part of the South Fork of Big Wash watershed.

The south fork heads to Lexington Arch. If the creek is running (which it usually is not), you will need to ford it. The creek crossing is lined by willows, young cottonwoods, sagebrush, and rabbitbrush. About 0.7 miles (1.1 km) later you may encounter a second ford, where a spring runs across the road and into a trough. This is a beautiful camping area in spring and fall, when the temperatures are not too hot at this lower elevation. Farther down the road is a big meadow, followed 0.5 miles (0.8 km) later by cliffs next to the road. A short road branches off just beyond the cliffs, leading to the canyons to the southeast. At 2 miles (3.2 km) from the fork, you can get a glimpse of the arch to the south before you enter the parking area. The road ends in this parking area on BLM land. The Forest Service built the trail to the arch, which is on National Park Service land. The hour-long hike over 1.7 miles (2.7 km), with 1,000 feet (300 m) of elevation gain, takes you to the impressive limestone arch. The trail ends at the arch, but the canyon beyond it is beautiful and solitary.

Mount Washington Area

High in the southern part of the park is the Mount Washington area. This includes not only Mount Washington, where you can drive almost to the summit at 11,658 feet (3,553 m), but also the 11,585-foot (3,531 m) Lincoln Peak, a beautiful bristlecone pine grove, and the Highland Ridge Trail. The easiest access is via an old jeep road from Spring Valley, although this is a white-knuckle trip that takes two hours from Baker. To reach the Mount Washington area by vehicle, start in southern Spring Valley on Highway 894, a paved road. The Mount Washington road begins between mile markers 5 and 6, opposite the old Kirkeby Ranch (still shown on topo maps), now signed as the Pickering Ranch. Like all the ranches in Spring Valley south of Highway 6/50, this ranch is owned by the Southern Nevada Water Authority.

The Mount Washington road is in good shape and passable for passenger cars up to the Pole Canyon adit of the Mount Wheeler Mine (chapter 20), at about 7,850 feet (2,390 m). Then the road starts getting much steeper, requiring a four-wheel drive short-wheel base vehicle to maneuver the tight switchbacks. This section was built in 1948 in order to move ore down the mountain. Before the road, miners tobogganed the ore down or took it down by mule. The road crosses a large burned area where a wildfire swept through in 1999. Although some people were concerned about it burning bristlecone pines, the wildfire opened up a great deal of habitat and the bighorn sheep population seems to be expanding. Some old miners' cabins near the Saint Lawrence Mine can be seen on the way, down a short spur. These demonstrate some very old construction techniques, such as using split logs for the roof. For those who like an exciting mountain bike ride, descending this road is a lot of fun. The area can also be reached by hiking up the North Fork of Big Wash on a trail that is obscured in places or hiking cross-country from Wheeler Peak or one of the canyons at the southern end of the range.

Most of the rocks are limestone, but from the summit of Mount Washington you can look north toward Wheeler Peak and see a myriad of rock colors. On the nearest ridge is a grove of twisted bristlecone pines. To the east are the remarkable cliff faces that line the upper sections of the North Fork of Big Wash.

A side road at about 11,200 feet (3,400 m) goes southeast over a ridge dotted with bristlecone pines to the trailhead for Lincoln

Cirque and Highland Ridge. The trail descends about 1.5 miles (2.4 km) into the cirque, which is especially beautiful in July, when the bright pink flowers of Parry's primrose (*Primula parryi*) contrast with the green vegetation and gray cliffs that rise many hundreds of feet. Several holes halfway up the cliffs are the entrances to caves. Some intrepid cavers rappelled down the crumbly rock face and entered them in the 1980s, finding vertical caves with moss and ice. No one has entered them since. Other caves in the area are also extreme, often filled with ice most of the year and requiring special techniques to plumb their depths. Despite these harsh conditions, recent inventories have found the caves to be home to a surprising number of invertebrates (Taylor et al. 2008).

Another seldom-used trail is the Highland Ridge Trail, which extends from Mount Washington south to Decathon Canyon. Most of the trail is not marked, so it requires route finding. It follows the high country and has stunning views as you traverse mountains, subalpine meadows, and bristlecone groves. This is excellent bighorn sheep habitat. The hike can be done in a long day but requires vehicles at both ends or a shuttle. It can also be combined with a Snake Range crest hike from Wheeler Peak. Wheeler Peak to Mount Washington is a very long day hike, with no trail once you leave Wheeler Peak, and no water available along the way unless you descend to Baker or Johnson Lakes. The views are spectacular, but this is extremely rough terrain and should be tackled only by experienced hikers.

Southern End of the Snake Range

The southern end of the Snake Range is rarely visited. The long canyons—Johns Wash, Murphy Wash, Decathon Canyon, and Big Springs Wash—are unknown even to most of the locals. With much of the underlying terrain consisting of limestone and dolomite, nearly all the precipitation that falls disappears, and there are no streams and only a handful of springs. Few minerals of value have been found in the area. For these reasons, no people live in or near these canyons, making them some of the wildest places in the Snake Range.

Partly in recognition of that, in 2006 much of the area south of Great Basin National Park was designated as the Highland Ridge Wilderness. The 68,627 acres (27,772 ha) are administered by the BLM.

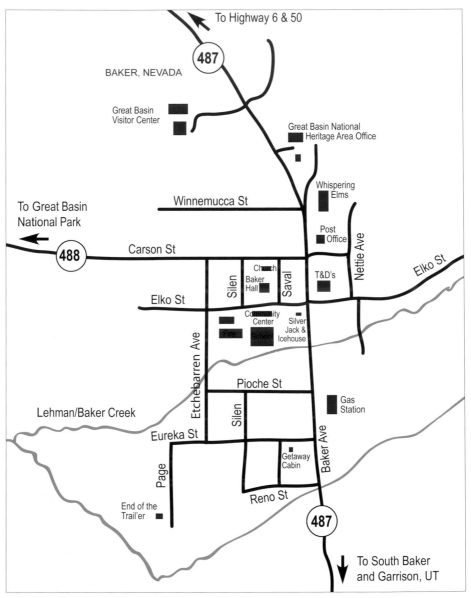

Figure 8-1. Map of Baker, Nevada.

GATEWAY TOWN

BAKER, NEVADA

The gateway to Great Basin National Park is Baker, Nevada, a small community of about two hundred people—if you count everyone who lives close by (figure 8-1). The town was settled in the 1880s and is the largest community in Snake Valley today. If you are visiting Great Basin National Park, you will likely be spending a night or eating a meal in this tiny town (appendix A).

Just to the north of Baker is the Great Basin Visitor Center, on the west side of the road. The visitor center opened in 2005 to help the park fulfill one of the purposes for which it was created: to interpret the entire Great Basin region. Exhibits in the visitor center include information about vegetation, wildlife, and culture, along with ongoing projects. A second building next to the visitor center holds the park library, which the public can visit with advance notice, and a classroom/meeting room.

Across the road are historic Forest Service buildings, painted white with green trim. This historic district includes an office, tack room, horse corral, house, well house, and fruit trees. This was called the Baker Guard Station, and a Forest Service employee lived at this location in a two-story house that was later moved to Ely. This land was transferred to the National Park Service in 1986, and some of the buildings are currently used for wildland fire operations and for the Great Basin National Heritage Area office.

The town of Baker, at 5,318 feet (1,621 m) elevation, was named after George W. Baker, one of the first ranchers. Although unincorporated, the town has developed a sewer and water system, and it also has an advisory board to recommend actions to the White Pine County commissioners. Trailers predominate in Baker because they are cheap and easy to bring in and few building codes need to be followed. The amazing amount of old equipment in many of the yards is due to the days when it was a long trip to get to town, so it was wise to save anything that might have the minutest possibility of being used again. The paltry precipitation and resulting lack of vegetation make all these treasure piles exceedingly visible to passersby. Nettie Baker, daughter-in-law of George Baker, named Baker's gravel streets after towns and people of Nevada.

Downtown Baker

The first store to open in Snake Valley was the Rancher's Store in 1892 (figure 8-2), owned and operated by Thomas Dearden Sr., who at the time of starting the store could neither read nor write. Nevertheless, he was successful enough that in 1905 he bought the store in Garrison from James and Clay Company and operated the stores in both Baker and Garrison. The original Baker store was in a 12' x 14' (3.7 x 4.3 m) log cabin, and later he expanded to a 16' x 20' (4.9 x 6.1 m) building brought from Black Horse; today it is the Silver Jack Inn and LectroLux Café (Quate 1993, 174). One of Tom Dearden's grandchildren recalls a humorous event in the store. One day his grandfather received a shipment of pocket watches. The local Indians were fascinated by them and demanded to know what good they were and how they operated. Tom Dearden explained the watches and showed them where the hands were when it was eight o'clock and five o'clock. He sold some watches to them. Many of these Indians were working on the Baker Ranch helping with the hay. From that time on, Mr. Baker never could convince them that it was all right to start working before 8:00 a.m. or continue past 5:00 p.m. It made no difference if only two forkfuls of hay were left to put on the stack; at exactly five o'clock, the workday stopped (Robison 2006b, 258).

Figure 8-2. The Rancher's Store, operated by Tom Dearden, was the first store in Snake Valley. This photo was taken about 1900 and shows from left to right: Ester Dearden Smith, Thomas Dearden Sr., Daisy Dearden, and Lester Jerome Robison with his horse and dog.

Across the street is T & D's, named for the owners, Terry and Debbie Steadman, who operate a convenience store, restaurant, and bar. They have decorated the interior with large photos of historic life in Baker. The building was originally built as a garage and had a gas station outside it.

The building that currently houses Happy Burro Trad'n Post, across the street from T & D's and the Silver Jack, was originally a Forest Service building that was moved to Baker. Two memorable owners were Lil and Art Brumley. Art had a great party trick. He would pop out his glass eye at the bar when he had to go to the bathroom and tell his customers that way he could always have someone watching the place (Koyle 2002). When Art got tired of people at the Outlaw Bar, he would take out a pistol he kept under the bar and fire a shot into the floor. It did not take long for people to quit partying and go home (Schlabsz 2007). Lil and Art kept their money between the mattress and box spring on their bed, and everyone knew that.

Because both of them partied hard and often passed out, it was only by miracle or thanks to kind locals that they avoided being robbed. Usually after they had hit the floor, someone helped put them to bed, continued to run the place until the party was over, and then hid the money, locked up, went home, and the next day went back and told Art and Lil where the money was (Schlabsz 2007).

Art eventually died of too much drinking, and Lil was left to run the place. She finally got lonely and moved back to Minnesota, so Chuck and Reita Berger bought the bar, even though they knew nothing about bartending and Reita did not drink alcohol. Nevertheless, they ran it for the next twenty-five years using the new name "The Outlaw." That name, in addition to the good hospitality, helped make The Outlaw a popular place for a large group of motorcycle riders. Each year, around the Fourth of July weekend, nearly five hundred bikers descended on the town of Baker. They tied ribbons on light fixtures in bars that they deemed to be okay. The few days they stayed were chaotic, with long hours at The Outlaw. The bikers camped up in the National Forest along Baker and Lehman Creeks, and because so many of them were in the area, the National Park Service had a SWAT team come in each year to help with crowd control. One time a ketchup and mustard fight broke out at The Outlaw. Reita had previously put all the glass ketchup bottles away so that no one could get hurt, but the plastic ones provided plenty of squirting power. Several people started squirting the condiments around the inside of the bar. Reita, tired from working such long hours and not wanting to see her business destroyed, demanded in a no-nonsense voice that they stop right then, threw them rags, and told them to clean it up immediately. They obeyed, and the bar was soon cleaned up. Then, from the back room of the restaurant walked two deputy sheriffs and the head of the NPS SWAT team. Reita asked them where they had been just a few minutes before and they replied they had been there watching the whole thing. Reita asked why they had done nothing to help her, and they said she had handled it perfectly; they could not have done any better.

In twenty-five years of business, only one fistfight broke out in the bar, and no one ever had to call the police. Reita said she could always spot the troublemakers and deal with them before any problems began.

When the crews came around trying to determine where to put the MX missiles, some people thought they would have to vacate

Figure 8-3. Photo taken from the gas station of the annual Snake Valley Festival parade. The festival is usually held the third weekend of June and includes lots of fun events.

Baker, and a bunch of locals gathered in the bar one night. The topic of discussion was how to start a new Baker and whom they would like to leave out of that new town. After a long conversation, the consensus was that every single person in town, no matter how annoying or bothersome, was needed to make Baker what it was (Berger 2006).

Farther south is the Sinclair gas station, which is the only place in downtown Baker to get gas and diesel. An RV park, laundromat, and showers sit behind the gas station (figure 8-3). At the north end of town sits the Whispering Elms Motel, Campground, and RV Park; and the Great Basin Lodge, a bar.

The Post Office

The first Baker post office was started in 1892 by Charles and Robert Peck in their home, located to the west of the main road in Baker.

Charley served as the first postmaster for fifteen years. Later a new post office building was built on Main Street. The back of the post office was a gathering place for several of the women who liked to quilt. It also had a lending library that was frequented by the townsfolk. Next to the post office was a large rose garden, which still exists today. Mail came from Ely on Monday, Wednesday, and Friday, and from Milford on Tuesday, Thursday, and Saturday. For many years the mail truck was a red Chevy pickup with a high camper on it. Leon Rowley was the driver, and he hauled not only the mail but supplies for the store in large insulated canvas bags with dry ice, parts for the ranch or the garage, medicine, small animals, trees, and anything anyone needed (Schlabsz 2007).

The new post office, built on the site of an old pond, was dedicated in 1986. The first postmistress there was Virginia Eldridge, who began in 1973, retired in 1990, and was succeeded by her daughter Daisy Gonder, who then served for twenty-one years. The post office is a frequent informal gathering spot in town, and any and all area news is placed on the bulletin board. It is not uncommon to see signs for services offered, vehicles for sale, wedding invitations, park events, job announcements, and articles stating someone's viewpoint.

The Law in Baker

Baker, as an unincorporated community, is patrolled by the White Pine County sheriff's office and the Nevada State highway patrol from Ely. In the past, Baker had deputy sheriffs and justices of the peace that lived right in town. Deputy sheriffs are hired by the elected county sheriff and must have some law enforcement training. In Nevada, a justice of the peace, or JP for short, can be a layperson, as long as that person attends two weeks of training in Reno and passes a test. The justice of the peace is an elected position unless the seat is unfilled, and then it can be appointed by the county.

Justice of the Peace

George T. Smith was the first justice of the peace in Baker, from 1897 to 1917, and then again from 1928 to 1941. He was also the first janitor of White Pine High School in Baker, from its start in 1930 until 1937. Meanwhile, his wife, Esther, cooked at the Baker Ranch, Mira Monte Hotel, and Lehman Caves Boarding House. While George was working in McGill for the eleven years between his two justice of the peace appointments in Baker, Esther raised eleven children in Baker and saw George only two or three times a year (Quate 1993, 221).

The next record of a justice of the peace is in 1964, when Betty Baker ran unopposed. During her eighteen years as JP, she married eighty-six couples. She held court in the entry room of her house, dealing with traffic violations and misdemeanors. During elections, voting booths were set up in her living room. When Betty retired, Barbara Sand served from 1982 to 1986.

When Barbara decided to resign, several people called Val Taylor at Home Farm, a commune near Baker, and urged her to take the job. She was not particularly interested in legal matters but needed the extra income, which at that time was one hundred dollars per month. One dilemma was where to hold court. Betty Baker had used her house and Barbara Sand her barbershop. The county commissioners were not comfortable letting Val hold court at Home Farm, because some looked upon it with suspicion and called it the Funny Farm. One commissioner suggested using a classroom in the old Baker Hall, and Val was able to get furnishings from the county maintenance warehouse without a problem.

She took the two-week class in Reno but found that she rarely had to use her training because legal business was slim, with only one or two cases a year, and about seventy to one hundred traffic tickets a year. She was pleased that rural justice was not bound by pomp and ceremony. Instead, the parties would sit down and say, "Let's work it out."

During her twenty years as JP, Val conducted ninety-six weddings in a variety of locations. She retired in 2006, which was the end of the justice of the peace position in Baker (V. Taylor 2006). One of the reasons for having justices of the peace away from the county seat was that it was an imposition to travel all the way to Ely. Nowadays, with good highways and comfortable vehicles, the trek is no longer what it used to be. In addition, for any important cases, Val had to go to Ely anyway to use the services of the court recorder. It appears that this rural icon will now remain a Baker memory.

Deputy Sheriff

Records are unclear about who the first deputy sheriff was in Baker. Between the Great Depression and World War II, Bryan Samuel Robison served as deputy sheriff, then went on to serve the same position in McGill, and finished his career as chief of police in Ely. George Leesburg was the deputy sheriff in the late 1950s and early 1960s. He liked to party, so most of the time, the police car, a black and white Ford with one red light on top and a spotlight on the side, sat in front of one of the local bars (Schlabsz 2007).

At one point, Archie Robison was the deputy sheriff. One night some local boys decided to play a prank. They disassembled a Model T, took the pieces up on the roof of a nearby building, and reassembled it. Full of good humor, they returned to the ground in the dark of night only to find that the deputy sheriff had been watching them for some time. He made them go back on that roof, take the Model T apart again, and reassemble it back on the ground (Schlabsz 2007).

Later, Deputy Sheriff Calvin Long spent several years in Baker and was compared by some to Barney Fife. He managed to run the ambulance into the post office and was caught by people peeping in windows to look for crime. One story about him involves the crew that was building Wheeler Peak Scenic Drive. One night, a worker drove a piece of heavy equipment into town and parked at the Hitchin' Post bar. Calvin decided that it would be unsafe for the driver to get behind the wheel after imbibing at the bar, so he impounded the vehicle by chaining it to a power pole. He neglected to tell the driver this, and when the driver started up the vehicle and pulled away, he pulled the power pole behind him and thereby disrupted power in town for a bit (Berger 2006).

Deputy Sheriff Mickey Kerns was also a character. One time he responded to an automobile accident but got a little too close to the scene. His car caught on fire, and because he had ammunition and firearms in the back, no one could get close enough to put the flames out and instead witnessed an impressive display (Schlabsz 2007).

Schools

Currently the Baker school houses third through sixth grade. Children in southern Snake Valley attend kindergarten through second grade in Garrison, Utah, and seventh through twelfth grades at EskDale, Utah. White Pine County, Nevada, and Millard County, Utah, have had a mostly beneficial agreement for decades, including providing buses for students on both sides of the state line. Until the high school in EskDale became public in 2004, students usually went

Figure 8-4. The old Baker schoolhouse from pioneer days is now found at the White Pine Public Museum in Ely (http://wpmuseum.org/).

to either Ely, Nevada, or Delta, Utah, and lived in apartments or with relatives in order to finish their secondary education.

The first schoolhouse for the Baker area was a 20′ x 20′ (6.1 x 6.1 m) building with a dirt roof (figure 8-4).It was built in the early 1890s, about 0.2 miles (0.4 km) southeast of the Bryan Robison Ranch on Strawberry/Weaver Creek. At first, school was held from October to May, but due to the difficulty of traveling in the cold and snow in winter, the school term was changed to summer. About twenty-five to thirty students attended, with one teacher. Some students traveled 7 miles (11 km) from Baker and other outlying ranches (Quate 1993, 136). In 1910 the first school was built in Baker, and dances for the southern part of the valley were often held there; they lasted from evening to sunrise, with dinner at

Figure 8-5. Cows have been an integral part of
Baker since Euroamerican settlement in the 1870s.
Jeff Davis Peak is in the background.

midnight. Because space on the dance floor was limited, each person paid for a dance number upon entry and, when that number was called, took their turn dancing (Quate 1993, 124).

The school in Baker, with its bell, nearby outhouse, and the teacherage (house for the teacher) operated until 1966, when it was consolidated with the Garrison school. The Baker school reopened in the fall of 1976 and has been open since then. Patsy Schlabsz remembers going to first grade at the old school. The teacher came in with a thermos full of coffee—although the students suspected that it was not all coffee, because she often fell asleep. After a few hours, the older boys grew tired of playing outside and threw rocks at the bell to wake up the teacher, and class finally started. Sometimes the water pump for the well stopped working, and the kids went to the garage in downtown Baker to get a drink. The fuel tanks leaked and the water tasted terrible, so when they had advance notice, the kids brought extra drinks from home (Schlabsz 2007). The old school was torn down when the new school opened in 1990 with modern technology, although the old bell was preserved and stands outside the new school.

At one time, from 1930 to about 1945, there was a high school in Baker, located in the pink building a block back from Main Street (L. Wheeler 2007). Nettie Baker donated the land, and the two-room school with a gym/stage was constructed. The first graduating class was in 1930, with seven graduates. After the high school closed, the LDS Church bought the building and used it as their church for many years. They also had regular potlucks and dances, and square dances called by Pop and Grace Wursderfer were popular for many years. The building was also the town cinema, showing Western movies, Gidget movies, and Elvis Presley movies (Schlabsz 2007). After the LDS Church constructed a new building in Garrison, the White Pine School District bought the building. Today it is called Baker Hall and is still used for a variety of events, including school plays and sports.

Near the school are two blue metal buildings, the larger housing the town's volunteer fire trucks and the smaller an ambulance and rescue truck. A low tan building next to the old tennis/basketball court is the community center. It is used for community meetings, English classes, and a variety of other functions ranging from baby showers to senior lunches. The nearby Baker Community Church was built in 2011 and holds multi-denominational services every Sunday.

Baker Ranch

To the east of town is Baker Ranch, the largest ranch in the area and one of the largest employers. The ranch is a cow and calf and feeding operation and has diversified to grow large amounts of alfalfa, corn, oats, and barley (figure 8-5). Hay is sold mostly in Nevada and California and also exported to other countries. The ranch also operates a small ready-mix cement plant.

Baker Ranch was first developed in the 1800s by the Baker family, who came from Missouri. They were intending to work near the Ward Mine by Ely but took a wrong turn and ended up traveling to farmland next to what was called Firbush Creek (now Baker

Photo courtesy Great Basin National Park

Figure 8-6. The Mira Monte Hotel in Baker, built about 1915. Photo
taken in 1920. The foundation can be found to the north of the
Sinclair gas station.

Creek). Some of the family stayed and worked on the ranch, while
George and one son went on to the Ward Mine and got a contract
to haul salt from the salt marsh 30 miles (50 km) north of Baker.
They hauled salt for two years with two sixteen-mule teams. Then in
1878 George W. Baker took a lease on the farmland and they raised
hay, grain, and vegetables and hauled them to Pioche to sell. In five
years, they bought the land and stopped freighting, turning more
of their attention to stock and farming. They expanded the ranch
to about 2,000 acres (800 ha) by taking homesteads and purchasing

land from other settlers. The Bakers expanded their cattle holdings until they had about six hundred, in addition to one hundred horses. From April 1 to September 30, they grazed in the Snake Range. At the end of September, the cattle were gathered and the calves weaned. Then they moved the cattle over the course of two days to the winter range near Skunk Springs in Tule Valley. Most of the calves were born from January to late March on the winter range, and when it came time to move the cattle back to the summer range, it took five to six days on account of all the young calves (Quate 1993, 103–7, 115).

Some Indians lived in and near Baker. One family, Baker Charley and Susie Charley and their four children, worked for the Bakers until about 1910, when they moved to Ibapah. It was common for an Indian to take the name of his employer. In 1890 a fandango was held in Baker that lasted about ten days. Fandangos were dance festivals that were typically held in late August or September, just before the pine nut harvest. After 1914, only one Indian family remained in Baker, the Joe and Mamie Joseph family, with eight children. In the 1920s, a typhoid fever epidemic killed Joe, Mamie, and three of the children. One of the surviving children, Orvil Joseph, worked for the Deardens in Garrison until 1960 (Quate 1993, 139–141). Some of the Josephs are buried in the Indian cemetery on the northwest side of Baker.

In 1904, George W. Baker died, and the land, money, and livestock were divided among his children. They ran the ranch for another ten years, with some of the Bakers living in a five-room house behind the present-day Sinclair gas station. Once they left in 1914, the house was not lived in again. One son was named Phillip but called "Doc." His wife, Nettie, was the "doctor" of the valley, having learned medicine from her father-in-law. She delivered many babies and treated many ailments. After Joe Dearden bought a Ford car in 1910, patients could be taken to the doctor or a doctor brought to them much faster (Quate 1993, 108–10; Schlabsz 2007).

From 1914 to 1921, Guy Saval ran the Baker Ranch for the Aztec Land and Cattle Company. Because of his Basque background, he hired many Basques, and some people called Baker "Basque Town" (Unrau 1990, 206). He expanded the ranch and built the two-story Mira Monte Club, a saloon and hotel, in Baker, (figure 8-6). Numerous parties were reported during the Basque Town era. In 1916, a rodeo was held every other Saturday afternoon and a dance at night in the Baker school. Alcohol was banned in the schoolhouse, and it was a two-block walk from the school to the saloon. Instead of making this trip several times during the night, many men brought bottles of whiskey and hid them outside the schoolhouse. Also outside the schoolhouse were Indians, who came and watched the dance through the windows. Some were also cognizant of the whiskey hiding spots and partook of the stashed alcohol. Often a fight would start, and after things started getting out of control, a deputy sheriff was appointed to Baker (Quate 1993, 134–35).

In 1921, Guy Saval left and Otto Meek took over the ranch. Meek had friends from Hollywood and convinced the right people that a movie ought to be made in Snake Valley. The movie *The Covered Wagon* was filmed near Pruess Lake (chapter 17). Later he attempted to get his Hollywood friends to vacation in Snake Valley, promoting Meek's Dude Ranch, with all the modern amenities plus the attractions of a ranch in Snake Valley: polo, fishing, a clubhouse, horse-riding lessons, and more. Some of his attractions were not feasible, but the glossy booklet promoting the dude ranch was analogous to the Hollywood promotion seen today. However, these attempts were not sufficient to win Hollywood interest, and Meek sold the ranch a few years later.

After a series of owners, Harold Raymond bought the ranch in 1956. He came from southern California with no previous ranching experience, so he hired Art Brumley to help out. Art was quite a character, having previously worked as a one-eyed pit boss in Tonopah. His agriculture experience consisted of working around racetracks. Art had a bit of an alcohol problem, and it did not help that he and his wife, Lil, ran a bar in downtown Baker. When the crew gathered in the cookhouse for breakfast in the morning, they asked Art what they should do that day. Art told them he did not care what they did, but to just "be sure to make a lot of dust so they can see you're doing something from uptown" (D. Baker 1999). During the last year Harold Raymond owned the ranch, he bought Charolais cattle, but they got bangs (brucellosis) and had to be slaughtered. He then bought ten thousand lambs but could not feed them. He wanted to sell the ranch (D. Baker 1999).

Fred Baker, from Delta, who was no relation to the first Bakers but who had worked as a ranch hand on Baker Ranch in the 1920s, was running Silver Creek Ranch in 1954. He leased Baker Ranch from Mr. Raymond. Fred's wife, Betty, remembered that Fred told her not to take too much stuff because they probably would not be there very long. In 1959 they moved into the main ranch house with scarce furnishings. Two years later, Mr. Raymond offered Fred, Betty, and their son Dean the ranch for purchase (D. Baker 1999).

Over the years, Baker Ranch expanded, adding Strawberry Creek Ranch and the old Glen Bellander Ranch on the north side of Baker. Dean's three sons entered the business and have since taken over, adding additional ranch land in Garrison, Burbank, and the Flat, north of the Border Inn. The current Baker family has been working Baker Ranch for over fifty years and produces over one million pounds (450,000 kg) of beef and several thousand tons of hay per year (D. Baker 1999).

Dean believes that the range is in better condition today than when they took over the place. The BLM has increased the animal unit months (AUMs), and he sees an increase in wildlife, especially pronghorn. He recalls that only twenty head of pronghorn used to live in the fields at Silver Creek, because the range was so bad when the Bakers bought it. Now it is easy to see two hundred scattered over the range (D. Baker 1999).

South of Baker

Heading south out of the "downtown area" of Baker, you cross about 1 mile (1.6 km) of open land and then enter South Baker, where about forty people live. About 1 mile (1.6 km) south, a flagpole marks the Baker Cemetery, which is relatively new, with the first person interred in 1994. Before this cemetery, many people were buried in the Garrison Cemetery behind the LDS Church or in small family cemeteries scattered around the valley, or they were cremated and had their ashes spread over their favorite area.

Just across from the turnoff for the cemetery is the turnoff for the old dump. Stories abound about the wonderful times spent visiting the dump to find discarded treasures. Due to sanitation laws, the dump was closed in the 1990s. Since then, it has been turned into a shooting range. Bring your own targets, tape measure, guns, and anything else you might need.

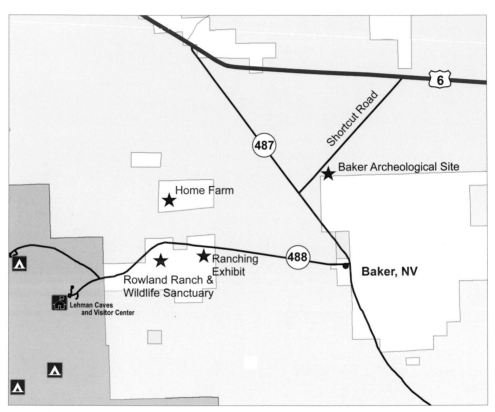

Figure 9-1. Map of attractions near Great Basin National Park.

GETTING TO GREAT BASIN NATIONAL PARK

Getting to your destination can be half the fun, and there are some quick, enjoyable stops on the way to Great Basin National Park (figure 9-1). These are all close to the principal roads that lead to the park boundary.

US Highway 6/50

Highway 6/50 is the main highway that connects Great Basin National Park with the outside world. It enters Snake Valley from the east at Utah mile marker 24, continues 38 miles (61 km) across Snake Valley (figure 9-2), climbs up and over Sacramento Pass, and then crosses Spring Valley and ascends Connor Pass.

Although US Highway 6/50 is combined through Snake Valley, Highway 6 and Highway 50 are considered separate highways and have distinct starting and ending points. US Highway 6 starts on Cape Cod in Massachusetts and travels to Bishop, California. First proposed as a major artery across the nation in 1926, the route was finally completed in 1937. At that time it stretched to Long Beach, California, making it the longest route in the United States, at 3,652 miles (5,877 km). Most of US 6 was designated as the Grand Army of the Republic Highway in honor of Union veterans of the American

Figure 9-2. US Highway 6 & 50 stretches into the distance as it bisects the valley.

Civil War (http://www.route6tour.com). It was not until 1952 that the last part of the route, between Baker, Nevada, and Delta, Utah, was paved. As *Business Week* pointed out in its issue of October 11, 1952, the paving was much needed:

> It was designated a transcontinental highway in 1937. Technically, it was. You could get from Princetown to Long Beach on it if you chose to try. But from Delta, about 80 mi. east of the Utah-Nevada border, to Ely, some 80 mi. west of the border, you ran into trouble. Much of this stretch of road was nothing but a wagon trail—rutted, filled with dust. It was one of the worst chunks of federal road in the country.

US Highway 50 extends 3,073 miles (4,946 km) from Maryland to California and has the distinction of being one of the last intact transcontinental highways. Like Highway 6, it was planned in 1926. In 1986, *Life* magazine ran an article about US 50, advising travelers to avoid it entirely, as it was devoid of many services. This article fueled Rich Moreno, the director of public relations for the Nevada Commission on Tourism between 1985 and 1992, to create a promotional "I survived Highway 50, the Loneliest Road in America" campaign in July 1986. The tongue-in-cheek campaign was so success-ful that the Nevada legislature was persuaded to designate Highway 50 "The Loneliest Road in America," and since then the campaign has inspired numerous bumper stickers, T-shirts, songs, and more (http://www.route50.com). The campaign lives on: travelers can pick up a Survival Kit from one of the businesses along the route, and if they obtain enough stamps from Highway 50 businesses, they receive a certificate from the Nevada Commission on Tourism. The kit also has games to play to help make the route more survivable.

Parts of US Highway 50 in the West follow the old Lincoln Highway, the first transcontinental highway in the nation. In Snake Valley, the Lincoln Highway follows the Pony Express Trail, which is located about 60 miles (100 km) to the north of the current US 50 and goes through Callao (see chapter 13).

It should also be noted that the current highway is south of the original gravel highway through Snake Valley. That route entered via Cowboy Pass, then cut down to Knoll Springs and across to the Robison Ranch, where there was a gas pump; then went to Silver Creek, which had another gas pump; then passed on the north side of Strawberry Creek until meeting up with today's highway about where the Weaver Creek sign is. This route avoided extra creek cross-ings and was used until the route through Kings Canyon was made in the early 1950s.

The Border Inn

At night you may be able to spot some lights in the middle of Snake Valley marking a small establishment (figure 9-3). This is the Border Inn, which straddles the state line, with the motel and gas station on the Utah side (with lower gas taxes) and the restaurant, bar, and slot machines on the Nevada side (with looser liquor laws and legal gam-bling). The Border Inn has been around for a while, although not always with that name. In 1952, Johnny "The Sheik" Sidowski and his wife, Amelie, bought a patented mining claim and built a busi-ness they called The Stateline. Johnny was so paranoid about being robbed, he would wait on his customers with his gun drawn. The fact was that *he* conducted the highway robbery: he charged passersby a dollar per gallon for water (Koyle 2002).

Martin and Jean Baker later ran the newly named Border Place for sixteen years. It consisted of one building with eight stools, a

Figure 9-3. The Border Inn provides a welcome respite for travelers.

rock-covered bar, and restrooms on the Utah side. In 1962, Martin moved the old visitor center from Lehman Caves and used it at the Border for living quarters (Koyle 2002).

In 1977, Denys Koyle and her first husband, Alex Perea, bought the Border Place. They remodeled the log house and made a cozy atmosphere for the business, adding five slot machines and a twenty-one table. In 1981, an arsonist burned the log house to the ground. Denys, who had taken over the business, had a chance to sell the place and did, but the buyers did not care for it, and in 1985 she repossessed it and rebuilt. In June 1986, the current building opened, along with eight motel rooms, additional slot machines, and updated gas pumps (Koyle 2002). With a remodel in 2008, the Border Inn now offers a motel with twenty-nine rooms, an RV park, bar, restaurant, party room, slots, pool table, gas, and diesel.

Baker Archaeological Site

Between the Border Inn and the town of Baker is the Baker Archaeological Site, accessed via the Baker Shortcut Road. This is one of two Fremont villages excavated in Snake Valley. Brigham Young University began a systematic excavation of the site in 1990. By the end of the field season, they realized that the village was considerably

Figure 9-4. The slate owl figurine was one of many artifacts found at the Baker Archaeological Site.

larger than they had anticipated, so they continued the excavation for the next three field seasons (Wilde and Soper 1993, 8).

In the middle of the village, they found a large building that was built partly underground and was surrounded by a number of other structures. It appears that the orientation of the village may have been planned to include the horizon calendar, with some doorways oriented so the summer solstice would allow the sun to shine into the building. Planting and harvesting times may have been indicated likewise (Wilde and Soper 1993, 28, 31).

Many artifacts were found at the site. Lithic artifacts included hundreds of projectile points, most of them made from obsidian; chipped stone; and grinding stones, including metates and manos used to grind pinyon pine nuts and maize. A slate owl figurine was one of the most decorative artifacts found (figure 9-4). It may have been made with slate from Wheeler Peak. It has indentations for the eyes, carved grooves and notches for wing feathers, and two drilled

Figure 9-5. Curbs mark the buildings at the Baker Archaeological Site to show the layout of this ancient Fremont village, believed to be inhabited from 1220 to 1295.

holes, possibly to allow it to be worn as a pendant. This owl may have been carved to represent a mountain feature to the east that resembles bird or bat ears. The owl figurine has become a symbol for the Baker Village. Many ceramic artifacts were also found. While most of them were plain, about 10 percent were painted. Tens of thousands of bone artifacts were recovered, including bones from bison and elk (Wilde and Soper 1993, 43, 48, 50).

You can take a walking tour of Baker Village. Although the excavations have been covered up, adobe curbs have been constructed around the outlines of the buildings so that you can get a feel for their size and orientation (figure 9-5). A helpful guide explains the surroundings along the self-guided trail. Shaded picnic tables and a pit toilet are also available. Like all archaeological sites on public land, this one is protected by law. You are not allowed to remove anything without a permit, so take photos, but no other reminders of your visit.

Figure 9-6. Post Impression Art: "The Grate Basin." The creativity of locals and visitors is displayed along Highway 488.

Nevada Highway 488: The Road West of Baker

The paved road that leads up the hill from Baker toward the South Snake Range is usually called the Cave Road or the Park Road, because it leads to Lehman Caves and Great Basin National Park. The official designation today is Nevada Highway 488.

Along the fence posts is an array of artwork (figure 9-6). Started by Lewis "Doc" Sherman in the 1970s to express his creativity and liven up the scenery, the artwork continues to change. With much of the art attached to fence posts, it is aptly called "Post Impression Art." Some of Doc's creations include *The Permanent Wave Society*, *Unicycle in the Sagebrush*, *Too Tall Tony* (figure 9-7), and others. Anyone is welcome

Photo courtesy Alana Dimmick

Figure 9-7. Too Tall Tony did not make it entirely into his grave.

to add artwork that is in good taste. Recent additions include the *Grate Basin*, a washtub with a grate next to it, and *Barb Wire*, a creation of a lady dressed in barbed wire.

Ranching Exhibit

About 3 miles (5 km) up the road is a small open-air shed, the site for a ranching exhibit that was inaugurated in 2004. It provides a good view of the ranches in Snake Valley, allowing visitors to see the circles of the pivot irrigation systems, the wet meadows used for pasture, and the expanse of winter range. A stop at the ranching exhibit is highly recommended in order to see the exquisite metalwork decorations depicting scenes of farm life and a cattle drive, created by local artisans Bill and Kathy Rountree (figure 9-8).

One of the panels in the ranching exhibit mentions the Eastern Nevada Landscape Coalition. Formed in 2001, the coalition's mission is to restore the dynamic and diverse landscapes of the Great Basin for present and future generations through collaborative efforts. Projects include restoring grasslands, sagebrush habitats, and riparian areas, as well as conducting inventories of roads, mining areas,

Figure 9-8. Some of the metalwork at the ranching exhibit; The North Snake Range is in the background.

and springs. More information is available on their website (http://www.envlc.org).

To the east and southeast is a large expanse called the Ferguson Desert, after an early settler. This was one of the most widely grazed areas in Utah in the late 1800s. Today sheep and cattle still graze here, but in smaller numbers.

In the early days of livestock grazing, the range was wide open, and Snake Valley was used primarily for winter sheep grazing (figure 9-9). Sheepherders, responsible for flocks of about two thousand sheep, raced from areas near Provo, Nephi, and Fountain Green, Utah, in October to get to the best grazing areas. They moved throughout the West Desert during the winter, returning to the summering grounds in April.

In 1900, the average sheep yielded 6 pounds (2.7 kg) of wool, but in 1946 this increased to 13.5 pounds (6.1 kg) of wool. Other changes over the years included fencing the ranges, allowing sheep to stay longer on the winter range, and, beginning about 1925, motorizing

Photo courtesy Russ Robison and the Swallow Family

Figure 9-9. Early sheep wagons were pulled by horse teams.

the sheep outfits. This resulted in being able to pull camp wagons by truck and thus haul more supplies, and it put several small stores out of business, including those at Ibex, Black Rock, and Clear Rock, Utah (Nielsen 1947, 64).

The competition for grazing areas on federal lands intensified, exacerbated by the drought of the early 1930s. Most grazers recognized the need for a better system of grazing use. The Taylor Grazing Act of 1934 was enacted to help solve this problem. Under this act, local grazing boards under the Grazing Bureau were established to allot permits. Range fencing began and was largely completed by the 1970s (Bluth 1978, 162). Additional improvements included building reservoirs and drilling wells. The Grazing Bureau eventually became the Bureau of Land Management (BLM) and shifted focus from solely grazing on federal lands to multiple uses.

As sheep prices declined over the years, cattle became more common on the range. The original cattle run in the Great Basin area were longhorns, which were brought from Texas. Over time, breeds that were better adapted to Snake Valley and easier to take care of were brought in. Today the most common breeds are Angus, Hereford, Charolais, Simmental, and mixes of these. Roughly four thousand cattle and ten thousand sheep now graze each year in Snake Valley

Figure 9-10. Home Farm is home to the School of the Natural Order.

(Craig Baker, personal communication, 2007). Both livestock owners and land agencies pay more attention to range health, and as a
result, the range has greatly improved over the last fifty years and
allowed expanding wildlife use.

Every year since 2001, the Border Inn has hosted a sheepherder's party in January. The party celebrates the sheepherders' way of
life, and old-timers share their stories. Traditional food is served,
and, starting in 2007, a sheepherder's ball is also a focal point. Since
sheepherders generally live such solitary lives, the party is a major
event for those who traverse the distant hills.

The School of the Natural Order/Home Farm

Just past the ranching exhibit is a sign marking the road to the
School of the Natural Order (figure 9-10). Located on Home Farm,
the school is a commune started by Dr. Ralph M. DeBit, also known
as Vitvan, "one who knows" in Sanskrit. In 1957, the school moved

to Snake Valley from California, where it had been incorporated in 1946. A combination of Eastern philosophy, modern field theory of physics, and general semantics forms the basis of beliefs. Vitvan was willing to share his road map to life but told students that they had to do their own work to "take the journey."

Many people in the valley were wary of this new group. Some thought it was a nudist colony, others a California cult. Vitvan instructed members to answer questions. Marj Coffman recalls going into the post office and telling the people gathered there that they (the group members) wore lots of clothes; after all, they were from California and it was really cold here (Coffman 2006)!

As students came to the valley, some filed for 5-acre (2 ha) tracts of land between the national monument and Home Farm. Many students got jobs in the community, becoming fully integrated as they served on parent-teacher associations, ran businesses, and joined community groups. Today all the members who live on Home Farm pay room and board but have control over their own money. They are expected to share chores. The fascinating book *People of the West Desert* provides a closer look at this communal life (Denton 1999).

Although Vitvan died in 1964, the school still sells his teachings via audio lessons and books on their website (http://www.sno.org). A newsletter is sent out every two months to students across the country. Those belonging to the school emphasize that it is not a cult. It is not centered on the personality of the leader but rather on his teachings. Classes and retreats are held on a regular basis so that members can return to the peace of Home Farm and join in the daily group meditations (V. Taylor 1996).

History of Home Farm Property

What is today called Home Farm was originally settled in the 1800s. For thirty-three years, it was known as the Fielding Ranch. John Fielding worked for many years at Lehman Caves National Monument and, along with his nephew Tom Sims, discovered the Lost River Passage in the cave (chapter 4). Occasionally he took pack horses up Lehman Creek to the glacier, chipped away ice, and brought it back and made ice cream. His wife, Emma, had passed away young, so their daughter Virginia helped out a lot. Virginia took the sheep and cows to Baker Creek to graze in the morning and returned them to the farm in the afternoon. Despite these responsibilities, she graduated from Baker

High School in 1933 with a graduating class of six students. In 1938, she married Joe Eldridge on the front lawn and went on to raise a family in Snake Valley (Gonder 2002) and become the postmistress in Baker.

In the 1930s, a severe drought hit Snake Valley, and the mountain creeks dried up before reaching the valley. All the springs near Baker dried up, and the closest reliable place for the community to find drinking water was the springs at Fielding Ranch (Dean Baker, personal communication, 2007). In 1957, John Fielding sold his ranch to the School of the Natural Order, which renamed it Home Farm.

Rowland Ranch

About 1 mile (1.6 km) past the turnoff for Home Farm is a driveway on the left with a mailbox for Circle M Ranch. The driveway (Circle M Ranch Road) leads past Rowland Ranch, which was at one time owned by Absalom Lehman, developer of Lehman Caves. He moved here in 1870 with his wife, Olive, from his ranch on Weaver Creek, where they had lived since 1866. Rowland Ranch had large meadows and a better water supply than Weaver Creek. The stream coming east off the slopes of the big mountain would soon be known as Lehman Creek.

In a letter home to Ohio in 1871, Olive admitted that she had not seen another white woman in a year's time, but she was content with her work and new home. She apparently did not know about Mrs. Hockman, living nearby in Burbank, who also went a year without seeing another white woman. Later in 1871, Olive gave birth to twelve-pound Laura, and in 1874 to Frank (Lambert 1991, 35).

As the children grew up, they often played with Indian children in the area, including Indian Charley, who was raised by Ab's brother, Ben, and his wife, Mary, who had settled in Baker. When he was small, Charley often rode a dog from Baker up to Lehman Ranch and apparently took pride in his good English, often correcting his playmates if they misspoke (Trexler 1966, 8).

Laura Lehman Mellanbrock recalls life as a young girl on the Rowland Ranch:

> The water fell over the wheel, ran through the calf pasture and down into the valley. Father put a screen in the stream, and in places the banks had washed from under the blue grass, and

it would hang into the water. Behind this, the fish would stay. Mother would say, "Run out and get six or eight," or as many as she wanted. We children would put our hands down into the water with fists doubled up and thumbs sticking out, and the fish would bite the thumb. Then we would press the thumb against the forefinger and pull the fish out. (Read 1965, 136)

Olive's health was deteriorating, so in 1883 she and the children went back to Ohio, where several of her sisters lived. Her health did not improve and she passed away that same year. Shortly thereafter, it is thought that Ab found the cave about 1.5 miles (2.4 km) to the west of the ranch and then established Cave Ranche near the entrance of the cave to be closer to it.

In October 1887, Ab put an ad in the *White Pine News* advertising his old ranch for sale. It included 600 acres (240 ha), with enough water to irrigate 500 acres (200 ha); 6 miles (10 km) of fencing that divided hay meadows, pastures, orchards, and cultivated fields; a young orchard of eight hundred trees bearing a variety of fruits; and an assortment of outbuildings, including stables, blacksmith shop, carpenter shop, butcher shop, corrals, and a rock milk house (Lambert 1991, 43). In short, it was a well-tended dairy ranch and produce farm.

In 1891, Lehman finally found a buyer, Charles Rowland. Charles and his wife, Elvira, and their six children operated the ranch until 1911, and it is the Rowland name that has since been associated with the property.

In 1976, Baker Ranch bought most of Rowland Ranch and still owns it today, using it for grazing. Many of the old buildings that Ab Lehman and other ranchers put up over the years still stand, or at least remnants of them do. Catalpa (*Catalpa speciosa*) and tree of heaven (*Ailanthus altissima*) trees rise high over the old Lehman homestead. Because this is private land, it should be visited only with permission.

David E. Moore Bird and Wildlife Sanctuary

On the north, west, and south sides of Rowland Ranch are three parcels of land owned by the Nevada Land Conservancy that make up the David E. Moore Bird and Wildlife Sanctuary, which is also designated by the Audubon Society as an Important Bird Area. The wet meadows, in combination with Rowland Springs Creek, Lehman Creek, and Baker Creek create good habitat for many birds and other wildlife. In addition, the sanctuary is in a transition zone between the pinyon/juniper forests and the sagebrush steppe community. No hunting is allowed, but bird-watching and wildlife viewing are encouraged. Birds to look for are the long-billed curlew, long-eared owl (*Asio otus*), Wilson's snipe (*Gallinago delicata*), and greater sage-grouse, which have historic leks (breeding grounds) here.

The North Snake Range from the Wheeler Peak Scenic Drive.

Part 3

Other Destinations near Great Basin National Park

Although Great Basin National Park may be the biggest attraction in the area, many other interesting places exist nearby. The following chapters will travel clockwise around Snake Valley, beginning just north of Great Basin National Park in the North Snake Range, and concluding with Spring Valley.

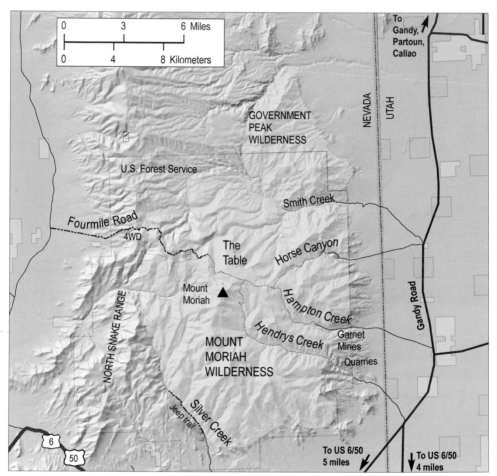

Figure 10-1. Map of the North Snake Range.

NORTH SNAKE RANGE AND MOUNT MORIAH WILDERNESS

If you like the scenery in the South Snake Range but want an even more remote experience, head to the North Snake Range on the other side of US Highway 6/50 (figure 10-1). Several hiking trails of different lengths are available (table 10-1), with the Mount Moriah Trail topping the range at 12,067 feet (3,678 m). Below the peak is the nearly 1-square-mile (3 km^2) Table, a high-elevation grassland. Beautiful isolated canyons support streams with Bonneville cutthroat trout. Old mines attract geologists and history buffs.

In 1989, much of the North Snake Range was designated the Mount Moriah Wilderness (figure 10-2). Additional land was added in 2006 for a total of 89,790 acres (27,770 ha), the majority managed by the Humboldt-Toiyabe National Forest. The BLM manages the remainder, along with the newly designated Government Peak Wilderness at the extreme north end of the range, consisting of 6,313 acres (2,555 ha). Although much of the range is designated wilderness, there is a network of roads that extends high up into the mountains adjacent to the wilderness boundary, with excellent campsites nestled in aspen groves.

Table 10-1. Hiking trails in the North Snake Range

Trail	Distance (miles) (one way)	Elevation change (feet)	Notes
Mount Moriah	1.6	11,000–12,067	From the Hendrys Creek junction to the peak. Must hike the Big Canyon, Hendry's, or Hampton Creek trails to access this trail.
Smith Creek	2.1	5,880–6,440	An old jeep trail continues farther but is extremely difficult to follow.
Big Canyon	3.1	9,900-11,000	To the Table via the west side
Hampton Creek	5.9	7,225–11,000	To the junction with the Hendrys Creek trail on the Table.
Hendrys Creek	9.9	5,900–11,000	To the Table.

Geology

The North Snake Range is a metamorphic core complex, meaning that the core of the mountain range consists of metamorphic rocks that have been uplifted. The overlying sedimentary rocks have for the most part eroded away, leaving the older rocks exposed. A fault called the Northern Snake Range Decollement, along which some of this uplift occurred, is exposed in this area. This low-angle fault can be seen along the canyon walls and on the Table.

A mixture of rock types is found in the North Snake Range. The northeastern part of the range shelters some limestone that has yet to erode totally away. Nevertheless, erosion has pockmarked the softer rock, making caves in the Smith Creek Canyon area. The northwestern and east-central parts of the range are primarily Prospect Mountain Quartzite. This area contains the beautiful rock quarried near Hendrys Creek and described in more detail below. The southern and southwest-central parts of the range are a mixed jumble of rock types, including tertiary intrusions in the Rock Canyon area and layers of dolomite, limestone, shale, and quartzite, to name a few (Hose and Blake 1976).

Figure 10-2. Mount Moriah Wilderness Area includes most of the North Snake Range.

Mount Moriah and the Table

The highest peak in the North Snake Range is Mount Moriah, at 12,067 feet (3,678 m). Spreading below Mount Moriah is the Table, a 7,000-acre (2,833 ha) high-elevation plateau dotted with ancient bristlecone pines. A herd of bighorn sheep is often found here, along with elk and deer.

In 2000, the 800-acre (320 ha) Mount Moriah Table Research Natural Area was designated by the US Forest Service as a high-elevation study area. It includes subalpine bristlecone forest, grasslands, and a minor shrubland community. The subalpine steppe grassland on Mount Moriah Table is dominated by blackroot sedge (*Carex elynoides*) and purple reedgrass (*Calamagrostis purpurascens*). This type of grassland is uncommon on the Humboldt-Toiyabe National Forest. Several bird species of special interest occupy the Research Natural Area, including peregrine falcons (*Falco peregrinus*), bald eagles (*Haliaeetus leucocephalus*), northern goshawks, flammulated owls (*Otus flammeolus*), and American three-toed woodpeckers (USFS 2007). The Forest Service designates Research Natural Areas to encourage further study of special ecosystems within the national forests.

Climbing Mount Moriah can be a short or long hike, depending on where you start. A road leads up the west side of the North Snake Range to within 4 trail miles (6.4 km) of the peak, but it is exceptionally steep and requires a four-wheel drive vehicle. This is an excellent way to get to some beautiful high-elevation terrain if you cannot hike far. To get there, drive about 5 miles (8 km) north of Baker, turn west on Highway 6/50, and go 14 miles (23 km) to near mile marker 81. Then turn north and go about 12 miles (20 km) to the Fourmile Road (FS Road 469) before turning east and continuing 10 miles (16 km) to the Big Canyon trailhead (see chapter 18 for more on Spring Valley). This trip, although only 42 miles (67 km), takes nearly two hours due to the rough roads. Along the way you will pass groves of aspens, beautiful primitive campsites, and exquisite views. The steep trail up the dramatic Big Canyon is well maintained and leads to the Table and trail junctions with Hendrys and Hampton Creeks from the east side of the range. These other trails are the long route up Mount Moriah and are described later in this chapter.

Silver Creek Road

One way to access the North Snake Range is via Silver Creek Road, which begins at Highway 6/50 near the intersection with Nevada 487. The bumpy road passes a Mt. Wheeler Power electrical substation and crosses Strawberry Creek (which flows in this section only during very wet years). About 2 miles (3 km) farther north, a side road heads off to the northwest to Silver Creek Reservoir, built by the Baker family in 1955. Located on private property, the reservoir is a popular place for locals to fish. The Nevada Department of Wildlife (NDOW) stocks it every year. A gravel road continues past the reservoir to the narrow, scenic Silver Creek Canyon. The road eventually deteriorates and becomes an old jeep trail. Old maps show hiking trails departing from the road up to the Mount Moriah area, but none are marked anymore.

The main road continues under cottonwoods and poplars that shade a couple of houses and then crosses Silver Creek, which is often dry at this location. This is Silver Creek Ranch. The Smithsons (Smittsens) homesteaded the area and then sold it in 1906 to the Bellander brothers: Albin, Alfred, and Axel. Axel lived in the upper house, Alfred in the middle house, and Albin in the lower house. In 1912, their wives and families moved out to the ranch. Their children attended school in a little log building about 1 mile (1.6 km) away. When Highway 6/50 came through this way, Silver Creek had a gas pump so that travelers could fill up (Quate 1993 192–94).

Ascending the creek drainage to the north, the road follows the bench along the North Snake Range. A turnoff marked with old tires leads up to Old Mans Canyon. This is also a good place to find bighorn sheep in the winter and pronghorn in the summer. Most of the bighorn sheep had disappeared from the area by the 1950s, so NDOW released more of them in the North Snake Range, and the Utah Division of Wildlife Resources released them in the Deep Creek Range in the 1980s. A second introduction took place in 2005 in the North Snake Range, consisting primarily of ewes and lambs.

Bighorn sheep prefer to stay on cliffy areas with low vegetation. They browse the high-elevation grasslands during the summer and move to slightly lower elevations when snow covers their food. The main predators of bighorn sheep are mountain lions, so bighorns like to stay near rocky ledges, where their sure-footedness gives them access to terrain that is prohibitive to lions. During the winter, NDOW flies over the Snake Range to look for ungulates and often sees big-horn sheep. Bighorn sheep in the North Snake Range often summer on the Table and winter in the Cove area. In the Deep Creek Range, Scotts Basin is favored summer range.

Hendrys Creek

Hendrys Creek is one of the more popular areas in the North Snake Range due to easy access, a maintained hiking trail, campsites, and good fishing. Hendrys Creek was named for a Mr. Hendry (also spelled Hendrie), who operated a sawmill in the canyon (Day and Ekins 1951, 535). The road to Hendrys Creek begins at the junction of Silver Creek Road [about 10 miles (16 km) from Highway 6/50] and Gandy Road [7.8 miles (12.6 km) from Highway 6/50]. About 3 miles (5 km) up the Hendrys Creek road, you enter the canyon.

Although Silver Peak Mine, near the head of the canyon, pro-duced lead, silver, and gold in 1925, Hendrys Creek is much bet-ter known for its rock than its minerals. The Star Dust or Probert quartzite mines began production in 1955 and consist of over twenty small quarries. You can see some of these quarries on the way up the canyon.

Hendrys Creek is one of the largest creeks in the North Snake Range. It was the refugium (safe area) for Bonneville cutthroat trout, providing adequate habitat to shelter them for the fourteen thou-sand years since Lake Bonneville dried up in this part of Snake Valley. The creek is the donor source for many other streams in both the North and South Snake Ranges.

A maintained trail, possibly the best in the North Snake Range, fol-lows the creek to the Table and Mount Moriah. It is about 10 miles (16 km) one way to get up to the Table and an additional 1.6 miles (2.6 km) to the summit. The beginning of the trail is at a barricade where the road used to ford the creek. The trail crosses the creek shortly beyond this, and then again multiple times. If you are hik-ing it during high water in June, be extra careful or you could be swept away. During the rest of the year it is often possible to cross the stream by rock hopping or wading through knee-deep water. The first 2 miles (3 km) of the trail are a slog on the old road across a sagebrush slope that can be very hot in summer. Then you start find-ing shade under some tall ponderosa pines and soon come to the wil-derness boundary marker. The canyon narrows and the walls become steeper, showing some of the beautiful quartzite rock that is quarried nearby. At about 3 miles (5 km), the trail passes a large waterfall (not visible from the trail, but you may hear it). Then the trail ascends more rapidly, passing old logging areas and the remnants of a saw- mill, including an old chimney. The old road ends here and the trail narrows as it leaves the forest behind and enters a large meadow. Here it is easy to lose the trail, but pick a route that goes up and you will reach the Table. Trees are blazed along the trail, so if you do lose it, look for the marked trees.

Besides the beautiful scenery along Hendrys Creek, the area has an unusual remnant of Native American culture. About 0.5 miles (0.8 km) south of Hendrys Creek is a large trap next to a ridge, one that is difficult to see except from a high vantage point. This trap was used by the Shoshone Indians to capture pronghorn. They put boul- ders in the shape of a *V*, with the wide end up high and the narrow end at the bottom. About fifty Indians were needed to make a drive, and they would often smoke themselves with sagebrush to disguise their human scent (Quate 1993 141).

Old Robison Ranch/Hendrys Creek Quarries

Continuing north on Gandy Road, you will come to a second road that descends from Hendrys Creek, and you may see dust trails from large trucks bringing stone down to the yard of Mt. Moriah Stone Quarries at mile 11.3. This is the site of the old Robison Ranch and is now a productive rock quarry. Several companies mine the quartz- ite out of the Hendrys Creek area, with Mt. Moriah Stone operating the largest quartzite quarry in the western United States. Mt. Moriah Stone claims include 1,200 acres (490 ha) of prime quartzite, layered 300 to 1,500 feet (90–460 m) deep (http://www.mtmoriahstone. com). The rock is often shipped to California and Utah for use in home construction. The quartzite is good building stone and also makes beautiful benches, tabletops, hearthstones, mantles, and land- scaping rock. It was used in the Brigham Young University library building and in the Federal Savings and Loan building in Illinois (Smith 1976, 57–58).

The water in Hendrys Creek rarely makes it down to Gandy Road in its regular channel due to diversions. When it does, the flood- ing washes a lot of gravel down the mountain benches. Heavy equip- ment is needed to keep the water in the channel and prevent it from flooding the road, and large piles of gravel are evident from the 2005 flood cleanup efforts.

Hampton Creek

The next creek north of Hendrys Creek is Hampton Creek, also home to Bonneville cutthroat trout. A steep trail accesses the Table, with an old garnet mine near the trailhead. Hampton Creek Road begins north of the old Robison Ranch on a marked road. On the first part of this road, greasewood is prevalent until you reach the Lake Bonneville shoreline, which is visible in two terraces to the north. Then the predominant vegetation switches to Mormon tea, shadscale, grasses, saltlover (halogeton), and rabbitbrush. Hampton Creek Road has especially sharp, shalelike rocks, so drive slowly to avoid a flat tire. At close to 4 miles (6.4 km) from Gandy Road, the road dips into a gully where some old cottonwoods appear to be dying. The road then follows a creek and reaches the Forest Service boundary at 4.6 miles (7.4 km). At mile 6.1 are a tank and a mill that was used for the garnet mines. The road ends at 6.4 miles (10.3 km) at the trailhead and a camping area.

Garnets are minerals, often dark red, that are used as the January birthstone. They are also used as industrial abrasives. The word *garnet* comes from the Latin *granatus*, which means "like a grain." The garnets found in Hampton Creek are the hardest and most common garnet type, called almandine, with the chemical formula $Fe_3Al_2Si_3O_{12}$. They are in an alluvial deposit that varies from a few to 100 feet (30 m) wide, which came from schist along the canyon wall that contains quartz, garnet, mica, and staurolite. The Hampton Creek mines (figure 10-3) processed garnets and sold them for some years, with test shipments made in the 1960s (Smith 1976, 57; Olson 2002).

You can still find many garnets in the area today. Look around the mining equipment or start up the trail. The Hampton Creek Trail up to Mount Moriah and the Table is extremely scenic and is shorter than the Hendrys Creek Trail because it is steeper. It is about 6 miles (10 km) to the Table and 1.6 miles (2.6 km) farther to Mount Moriah. The first mile (1.6 km) or so switchbacks through pinyon pine and junipers and allows some views of garnet mining. If you look down at your feet when the sun is shining, you can spot sparkles of light on the ground. Take a closer look and you are likely to see garnets scattered about.

Figure 10-3. A few structures still remain from the
days when garnets were mined near Hampton Creek.

Later, the trail follows the creek more closely. As with the other
creeks in the area, be extra careful of creek crossings during high
water, which usually occurs in June. Eventually the trail leaves the forest and continues into a beautiful meadow, which is a great camping
spot. Be sure to use low-impact camping techniques to preserve this
fantastic spot. It is not much farther now to get up onto the Table.

Horse Canyon

About 17 miles (27 km) up Gandy Road is a small red building (the
Beck place). On the west side of the road is a sign marking the route
to Horse Canyon. This small canyon is scenic and isolated and rarely

Figure 10-4. Smith Creek Canyon's cliffs, dotted with cave entrances, rise high above the canyon bottom.

visited, although the trail up Horse Canyon is theoretically one way to reach the Table and Mount Moriah. The trail is not always easy to follow due to infrequent maintenance and few visitors, so be sure to have a good map. If you like the feeling of really being out in the wilderness, this is a good place to go.

Thirty-three tons (33,000 kg) of lead-zinc ore were mined from the canyon and contained small amounts of silver and copper. The mining started in 1948 at what was called the Galena, Monitor Gulch, or Kaufman Mine (Smith 1976, 57).

Smith Creek Canyon

Smith Creek Canyon is one of the most dramatic canyons in the area, with walls rising nearly 3,000 feet (900 m) above the canyon floor and limestone liberally pocked with cavelike entrances (figure 10-4). To reach the canyon, turn at mile 17.2 on Gandy Road. From the turnoff you can see a gaping cave entrance high up on the north cliff wall, Smith Creek Cave, which, despite its large entrance, does not extend far into the mountain. A gravel road extends 5.6 miles (9.0 km) to the canyon (although the sign says 7 miles [11 km]), ending at the wilderness boundary. From there you can theoretically follow the trail along Smith Creek up to the Table, but it can be extremely overgrown after 2 miles (3 km). It is also possible to hike up Deadman Creek, a tributary to Smith Creek, but the old trail has mostly been overrun by vegetation, so plan on a slow, painful hike.

Smith Creek Cave has revealed important information about the area. In 1899, Josiah E. Spurr visited Smith Creek Canyon, noting many caves, but it was not until the summer of 1925 that the first archaeological surveys were completed by Willis L. and George A. Evans, who also conducted surveys in Baker and Council Hall Caves. In the 1950s, the Salt Lake Grotto (caving club) explored and mapped six caves in the canyon, including Smith Creek (Tuohy 1979, 6–13).

Excavations of Smith Creek Cave occurred in 1968, 1971, and 1974 (figure 10-5). Archaeologists found that the front portion of the cave had been inhabited periodically from twelve thousand to ten thousand years ago. The main activities appeared to be hunting sheep, bison, and a small camelid; and processing hides. From ten thousand to three thousand years ago, the cave was not frequently occupied. From three thousand years ago until the present, the cave was used more regularly by hunters who made the Rose Spring type of projectile points, some unidentified people who constructed grass-lined ovens, Parowan Fremont horticulturists, and others (Bryan 1977, 170, 195).

Paleontologists found the bones of a new species of mountain goat, called Harrington's mountain goat (*Oreamnos harringtoni*) in Smith Creek Cave. It was smaller than today's mountain goat, with a narrower face and thinner horns (Stock 1936). Paleontologists also found the remains of a gigantic vulture, with a wing span of 16–17 feet (5 m), possibly the largest North American bird capable of flight. It was originally named *Teratornis incredibilis* (Howard 1952) and has since been renamed *Ailornis incredibilis*. One can easily imagine this humongous bird taking off from the perch of the Smith Creek Cave entrance.

Using evidence from packrat middens, researchers found that bristlecones grew near the cave entrance 12,600 years ago but had disappeared by 12,000 years ago (Bryan 1977, 243). Today, bristlecones are found only several miles farther up Smith Creek Canyon, at higher elevations.

Several other caves dot this limestone canyon, including Charlie's Cave. This is a rock shelter near the end of the road. Charlie lived

Figure 10-5. Visitors to Smith Creek Cave peer into an excavation pit dug for archaeological and paleontological studies.

there year-round in the 1920s for several years and did some copper mining in the area. Tom Sims recalls his dad taking Charlie grub to help keep him alive (Sims 2007).

One of the tributaries to Smith Creek is Deadman Creek, named for the killing of a white man during the Indian war panic of 1875 (see chapter 17 for more information). During drought years, Deadman Creek does not flow into Smith Creek (Sims 2007).

Deadman Creek has an additional tributary, Deep Canyon, and both of these creeks plus Smith Creek contain reintroduced Bonneville cutthroat trout. Smith Creek occasionally has enough water to run into the valley, where it irrigates Smith Creek Ranch, found at mile 20.7. Smith Creek Ranch was first called Smithville and housed the Smithville post office from 1894 to 1911. During the drought of the 1930s, the creek dried up, and sand drifted so high that people could walk over the fences (Sims 2007).

Marble Canyon

The extreme north end of the North Snake Range is far off the usual itinerary. A network of roads leads from the Gandy area across the mountain range and into Spring Valley. One of the more interesting canyons is Marble Canyon. In 1891, the Marble Monster and Marble Vale claims were staked to mine marble, with additional claims made in 1908. The US Geological Survey examined the canyon in 1907 and found the marble was a member of a series of metamorphic, pre-Cambrian rocks that extend up the canyon for 2 miles (3.2 km) between metamorphic schists. The color varies from white to pink to mottled, but most of it is dark bluish-gray. White marble is found in a 35-foot (10.7 m) layer in the western portion of the canyon. No records of production exist, but at least some marble was used for headstones in the Garrison Cemetery, including one for Isaac Gandy (Darton 1907; Smith 1976, 57).

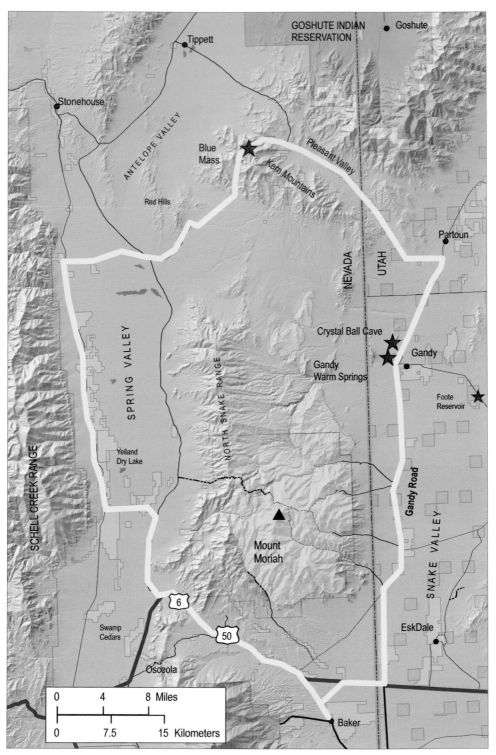

Figure 11-1. Map of Gandy loop.

GANDY WARM SPRINGS, CRYSTAL BALL CAVE, AND BLUE MASS SCENIC AREA

The Gandy, Utah, area (figure 11-1), is about forty-five minutes north of Baker and can be visited in a pleasant half-day trip from there to see warm springs and a scenic cave. For a full day loop trip, after visiting Gandy, head east to some springs with interesting fish and frogs and on to the Confusion Range (chapter 15). Or drive northwest to Blue Mass Scenic Area in the Kern Mountains to see some beautiful granite rock spires in an idyllic spot.

Gandy Warm Springs

Gandy Warm Springs begins as a natural spring emerging from a cave at a constant temperature of 81°F (27°C; figure 11-2). Several other springs join the main one, and the water flows down Warm Creek toward the east, where it is used for irrigation and eventually drains into the south end of Gandy Salt Marsh.

The warm springs are reached by driving 26.2 miles (42.2 km) north of Highway 6/50 on Gandy Road, which begins 0.5 miles (0.8 km) east of the Border Inn. Then take the road northwest across

Figure 11-2. Gandy warm springs emerges from the southeast side of Gandy Mountain. The water temperature is about 81 degrees Fahrenheit.

from a simple sign reading "Gandy." Keep driving about 2 miles (3 km) to the south part of Gandy Mountain, where a number of springs emerge from the mountainside, and turn right on a well-rutted road. If you get lost, just keep looking for riparian vegetation—there is not much water in this area, so it will not take long to find. The warm springs are a popular water hole for locals and are used for baptisms by members of the House of Aaron from EskDale.

The depth of the water near the springhead varies depending on how high the rock dams are. Some people raise the dams to allow better soaking, while others lower them to enter the cave. This is a dreadfully dangerous cave; one man died here in 2004. If you must enter, go with other people, wear proper caving equipment, including a helmet, and take several lights. The low ceiling makes it extremely easy to hit your head and become disoriented, and the water moves surprisingly fast in the cave. In addition, there are sections with less than 2 inches (5 cm) of breathing space in the 40-foot (12 m) recess.

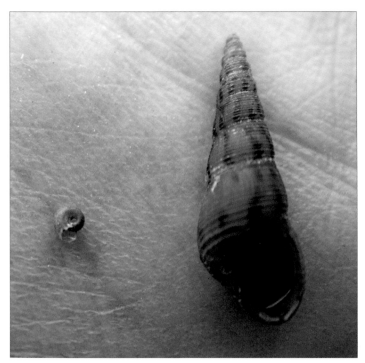

Figure 11-3. A Great Basin springsnail is much smaller than the introduced red-rimmed melania snail. Both are found in Gandy Warm Springs.

If you look closely at the water in Gandy Warm Springs, you may be able to see small fish darting about. These are speckled dace. The speckled dace here are home to a little parasite, *Centrocestus formosanus,* which affects their gills (UDWR 2004). The parasite is not native to the area; rather, it is present due to another nonnative species, a snail called the red-rimmed melania (*Melanoides tuberculatus*). This snail competes with the native snails, leaving them less food and space (Benson 2007). The red-rimmed melania is about 1–2 inches (2.5–5 cm) long, with a pointed end and several whorls (figure 11-3). It is native to Africa and Asia and was brought to the United States for the aquarium business (UDWR 2004). It was introduced into Gandy Warm Springs by someone dumping their aquarium into the spring water.

The red-rimmed melania is very common in the warm water, while the native springsnails are becoming increasingly difficult to find. This is unfortunate, because Gandy Warm Springs is the only home to the glob-nosed springsnail (*Pyrgulopsis saxatilis*).

Springsnails of the genus *Pyrgulopsis* are found in greater numbers in the Great Basin than anywhere else in the world. The diminutive snails are black and slightly larger than the period at the end of this sentence. Because of their lack of locomotion, they indicate that the water source where they are located has been around for a long time, possibly as long as ten thousand years. During thousands of years, some of the springsnails have been so isolated they have evolved into new species, like the ones here. Three other species of springsnails are found in the area at various springs. They favor fairly warm water with high conductivity and a low gradient and are often found on watercress (*Nasturtium officinale*).

The springsnails at Gandy Warm Springs are currently threatened by both nonnative snails and possible dewatering due to large-scale groundwater pumping in Snake Valley. Because this species is found nowhere else, if it disappears, it will be gone forever.

Crystal Ball Cave

Although the warm springs attracted Indians and early settlers, a second attraction in Gandy was not found until January 1956, when George Sims was looking for some sheep. He was riding on the northeast side of Gandy Mountain when he came to a small opening and looked in. He saw that it was very deep, so he went home and later returned with his brother-in-law Cecil Bates and some of their sons. They crawled in with flashlights and lanterns and found an array of cave formations and vast crystal deposits (figure 11-4). Jerald Bates remembers that this was the first hole his uncle found that was worth going into; over the years they had been sent into multitudes of little holes. The cave was so big that Jerald was worried when they first went in that they might get lost. When they got far enough from the entrance that the natural light was dim, he made tracks to make sure they could find their way out (J. Bates 2007). George named the cave Crystal Ball Cave, and along with his brother Tom Sims and brother-in-law Cecil Bates staked mining claims to the cave and began working to improve access. Tom Sims helped make the entrance large enough to walk in and wired the cave for an electrical light system, which was later removed. They tried to get the cave into the national park system, sending a letter to the secretary of the interior in 1957, but this request was rejected. In 1957, a second cave was found, called Gandy Mountain Cave (M. Bates 1994).

Figure 11-4. Crystal Ball Cave is a stunning cave filled with large crystals located in Gandy Mountain. The Bates Family provides tours of the cave.

Crystal Ball Cave is well worth the effort to see. It formed by slightly different processes than the more-visited Lehman Caves; thus it looks quite distinct. After about 500 feet (150 m) of cave passages were dissolved out of limestone rock, water filled the cave. This water was supersaturated with calcium carbonate, which settled out of the rock on the interior surfaces in the form of crystals. Gradually the water level dropped, and weathering and earthquakes caused some of the rocks to fall. Water began seeping into cracks above the cave and dissolved the limestone, redepositing it into cave formations (Heaton 1985).

When you walk into the first room and see it entirely coated with crystals called nailhead and dogtooth spar, you feel as if you are inside a geode. The cave also has a variety of speleothems, including stalactites, stalagmites, soda straws, cave popcorn, and more. The tour is not lighted and is over the natural cave floor, so take a flashlight and wear comfortable walking shoes. The hardest part of the tour is walking up to the cave entrance, which is about a 400-foot (120 m) climb.

When you exit the cave, be sure to take in the excellent view of Snake Valley and the Gandy Salt Marsh and playa across the valley.

One of the most astounding things about Crystal Ball Cave is its paleontology. The cave has been accumulating bones for at least twenty-three thousand years and was in close proximity to Lake Bonneville. Species found in it include several horse species, saber-toothed cats, camels, bison, skunks, bighorn sheep, musk oxen, and marmots (Heaton 1985).

On the east side of the mountain is a line of Lombardy poplars planted by early settler Almond Rhoades. They mark the driveway to the Bates's house, which is reached by the turnoff at mile 26.9 on Gandy Road. The site stewards for the BLM-managed cave, Jerald and Marlene Bates, give guided tours of Crystal Ball Cave by request. It is best to contact them in advance at 435-693-3145 to make sure they will be home. If you are feeling particularly adventurous, inquire about touring Gandy Mountain Cave. Entered via a small culvert, this cave requires some belly crawling, but it is well worth it to see the beautiful formations.

Gandy (Smithville)

Gandy, first known as Smithville, is spread out near the solitary mountain called Gandy Mountain (or Spring Mountain), the landmark for the community (figure 11-5). It was settled in three sections, beginning in 1887 with four families settling on the east side, two near the salt marsh, and some near Warm Creek (M. Bates 1994, 8–9).

Soon after Smithville was settled, a small Goshute Indian encampment was established on the outskirts, sharing Warm Creek. The Indians farmed, made baskets and water jugs from small willows, and moccasins and gloves out of deerskins. They lived in wickiups and moved often. During the fall, they gathered pine nuts from the surrounding mountains. They also held dance festivals, known as fandangos, with visiting Indians that would last for days. One story about Indian customs involves a woman named Nische, who was married to a white man, Fred Atkinson. They had converted an old schoolhouse into their home, but when Nische became pregnant, a tent was put up behind the house and she moved into it. She did this because if she died, everything around her would have to be burned, and she did not want to risk having their house burned down. Relatives and

Figure 11-5. Gandy Mountain is a solitary mountain that is the landmark for the community of Gandy.

friends played the drums night and day in preparation for the birth of their child (Sims 2006).

From 1887 to 1889, no mail service reached Smithville, and the locals took turns getting the mail from Muncy Creek, Nevada, on the other side of the Snake Range. In 1890, a post office was established, but in 1894 it was moved to Smith Creek Ranch, which was also called Smithville. In 1906, a new post office was established near Warm Creek. Because the name Smithville, Utah, was already in use, a new name was needed. The townspeople decided to use the name Gandy, in honor of the oldest resident, Isaac Gandy, who had bought Rhoades Ranch in 1898. Isaac Gandy served as postmaster for twenty years. The Smithville post office at Smith Creek was discontinued in 1911, but the Gandy post office was in use until 1940 (M. Bates 1994, 10, 43).

Until 1917, school at Gandy was held in a tent. Then a school building for about twenty students was built close to the post office. In 1925, the teacher taught at the Sims place at Smith Creek for half the day and in Gandy for half the day. This was not the best for either the teacher or the students, so in 1927, the school board decided to hire a teacher who owned a car so that he could take the Sims and Simonson children to Gandy. Tom Sims recalls being one of those children, along with five or six others, traveling down the road in the Model T (Sims 2006). The school was periodically opened and closed during the next fifteen years, depending on the number of students. From 1944 to 1948, students attended the Baker School. In 1948, the Gandy School building was moved closer to Warm Creek Ranch because more students were there. In 1952, the school population swelled when oil drillers worked east of Gandy and sent their children to the school. The Gandy School closed in the early 1960s (J. Bates 2007).

Apart from school, children spent a lot of time helping with chores such as haying, milking the cows, and irrigating. They also gathered wood, and Jerald Bates remembers that they procrastinated doing this task until late in the day. When they went out to get wood, they often heard coyotes howling. The older children quickly ran into the house, locking the youngest brother outside. Of course, they would not necessarily be able to stay in the house for long, because the lack of indoor plumbing necessitated trips to the outhouse. The kids also had fun trapping, fishing, and wandering. They rode horses and chased mustangs in the hills, taking lunch and a quart jar of milk, which by lunchtime would have pieces of butter floating in it (J. Bates 2007).

Marlene Bates remembers hunting rabbits, going to the cave, hauling piles of hay onto the wagon and tramping it, and joining with a bunch of children for a chickery. A chickery involved going and stealing a chicken or two and then cooking them—although many of the parents willingly provided the chickens. Some of the games they played were called Sardines and No Bears Out Tonight, variations of today's hide-and-seek (M. Bates 2007).

Gandy Salt Marsh

East of Gandy lies Gandy Salt Marsh, a unique place not only in Snake Valley but also in the world due to the numerous springs supporting frogs and fish in such a hostile environment (figure 11-6). The salt marsh was created after Lake Bonneville gradually receded. A natural dike stopped water from flowing farther north in Snake Valley, allowing the salt to precipitate out. The water comes from a combination of sources, including Warm Creek, various springs, and mountain runoff, and collects in what is known as Salt Marsh Lake.

Figure 11-6. A spring in Gandy Salt Marsh may contain fish and frogs despite the harsh environment around it. The Foote Range is in the background.

The lake varies greatly in size during the year, from about 500 acres (200 ha) to over 2,000 acres (800 ha).

Although salt might not sound glamorous, it attracted plenty of attention when the first miners came to the area. Salt was used in mining to flux out the ore, basically removing the impurities and concentrating the ore. The salt was transported great distances, including 70 miles (113 km) to the Ward Mines in Steptoe Valley (near today's Ely) and 150 miles (241 km) to the mines near Pioche, Nevada. What makes this even more remarkable is that the roads were extremely rough at that time. Few towns existed where the wagons and oxen or mule teams could stop. In addition, after high water new places to ford the creeks had to be found.

Gandy Salt Marsh was such an important destination in the late 1800s that a small town was established on the western shore of the lake and called Smithville, Utah, the third location with that name. A post office operated, with the mail brought from Pioche. A salt works was developed to extract salt from Salt Marsh Lake. Gravel was laid down across the salt marsh into the lake, and then small cars on wheels went out and collected the salt. Salt was hauled with two sixteen-mule teams, and they put about 1,800 pounds (816 kg) of salt on each of three wagons coupled together (Quate 1993, 104–5). Eventually the railroads took over hauling salt to the mines and the salt works were abandoned. Today all that remains of Smithville are one tree and a foundation obscured by the nearby greasewood. The foundation at one time supported a two-story building.

Gandy Salt Marsh seems extremely inhospitable but in fact is home to two sensitive species in Snake Valley, the Columbia spotted frog and least chub. Probably one of the reasons these animals have survived so well is that the area is extremely difficult to access. The slightest bit of moisture makes the soil extremely sticky, clinging to shoes and bogging down vehicle tires. Wetter areas have vegetation that grows over 6 feet (2 m) high, obscuring the view. Small areas of water are deceiving, since many are very deep, up to 15 feet (5 m) in places. If you do not carefully watch your step, you can suddenly fall into one of these small pools and be trapped. The numerous cow carcasses throughout the marsh testify to the difficulty of surviving in this area. Nevertheless, least chub have found homes in some of the one hundred or so small springs. Every year, the Utah Division of Wildlife Resources (UDWR) conducts surveys for least chub and Columbia spotted frogs to determine their status.

Figure 11-7. Foote Reservoir was constructed around Bishop Spring to hold additional water.

East of Gandy

Although Gandy Salt Marsh is difficult to access, there are a couple of places that are near a good gravel road that also have frogs and fish. About 8 miles (13 km) east of Gandy is Foote Reservoir, an impoundment around a large spring called Bishop Spring (figure 11-7). Surrounding the reservoir are many Russian olive trees, although some have been removed in recent efforts to control them. During late summer, the deerflies can be unbearable. Bishop Spring is about 15 feet (5 m) deep and clear and is a reliable source of water. The water not used for agriculture flows into Bishop Marsh. This large marsh is home to least chub, Columbia spotted frogs, and northern leopard frogs, along with a great variety of birds. Although not far from Gandy Salt Marsh, this marsh has a different character, with more dry knolls separating the wet areas. It also has unexpected deep areas and some exceptionally sticky mud.

Less than 0.5 miles (0.8 km) east from Foote Reservoir is Twin Springs, two springs that emerge close to one another. Look closely in the springs and you may notice little fish. This is one of the best places to easily see Utah chub and least chub. Both of these species form shoals, or groups of fish. The Utah chub prefer deeper water, while the least chub will often swim closer to the surface. The north spring is fenced off from cattle, while the south spring is open. Increasing numbers of Russian olive trees are growing near both of them.

An unusual population of garter snakes is found nearby; they are all black, or melanistic. This is due to a recessive gene that has become prevalent in this population. There are only a handful of other places in North America where this has occurred (King 2003). Snakes are protected in Utah and Nevada, so if you want to do more than take a picture of one, you need to get a collecting permit.

Blue Mass Scenic Area and the Kern Mountains

The Kern Mountains to the northwest of Gandy have begun to get more visitation in recent years due to rock climbers and nature lovers learning about the interesting granite spires in the Blue Mass Scenic Area, administered by the BLM.

Pleasant Valley, on the north side of the Kern Mountains, was the mail route for the Overland Stage Company from 1859 to 1860. Henry "Doc" Faust was the stationmaster, and he heard that newspaper editor Horace Greeley of "go west, young man" fame was coming his way. Doc hid all the candles so Greeley would not be able to read or write in the evening but instead would be forced into conversation about the outside world. The plan was successful, with Greeley giving interesting accounts of his travels. He did find time to write about the West Desert, though. He described it as "desolate," "irredeemable," "the forlornest spit I ever saw," and "doomed to perpetual barrenness." He noted that the water was brackish and sulfurous and that even the mules practiced "great moderation in the use of it." When he was at the south end of the Deep Creek country, he stated, "If Uncle Sam should ever sell that tract for one cent per acre, he will swindle the purchaser outrageously" (Greeley 1860).

As early as 1859, employees of the Overland Stage Company recognized silver and gold ores in the area, but it was not until 1868 that the first claim was made, the Mammoth on the south side of Pleasant

Valley. The Pleasant Valley Mining District was organized in April 1869. A month later, men from Kern County, California, found silver-bearing veins and organized the Kern District. This name was later applied to the mountains. In 1872, the mining district was renamed the Eagle District, and this is the primary name for the mining area in the record books despite later name changes (Smith 1976). Tungsten was later found and mined, principally during the World Wars, when prices were high. Mining remains are still present at the aptly named Tungstonia, on the south side of the Kern Mountains.

George Sims discovered the tungsten at Tungstonia (figure 11-8). Before building a house, George and his partner, Casman Olson, lived out of a tent by the mine. After returning from a trip, they found that the tent and supplies had been stolen. They used their tracking skills to track the culprit up and over the Kern Mountains into Pleasant Valley. When the next morning dawned, the culprit awoke to George Sims holding a six-shooter straight to his head. The thief told George and Casman to load up the supplies he had stolen. They happily obliged. Then they took off the thief's shoes and told him that he would be able to find them several miles away and that he had better start walking. Apparently he never forgot his barefoot walk out of Pleasant Valley, complaining later that it was one of the worst experiences of his life (Sims 2007). Tungstonia produced enough ore that in 1917 there was a mill working three shifts, and they sent the concentrates north to be transported by the Deep Creek Railroad (Read 1965, 130).

Miners came and went, but ranchers stayed longer, planting fields and building schools. Some cabins near Blue Mass Scenic Area, at the west end of the Kern Mountains, belonged to two Henriod brothers, who raised sheep in this idyllic spot. A small creek winds through lush vegetation under the towering, eroded granite rocks. Wildflower displays can be spectacular, and rock climbers are slowly discovering this area and putting up new routes. Plan on at least a day to visit Blue Mass, as it is about 70 miles (113 km) north of Baker and it takes nearly three hours to get there. One loop route that can often be traveled in a regular car (with good tires and a good spare) is to go up about 38 miles (61 km) on Gandy Road to the road signed Pleasant Valley, and then drive 10 miles (16 km) to reach the state line, and another 11 miles (18 km) to Grass Valley Canyon Road. Head south to Blue Mass (figure 11-9). After stopping and enjoying the scenery in Blue Mass, you can continue south on Grass Valley

Figure 11-8. This mining structure at Tungstonia is a reminder of the small mining town that once existed here.

Figure 11-9. Blue Mass Scenic Area is a combination of granite rocks, a trickling stream, and solitude.

Canyon Road about 13 miles (21 km), and then southwest for about 11 miles (18 km) on White Pine County Road 37 until you reach paved Highway 893 in Spring Valley. Drive 22 miles (35 km) south on the pavement. (See chapter 18 for more on Spring Valley.) To take a shortcut back to Baker, turn east on a good gravel road and drive 5 miles (8 km) to cross the valley, then south for 8 miles (13 km) to reach Highway 6/50 near mile marker 81. From there it is about 19 miles (31 km) back to Baker.

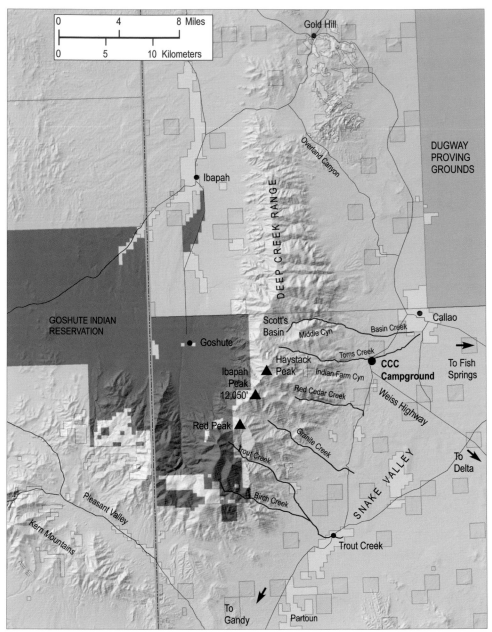

Figure 12-1. Map of Deep Creek Range and Gold Hill.

Deep Creek Range, Partoun, Gold Hill, and Goshute Indian Country

The Deep Creek Range, an hour north of Baker, is a great destination for backpacking, climbing 12,087-foot (3,684 m) Ibapah Peak, fishing for Bonneville cutthroat trout, and admiring the varied geology (figure 12-1). Along the way you travel through the remote communities of Partoun and Trout Creek.

The Deep Creek Range was overlooked by early foresters during the creation of the national forests, despite its high elevation and variety of tree species, including pinyon pine, juniper, white fir, aspen, Douglas-fir, limber pine, and Great Basin bristlecone pine. The BLM thus administers this fascinating piece of land (figure 12-2), much of which has been a Wilderness Study Area since 1990. Many of the canyons are easily accessed from Gandy Road (Snake Valley Road), which parallels the mountain range.

Figure 12-2. The dramatic Deep Creek Range is full of interesting places to explore.

Geology

The Deep Creek Range contains an interesting mix of rock types. The northern portion, near the Gold Hill area, has base layers that are roughly three hundred million years old, the Mississippian Chainman Shale and Permian limestone, both containing fossils. About thirty million years ago, during the Tertiary period, the area became very active, with granite and volcanic rocks thrusting upward into the softer, overlying rocks. This violent geologic history brought various minerals to the surface along with the igneous rocks, helping to make it a mining mecca for the last century and a half. Farther south, from about Overland Canyon down to Middle Canyon, the rock layers are exposed in bands going from north to south. They span a wide variety of ages. These formations consist of a thick layer of Cambrian Prospect Mountain Quartzite, the older and even thicker Precambrian McCoy Creek Group, a variety of Cambrian and Ordovician Formations, and then the younger Devonian sedimentary rock. For the nongeologist, one of the easiest rock layers to identify is between Middle Canyon and Trout Creek, where the rock consists of Tertiary granite intrusions (figure 12-3). The hard, white granite is well exposed and scenic, and one of the canyons is descriptively named Granite Canyon. South of Trout Creek, the rock is primarily

Figure 12-3. Granite rocks are common in the central part of the Deep Creek Mountains.

Precambrian McCoy Creek Group, along with some Tertiary deposits. Red Mountain, made of iron-stained rock of the McCoy Creek Group, is easy to spot because of its size and color (Hintze 1997).

The Deep Creek Range is high enough that it supported glaciers until several hundred years ago. These glaciers were in Toms, Indian Farm, Red Cedar, Granite, and two unnamed canyons on the west side of the range.

Partoun and Trout Creek

Before reaching the Deep Creek Range from the south, you pass through two small communities, Partoun and Trout Creek, where the largest landmark is the West Desert School. Partoun was originally established by Dr. Maurice Lerrie Glendenning as a House of Aaron community. Dr. Glendenning incorporated the Order of Aaron, which follows Old Testament teachings, in 1943. In 1949, he and his followers homesteaded about thirty 160-acre (65 ha) lots, built homes, drilled wells, cleared land, and erected a church. Life for the early homesteaders was not easy, especially because many had never worked the land before and money was scarce. Because farming did not pay all the bills, it was very common in the early days of Partoun for the women and children to stay at the homestead while the men went elsewhere to make enough money to support their families. The children needed to go to school, but the nearest schools were in Callao and Pleasant Valley, each over 20 miles (32 km) away. The community asked the Tintic School District superintendent to establish a school in Partoun, offering church buildings as temporary classrooms. In the fall of 1949, fifteen students enrolled, and by the end of the school year, the number was up to twenty-nine, in the first through the ninth grades (M. Bates 1994, 86–87).

In September 1950, the students began school in a new building with a second teacher. A small store and gas station opened in the community (M. Bates 1994, 87). It was difficult to get enough water for these small developments. Bart Wright remembers doing wind dances as a child to get wind to turn the windmills to pump water out of the ground (Wright 2006). Due to this lack of water, many of the House of Aaron members decided to move about 30 miles (48 km) south in 1955 and establish another community, which they called EskDale (http://www.eskdalecommunity.com). However, some original homesteaders decided to stay in Partoun.

Despite many of the House of Aaron students leaving, the Partoun School continued. Due to dwindling student numbers in other areas, it became the principal school in North Snake Valley. The name was changed to the West Desert School in 1976, and a high school was built in 1980 (figure 12-4). At the first high school graduation, Utah governor Scott Matheson delivered the address, speaking about the proposed MX missile system (see chapter 15). The next governor to visit the area, Utah governor Jon Huntsman, would come nearly twenty years later to learn about another looming crisis—the southern Nevada water grab.

West Desert High School contains three classrooms, a cafeteria, computer room, and library. Its most impressive attribute is a

Figure 12-4. West Desert School is the largest building in Partoun. The school is nicknamed the Hawks.

regulation-size gym, home of the Hawks, built in the 1990s. Sports are important here, and most students participate. Approximately fifteen to twenty-five students attend the high school, coming from Gandy, Pleasant Valley, Callao, Trout Creek, Partoun, and isolated ranches.

Like all the communities in Snake Valley, Partoun is unique. The student body consists of an interesting mix of students belonging to the LDS (Mormon) Church, fundamentalist Mormon polygamist sects, and the House of Aaron. Teachers note that as long as the students do not try to convert each other, they get along well. Over the years, the number of students has stayed about the same, except when large polygamist groups come to the area. One group that settled in Pleasant Valley quadrupled the student body for a few years (Hill 2007).

Electricity today is provided by Mt. Wheeler Power, established in the early 1970s. Before then, generators were needed. An interesting tidbit about electricity between Gandy and Partoun involves Gandy Salt Marsh, which lies east of the power lines. Salt was mined here for many years in the 1880s, and a lot of salt is still available today. When the wind is blowing from the east, some of the salt is blown onto the power lines and sticks to the wires. The salt conducts electricity, and when it gets wet from snow or rain, it can cause the electricity to arc from the power lines to the power poles, setting them on fire. In early 2007, five power poles burned down this way (J. and M. Bates 2007). In order to prevent damage to the power lines and power poles, Mt. Wheeler Power offers rewards to anyone who reports problems in a timely manner.

Roads near Partoun were graded just once a year until the 1970s, when Wes Lewis was hired to run the grader for a year. He was responsible for grading over 450 miles (720 km) of roads, and for twenty years he did this job by himself. Then Juab County obtained more funding, and today two county highway department personnel are located in the western part of the county. As a result, the roads are wider, the main roads are graveled, and more signs, culverts, and delineator posts are installed (Lewis 2007).

The larger community, including Granite Ranch, has volunteer ambulance and fire departments. Although the nearest hospital is over 90 miles (140 km) away, the volunteers are trained to modern standards and know the latest techniques.

Trout Creek is located just 2 miles (3 km) north of Partoun and was settled by sheepherders and miners. It is difficult to see much from the road that winds through it due to the thickets of Russian olives that obscure the views. This used to be the site of a large meadow, but settlers brought in Russian olives and the nonnative trees expanded quickly, especially during wet years, taking over the native vegetation. North of the Russian olive trees, the road passes a church belonging to the Church of Jesus Christ of Latter-day Saints. The groomed grass and short stretch of pavement in front of the church is in stark contrast to the desert surrounding it.

Shooting near Trout Creek

An incident in the early days of this remote part of Snake Valley exemplifies the rough-and-tumble *Wild West*. According to a story in *The West* magazine, this is what happened: The Harris family, consisting of Mrs. Alice Harris, her sons Leland and Eugene, and a daughter, Beth, claimed squatters' rights to a one-room cabin that had been built by an earlier squatter, Henry "Pegleg" Miller. They also claimed the nearby meadows, which had been poorly fenced. Cattle from Trout Creek Ranch to the north, run by Jess Cone, and from Warm

Creek Ranch to the south, run by Jack Singleton, often found their way into these meadows. The Harrises issued threats and demanded to be paid whenever this happened. A truce was called during World War I, when many of the local boys went into the service. After the war, things went back to the way they had been. Then they got worse.

It was July 23, 1919, a hot summer day, and the Harrises corralled cattle belonging to both the big neighboring ranches. They sent ultimatums to both. Jack Singleton from Warm Creek Ranch was away on business, but Jess Cone of Trout Creek Ranch was home. He expected trouble, so he sent to nearby Callao to get Joe Sabey, the Juab County deputy sheriff. They went out to the Harris place, along with Jess Cone's twenty-year-old son and two young boys, who were to drive the cattle back after matters had been settled. When they arrived, Edward Tackman, who had been living with the Harrises and advising them to show their mettle to the larger cattle operators, had his rifle pointed at them. He declared he was a secret agent, but when Deputy Sabey demanded his papers, he had none. Mrs. Harris went over to Jess Cone, still mounted on his horse, and berated him. He laughed at her, and she started hitting him. While Deputy Sabey was following Edward Tackman into the house, Eugene Harris blasted Cone from the saddle with a shotgun. Then Leland Harris shot Deputy Sabey with his Army Colt .45. Cone's son and the two small boys put spurs to their horses and galloped away among a deadly hail of bullets. One of the horses was shot, but the boys escaped and arrived back at Trout Creek Ranch. No one there wanted to return to the Harris place, so they went to get big Sam Falkenburg. He had gone up to Gold Hill to get supplies, and while they were informing him of what had happened, they saw Eugene Harris roar by in an old jalopy. Sam Falkenburg found him in the telegraph office sending a message to his sister. Sam sent a message to the Juab County sheriff to meet them at Trout Creek Ranch. The Gold Hill marshal eventually showed up and agreed to accompany them back to the ranch. Upon arriving, they found that Jess Cone was dead, but Deputy Sabey was still alive. While waiting for the sheriff, who was delayed a day because he was waiting for a Salt Lake City reporter to accompany him, Falkenburg and the others turned back a mob that was ready to lynch the Harrises. The case went to court in Nephi, Utah, and after two weeks the jury convicted Eugene Harris. The family appealed and hired a better lawyer, and Eugene Harris was acquitted in the second trial, in 1921. Leland Harris never stood trial for shooting Deputy Sabey (Spendlove 1968).

The official court records have a slightly different account. Based on the testimony given in the Juab courthouse, it was summer 1917 when the Harris family arrived in Trout Creek. Jess Cone rode by and told them they had better move on. In July 1918, when the Harrises returned from town, they found that their horses had been shut in their cabin, their fences were cut, and sixty head of unknown cattle were in their pastures. These turned out to belong to Jess Cone. When he came to get them, he reportedly drew a gun on Eugene Harris and threatened all of them. On July 20, 1919, Eugene Harris and the Harris's employee Edward Tackman corralled trespassing cattle and rode to notify Cone. When they reached him, he became angry and swore and then struck Harris to the ground, unconscious. The next Tuesday, the family saw a cloud of dust approach their cabin and identified Cone. Knowing he always came armed, Mrs. Harris asked Tackman to meet Cone and ask him to disarm, as Tackman did not have as much history with Cone. She and her sons listened from the window as Tackman told Deputy Sabey he was in government service. Mrs. Harris knew that was untrue, so she went outside. Tackman told her that Deputy Sabey had said that he had deputized Cone. After further conversation with Deputy Sabey, Mrs. Harris told them to take the cattle and leave. Then in Eugene Harris's words, Cone rode over to his mother, "called her a vile name and told her to get out of the way or he would hit her. I grabbed my gun . . . he reached out, grabbed her by the nose, and said he would cripple her. Mother screamed, broke loose, and turned around and Cone reached for his gun and drew it out, and just then I shot." The Supreme Court ruled that this was self-defense and reversed and remanded the court decision back to the district court (Dalton 1922, 331–43).

Trout Creek Canyon

Trout Creek, a destination for hiking, fishing, rock hounding, and history, is near the southern end of the east side of the Deep Creek Range. The turnoff for Trout Creek Canyon, named for its Bonneville cutthroat trout, is marked with a sign on Gandy (Snake Valley) Road about 50 miles (80 km) north of Highway 6/50. About 4 miles (6 km) up the rough road, you reach mine tailings and then mining equipment along the creek. This is a gravity mill that was constructed in the 1950s to process the lead, silver, and zinc ore from the Trout Creek Mine. A bit farther up are a stone house and more tailings.

Tungsten was also mined from Trout Creek after being discovered in 1916, with peak production in 1977–78 (Nutt et al. 1990).

The perennial stream in Trout Creek Canyon is monitored about 4.7 miles (7.6 km) from the main road by a USGS gauging station that measures the water level and transmits the data via satellite to a website (http://waterdata.usgs.gov/ut/nwis/uv?site_no=10172870). The road ends shortly after the gauge at a campsite with aspen, pinyon and juniper, sagebrush, and water birch. This is the Wilderness Study Area boundary, and markers declare that the road, which crosses the creek, is closed to vehicular traffic at this point.

It is possible to go by foot or horse farther up the old road. One of the sights to see is the cabin built by an outlaw. One version of the story is that a man from Texas named Albert Ross Goodin worked on ranches and later became an outlaw, riding with the Jesse James gang. When the gang got caught, Goodin escaped. The gang thought he had turned them in and swore they would catch him and kill him. In fear, Goodin eventually moved to Utah and built a rock home high up on Trout Creek. The building had one window and one door and a roof of willow limbs covered with dirt. Later he moved to a small one-room log cabin farther downstream. He was an excellent shot and was also a bit paranoid. To protect himself, he built a series of fortresses around the cabin that were 5 feet (2 m) deep, 6 feet (2 m) across, and lined with flat rocks with peepholes around the top. He also supposedly built gun ports in the cabin's walls and in the corral. To add to his mystique, he apparently had hidden money from his outlaw days. One time, about 1923, Mrs. Clara Tripp of Callao needed a large sum of money, about $3,000, and did not know how to get it. Goodin said he would get it for her and went up near his cabin and returned with gold certificates for the entire amount. He became known to many of the locals as "Old Man Ross" and lived there until he was very old and had to be placed in a retirement home. Later, George Mack (or MacMillan) took it over (Rosenberg 2007).

Granite Creek Canyon

The Granite Creek Canyon turnoff is at mile 52.1 and goes to a spectacular granite canyon leading up to the highest peak in the Deep Creeks, Ibapah Peak, at 12,087 feet (3,684 m). The Douglass mailbox also marks this turnoff. The route up to Ibapah Peak via Granite Creek Canyon is the most common path, but not necessarily the easiest, with over 5,000 feet (1,524 m) of elevation gain and a 6-mile (10 km) trek one way from the trailhead at the Wilderness Study Area boundary. The route is rather straightforward, although it requires a long day trip or a backpacking trip. To reach the trailhead, at about 6,900 feet (2100 m), take the Granite Creek Canyon road approximately 5 miles (8 km) from Gandy Road. The end of the road is signed and blocked by large boulders. Continue by foot or horse up the old jeep road, which parallels the perennial stream that harbors Bonneville cutthroat trout. After about 3 miles (5 km), the road peters out and a trail that fades in and out leads up to the pass between Red Mountain to the south and Ibapah Peak to the north. Near this pass, cut across a large meadow into the trees toward the peak on the north. A narrow trail that looks more like a wildlife trail skirts through the trees and then follows the ridge up to Ibapah Peak, where a little rock shelter provides minimal protection from the wind. At the summit are the well-preserved remnants of a heliograph station, used in the 1880s to help map the area. The views from the highest point in Juab County, Utah, are outstanding, and if your legs have the strength, it is a wonderful traverse along the ridgeline to visit Haystack Peak to the north (figure 12-5).

Indian Farm Canyon

At mile 57.6 is the turnoff to Indian Farm Canyon. Named for Indian Tom, who farmed the area in the early days of Willow Springs (Callao), the canyon is absolutely beautiful and is a great place for primitive camping. The gravel road leads past an old stone building, which once served as a powder magazine for the Civilian Conservation Corps (CCC). The road eventually ends near the canyon mouth after 2.3 miles (3.7 km), but you can continue among the water birch, aspens, cottonwoods, pinyon pine, and Woods' rose up the canyon for about 0.5 miles (0.8 km) along a four-wheeler track, and then another 0.5 miles (0.8 km) on a faint wildlife trail.

CCC Camp

Just ahead on the east side of the Pony Express Road is the Callao Civilian Conservation Corps campground, marked by a grove of cottonwood trees shading picnic tables and fire rings. The CCC camp established here in the fall of 1938 was occupied during the warmer months until 1941 (figure 12-6). The small campground belies the

Figure 12-5. The crest of the Deep Creek Mountains is above the treeline. This photo is taken from Ibapah Peak looking north to Haystack Peak.

fact that this was a large CCC camp with about thirty buildings and over one hundred men. At first there was reluctance to put a CCC camp so far from city amenities, but after a letter from the Utah governor, the camp was established as a summer camp. The CCC helped build a road through Sand Pass, constructed terraces for erosion control, developed springs and reservoirs, made campgrounds, and built fences (M. Bates 1994, 257; P. Wilson 1999, 214). They also made stone monuments to commemorate the Pony Express stations (Bluth 1978, 164). After the CCC camp closed, the buildings were moved to other locations.

Toms Canyon, Middle Canyon, and Scotts Basin

At mile 58.1, about 2 miles (3 km) south of Callao, is a signed turn-off for Toms Canyon, Middle Canyon, and Goshute Canyon. Near the road are a reservoir and weir, operated by the Callao Irrigation Company. A concrete-lined flume built in 1948 helps carry water from Toms Canyon, Indian Farm Canyon, and Basin Creek to the reservoir, shepherding it across the alluvial debris to five ranches.

Take this turnoff and stay on the straightest road (there are many turnoffs) in order to reach the Middle Canyon trail. The steep four-wheel drive road narrows into a jeep trail in about 4 miles (6 km);

Figure 12-6. CCC camp near Callao

from there it is an additional 3 miles (5 km) up to Scotts Basin, named in honor of Utah governor Scott Matheson. Locals often shorten this to the Basin. The land was private and bought by the Nature Conservancy in 1989 and then donated to the BLM. Scotts Basin is about 3 miles (5 km) across and 2 miles (3 km) wide and is important summer range for livestock and wildlife. A prominent rock formation on the west side is called Chimney Rock; you can also see an avalanche path on the north side. This is a great place to spot wildlife such as elk, bighorn sheep, and deer. Another way into the basin is the jeep trail in the canyon to the south, Toms Canyon. The road is closed before reaching the basin by the Wilderness Study Area boundary, but it is possible to continue on foot. Toms Canyon is spelled Thoms Canyon on old maps and is named after a Goshute Indian.

Goshute Canyon

Goshute Canyon, 6 miles (10 km) west of Callao, was one of the most productive mining areas in the Deep Creek Range. Several areas of gold were found at the Eagles Nest Mine, Oro del Rey workings, Evelyn Mine, and Silver Queen property. Although most mines in Snake Valley have not been worked for many decades, Goshute Canyon was worked as recently as 1982, with 2,000 feet (600 m) of underground excavations developed. At that time, seventeen adits, five caved adits, one tunnel, two declines, four shafts, and two prospect pits were present. The value of the gold estimated to still be in the ground ranges from $143 million to $1 billion (Nutt et al. 1990)!

Gold Hill

Off the northern edge of the Deep Creek Range, in rolling mountainous terrain, lies Gold Hill, 23 miles (37 km) north of Callao. This mining town was the center of excitement through many boom and bust periods. Today, Gold Hill can almost be called a ghost town. With many remnants of past times, a handful of people still live here, helping to keep those memories alive.

In 1892, the town of Gold Hill was created, and Colonel James Woodman built a smelter here. He operated the Cane Springs and Alvarado Mines, which produced between $200,000 and $300,000 in three years. Miners poured into town, most of them living in tents. When the gold boom ended in 1895, it did not take long for them to pack up and move to the next location. The smelter was taken apart and also moved to the next mining boom town (Carr 1972, 38).

During World War I, more raw materials were needed and attention returned to Gold Hill, this time primarily for tungsten. Prices for tungsten, used in electric filaments and as a strengthening agent in steel, skyrocketed in 1916. The cheapest way to ship it out was to send it in small parcel post packages via the post office. Tons of tungsten were sent this way (Bateman 1984, 319). Freight wagons and stagecoaches hauled ore and the mail nearly 50 miles (80 km) to the Western Pacific Railroad, which had been completed in 1906. With old mines reopened and new mines staked, efforts to build a spur to the railroad strengthened (Carr 1972, 38).

In 1917, a spur line was built, connecting 46 miles (74 km) to the main line and cost $450,000. Two locomotives, a combination passenger coach, a freight car, and a water car made up the Deep Creek Railroad. The train traveled 10–15 miles per hour (16–24 kmph), and the locomotives could pull only three cars at a time (Bateman 1984, 315-316).

The years 1917 and 1918 proved to be the biggest production years in Gold Hill's history, with $1 million worth of ore leaving for the Salt Lake Valley smelters. The town of Gold Hill blossomed with three thousand people. A 40-acre (16 ha) site was plotted, complete with blocks, street names, and areas for a school, church, and library. Several stores opened, selling groceries, dry goods, and hardware. A gas station, assay office, and boarding house, as well as several saloons, hotels, and cafés all operated, and the *Gold Hill News* provided information to the town. The pool hall was the largest building in town and was used for town meetings. Despite quite a few respectable buildings, especially for the businesses, most of the residences were either simple tents or canvas-covered shacks. Outhouses were positioned over old mine holes to save digging a pit, but some of these mine holes were located in the middle of the street (Carr 1972, 38).

One memorable character in town during these boom years was Dr. Joseph Peck, who attended to the residents of Gold Hill and Ibapah, as well as other folks in the area. His engaging tale of life on the mining frontier is told in *What Next, Doctor Peck?* He mentions in his book the lack of decent drinking water in Gold Hill. Apparently, early mining had contaminated the groundwater supply, so it was necessary to drink bottled water or other bottled beverages. When Utah began its prohibition against alcohol in 1917, Gold Hill was a good place to go if you fancied some whiskey. It was easy to hide the stills in mine shafts, and lookouts could spot people coming miles away across the desert by their dust trails.

As World War I continued, the cotton fields in the southern United States were being overrun by the cotton boll weevil. Arsenic was needed to treat the fields, but because of the war, overseas supplies were not available. It turned out that Gold Hill had vast deposits of arsenic. The Gold Hill and US Mines produced $2.5 million worth of arsenic between 1923 and 1925. The demand for arsenic dropped sharply in 1925, when foreign supplies again became available, and the arsenic market collapsed (Ege 2005, 3–4).

In the early 1920s, anywhere from 500 to 1,500 people were in town. The Goodwin Mercantile was built as the second grocery and dry goods store in town and still stands (figure 12-7). They sold a lot of hay and grain to sheepmen. Water was piped from Oquirrh Springs, and electricity was supplied by a Delco generator. School started in 1919 and continued through 1937 (Bateman 1984, 319–23, 328).

From 1926 to 1940, mining of various ores continued, but on a smaller scale. Due to the reduced amount of ore, the Deep Creek Railroad stopped running in 1938 and the tracks were removed in 1939.

Figure 12-7. The Goodwin Mercantile in Gold Hill still stands today, although it has not sold goods for over 50 years.

World War II renewed the need for tungsten and arsenic, and the mines sprang back into action. The US Mine produced ninety-eight thousand tons of ore with 15 percent arsenic content. Tungsten came primarily from the Reaper, Yellow Hammer, and Lucy L Mines near Clifton, earning between $100,000 and $120,000 (Ege 2005, 3–4). Gold Hill businesses and the school reopened, a bowling alley was built, and electric street lights appeared for the first time. This boom did not last long, though, and the school closed in 1946 and the post office closed in 1949 (Carr 1972, 39).

Since World War II, very little mining has occurred in Gold Hill. Nevertheless, it has a remarkable past. The Gold Hill District was the largest producer of tungsten in the state. In addition, from 1892 to 1961, a recorded 25,900 ounces (730 kg) of gold, 832,000 ounces (23,600 kg) of silver, 10.9 million pounds (4.9 million kg) of lead, 3.5 million pounds (1.6 million kg) of copper, and 20,000 pounds (9000 kg) of zinc were removed from the area (Ege 2005, 3). A total of $6–10 million in ore is estimated to have been mined from the Deep Creek region (Bateman 1984, 319).

The Gold Hill Mining District is known worldwide for its rare and unusual minerals. Many rock hounds visit the area to collect from public land. Some areas are private and all signs should be respected.

The Goshutes

The western side of the Deep Creek Range is designated as the Confederated Tribes of the Goshute Reservation. The Goshutes are a band of Western Shoshone. Major Howard Egan was one of the first people to write about the Goshutes, and he noted that they had a variety of food sources. They held periodic cricket drives by moving the crickets to foot-deep trenches covered with grass straw and then set the straw on fire to suffocate the crickets. Bushels of dead crickets were gathered, dried, and ground into flour. When roasted and mashed, they reportedly tasted like peanut butter. They gathered ants from anthills in winnowing baskets, then parched the ants and mixed them with flour and salt. Rabbit drives were common. The Goshutes also caught gophers by flooding the burrows and hitting the animals on the head when they came out. Major Egan observed one woman catching twenty-five to thirty gophers in half an hour using this method. Native trout and chub were often caught by diverting the stream water and then capturing the fish in the pools. The Goshutes used eighty-one species of wild vegetables, including seeds from forty-seven, roots from eight, and greens from twelve. Pinyon nuts were a major source of food. They also ate all birds, except magpies, and bird eggs (Bateman 1984, 281–82).

We can get a much more detailed look at the Western Shoshones from Steven Crum's book *The Road on Which We Came: A History of the Western Shoshone* (1994). The Western Shoshones called themselves the Newes and covered a large area of the Great Basin, although Snake Valley was about the eastern limit of their range. They traveled in small, extended family groups because they realized that the Great Basin had limited natural resources and they could not overpopulate the country or concentrate in large numbers in one place for a long time. Regional pine nut festivals or dances were one reason to gather, and potential mates were identified on these occasions. Round dances were held to celebrate different seasons. Whites labeled these dances "fandangos," which is Spanish for "celebration or dance," and eventually the Shoshones also adopted the name and added other activities to these events. The Newes were known for their basketweaving (Crum 1994, 1–8, 40).

As more white settlers arrived in the 1850s, these groups felt their lifestyle being threatened. In the spring of 1859, Jacob Forney, superintendent of Indian affairs for Utah, wanted permanent farms to be developed for the Goshutes. Indian agent Robert Jarvis was instructed to set up a farm at Deep Creek. On March 25, 1859, Jarvis met with one hundred Goshutes from several bands and convinced them to try farming. The Goshutes were not pleased with all the new traffic through the area, with the Overland Stage and then the Pony Express cutting across their traditional lands. An attack at Willow Springs in 1860 resulted in three Goshutes being shot and scalped, which added to the resentment. When whites killed Indian women and children at a peaceful Indian encampment near Simpson Springs in 1863, the outraged chief and braves retaliated by killing all seven inhabitants of Canyon Station and burning it down. In 1863, a "Treaty of Peace and Friendship" was signed. The Goshutes would allow travel routes, military posts, station houses, telegraph lines, stagelines, and railways through Goshute country. In addition, they would allow mills, mines, and ranches and permit timber to be taken. The Goshutes agreed to ranch and farm. In return for driving away and destroying the wild game, the US government would pay the Goshutes $1,000 per year for the next twenty years. This treaty was ratified by Congress in 1864 and signed into law in 1865 by President Abraham Lincoln (Bateman 1984, 72, 80, 82).

In 1869, the Goshutes cultivated 30 acres (12 ha) at Deep Creek, growing wheat, potatoes, and turnips. Despite later attempts to move the Goshutes to a variety of places, including Fort Hall, Idaho; Uinta Valley, Utah; and even Indian Territory (today's Oklahoma), the Goshutes stayed put (P. Wilson 1999, 26–28). The Goshute Indian Reservation, consisting of 34,560 acres (13,990 ha), was established on March 23, 1914, on the west side of the Deep Creek Range. The reservation was expanded in 1939 and again in 1984 and now includes 112,870 acres (45,680 ha), with Ibapah as the main community (http://www.goshutetribe.com). A small convenience store is in Ibapah, and a guided hunting service provides elk hunting opportunities.

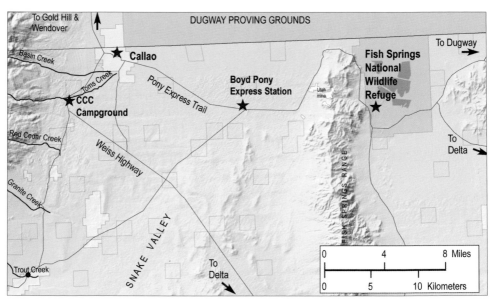

Figure 13-1. Map of Callao area.

PONY EXPRESS TRAIL
AND CALLAO

Three notable historic cross-country routes traversed the terrain near Great Basin National Park: the Overland Stage, the Pony Express, and the Lincoln Highway. Parts of these routes overlapped and can still be followed today. From Great Basin National Park, a good starting point is Callao, Utah, 65 miles (105 km) north of Highway 6/50 on Gandy (Snake Valley) Road (figure 13-1).

Callao is the oldest settlement in Snake Valley, and there were three periods when it had quite a bit of excitement: the Pony Express days, when it was called Willow Springs and was a resting station; the 1890s, when gold was discovered at nearby Gold Hill; and the 1910s and 1920s, the height of the first transcontinental highway, the Lincoln Highway. Since then, it has been a quiet refuge in the shadows of the Deep Creek Range. During non–boom times, residents rely on ranching and farming to keep the bills paid.

Beginning of Willow Springs: The Pony Express Days

In 1845, it took six months to get a message from the East Coast to California. Some thought it could be done faster, and a group of investors, William H. Russell, Alexander Majors, and William B. Waddell, joined together to form the Pony Express in January 1860.

They advertised that the Pony Express would deliver a letter from Saint Joseph, Missouri, to Sacramento, California, in just ten days. It accomplished this feat by using fast horses and expert riders. Many stations along the previously existing Overland Stage route were used, with additional "swing" or "relay" stations where riders switched out horses. At first they were located every 25 miles (40 km), but by the end of 1860 even more were added so that they were positioned every 10–12 miles (16–19 km). The riders stopped at a home station and the next rider took the mail. The first rider waited for the mail to arrive from the opposite direction and then took it, traveling twice in each direction each week, which enabled him to know about 100 miles (160 km) of the trail well. This knowledge came in handy during bad weather, when a rider did not have time to sleep at the station and could take a nap in the saddle instead (Bensen 1995).

A large number of horses were needed for this venture, and the Pony Express purchased between four hundred and five hundred mustangs, many of them above cost. They tried to get the best horses available. In addition, they hired two hundred men to run the stations and eighty riders. The advertisement for riders best explains the frame of mind: "WANTED: Young, skinny, wiry fellows not over eighteen. Must be expert riders, willing to risk death daily. Orphans preferred. Wages $25 per week." These wages were better than what the army was paying, so there was no shortage of applicants. Riding contests were held in some towns to get the best riders (Bensen 1995).

Tales of exciting adventure abound from the short-lived Pony Express, but the completion of the transcontinental telegraph in October 1861 eliminated the need for it, and it ended up being a financial disaster for the investors. Nevertheless, the willingness to cross so much land, the infrastructure and scheduling needed, and the temerity of the riders have made the Pony Express live on. The Pony Express route is now recognized as a National Historic Trail, managed by the Department of the Interior's BLM and National Park Service (http://www.nps.gov/poex).

Every June, riders retrace the entire route to remember the Pony Express days. They generally try to time the reriding with the full moon so that there is more light available in the isolated stretches in the middle of the night. Beginning in 2008, a GPS unit was included in the mochila, the traditional mail sack, so people at home could watch the progress of the Pony Express reride on the Internet (http://www.xphomestation.com).

Willow Springs Station

With its plentiful water, access to timber, and good agricultural land, the Callao vicinity was the only logical place for a settlement along the Great Salt Lake Desert portion of the trail. The station established in 1859 for the Overland Stage was also used by the Pony Express. The Willow Springs station consisted of three rooms with adobe lining, stables, and a rocked-up spring. Several dwellings and a store were constructed nearby, and a camp of Goshute Indians lived along the edge of town. Some families came to ranch and help supply the early stations with hay and wood. Besides Willow Springs, other nearby stations included Boyd, Fish Springs, Black Rock, and Dugway to the east.

Pony Express rider Elijah Nicholas "Nick" Wilson relates a first-hand account of the excitement that took place at the Willow Springs station. Nick had run away from his family in American Fork, Utah, when he was twelve years old, in about 1850, and lived with the Shoshone Indians for two years, learning their language and their ways. He also became adept at riding horses and used this skill to become a Pony Express rider. His home station at the time was Shell Creek, and his route was between there and Deep Creek. One day he rode to the Deep Creek station and the relief rider was not there, so he continued to the next station, Willow Springs, where he learned that the rider had been killed on the desert by Indians. About 4:00 p.m., seven Indians rode up to the Willow Springs station and asked for food. Neece, the station keeper, offered them a 20-pound (9 kg) sack of flour, but they demanded a sack for each of them. Neece threw the sack back into the house and told them to leave; he would not give them anything.

The Indians got angry and shot arrows at a lame old cow nearby. Neece grabbed his pistol and started shooting at them, killing two. Neece told Nick and the other two men there, Lynch and Pete, that they were "in for a hot time tonight." He knew there were more Indians up the canyon and that they would be coming as soon as it got dark. Just after dark they saw a big dust cloud over the canyon mouth 6 miles (10 km) from the station and knew the Indians were coming. Neece wanted to surprise them, so they went 100 yards (100 m) away from the station and lay down in the sandy knolls covered with greasewood.

Neece told the other men, "When you fire, jump to one side, so if they shoot at the blaze of your gun, you will not be there." They soon heard yells and the thumping of horses' hooves. When the Indians got close, all the men shot except for Nick, who was so excited that he forgot to fire. He kept shifting around and eventually landed in a small wash, where he stayed.

The shooting eventually ceased, and he raised his head to look around. He could see several humps of sand covered with grease-wood that looked like Indians on horses in the dark, so he stayed put. Later, he started crawling back to get his horse. He saw light shining through the cracks of the station and thought it was full of Indians until he heard them talk and realized that all three of his friends had survived. Several Indians had been killed and the rest had run. The Indians did not bother them again there but soon got revenge at Canyon Station (Wilson and Driggs 1991, 142–45).

Later, Nick got ambushed while riding for the Pony Express, but fortunately, one of the Indians knew him from when he had lived with the Shoshones, and they let him go. He was still not out of harm's way and at one point got shot through the head with an arrow and was left to die, but he survived an eighteen-day coma and went on to help with the Overland Stage (Wilson and Driggs 1991).

Advance of the Telegraph and Railroad

Although the mail was faithfully delivered, the advance of the tele-graph made the Pony Express short-lived, ending it in 1861. The Overland Stage continued until 1869, when the transcontinental railroad superseded it. The Willow Springs post office closed that same year.

In 1870, Wells Fargo sold its holdings at Willow Springs to George Washington Boyd. Boyd had first come to the area with Major Howard Egan to pick a route for the Pony Express, and the Boyd Pony Express Station to the east of Callao was named for him. Boyd then started supplying hay and wood to the Overland Stage and homesteading land with his son-in-law Enoch Wallace Tripp. Enoch, who was called E. W., came to Willow Springs about 1869 with his wife, Julia. They wanted to farm, and in order to get water to their fields, E. W. pulled the plow and Julia steered it to dig a diversion ditch across the bench (the sloping hills below the mountains) from Toms Creek. Eventually the family expanded to include nine children. E. W. wanted to have music in his house, so he brought a beautiful organ across the desert by wagon, taking two weeks to do so (Bateman 1984, 270–71).

Figure 13-2. The remains of the Overland Canyon Pony Express station.

Two of the Tripp sons, George Washington and Wally, often played with Goshute children, in particular a boy named Beasup, whose father worked for E. W. One day, Beasup decided he wanted to be white like Wally and George, so to help him they filled a tub with soapy wash water and tried to scrub him until he was white. The only parts that got white were the palms of his hands and the soles of his feet (M. Bates 1994, 125).

Following the Pony Express

From Callao, you can revisit Pony Express stations both to the east and the west. The Overland Canyon Pony Express Station (figure 13-2) is the next station to the west and can be combined with a visit to Gold Hill. In retaliation for the Simpson Springs attack (chapter 12), some Goshutes decided to attack the Overland Canyon station. The Indians hid in the mountains during the night and started attacking the next morning while the men at the station were eating

Figure 13-3. Boyd Station, one of the best-preserved Pony Express stations along the nearly two thousand mile route.

breakfast. Six men were killed almost immediately, and the station was looted and burned. One soldier got on a horse and attempted to escape. While he was riding away he was shot, but he made it to Willow Springs and managed to tell the story before dying. As a result of the attack, the station was moved 3 miles (5 km) east to a more defensible location (where the ruins are today). It is sometimes called Round or Rock Station because of the small round rock fort with gun ports. A corral and station house were also built at the location (Bateman 1984, 69, 72, 80). The next station to the west is Ibapah, but the next few stations after that are not well documented.

The next station to the east is Boyd Station (figure 13-3), just before the Fish Springs Range. This is one of the best-preserved stations and is a good place to stop on the way to the next station, at Fish Springs. The Pony Express Trail can then be followed on gravel back roads to south of Tooele, Utah, and is a back way to reach Salt Lake City.

Mining Boom

The discovery of gold in nearby Gold Hill and other places in the Deep Creek Range in 1892 created a second boom for the community of Willow Springs. Farmers and ranchers were again needed to provide food and supplies for these newcomers, and the little town became the center of activity. In 1892, a meeting about a post office for the area was held at C. J. Tripp's Six Mile Ranch. C. J. Tripp was appointed the postmaster and his house became the post office. They needed a new name since Willow Springs, Utah, was already taken. The name Callao was selected. One story says the new name was chosen because a visiting survey party saw the steep Deep Creek Range and was reminded of Callao, Peru. The pronunciation is quite different from the Spanish; the locals pronounce it *Cal-ee-oh*. In 1894, E. W. Tripp Sr. became the postmaster, and the post office moved to Willow Springs. The community changed its name to Callao to match the post office (Bateman 1984). The mining boom subsided in 1895, and the bucolic life in Callao resumed.

The Lincoln Highway: The First Transcontinental Highway

This town of many lives was revived when the first transcontinental highway, the Lincoln Highway, was routed through it. Although there were 2.5 million miles (4 million km) of roads in 1912, few of them connected and none traveled all the way across the country. Long-distance travel was accomplished mainly by railroad because the dirt roads were bumpy, dusty, and impassable when wet. Carl Fischer, who built the Indianapolis Motor Speedway and developed Miami Beach, Florida, had a vision: a coast-to-coast rock highway. He figured that the graveled highway would cost about $10 million.

By 1914, $5 million had been raised but little additional money was coming in. Most of the Lincoln Highway still consisted of poorly maintained dirt roads, although local consuls, or ambassadors, were chosen to help promote the highway and help travelers. Fischer decided to change tactics and started promoting a concrete highway as the superior way to travel. He figured that as people started enjoying the smooth concrete, they would press the federal government to make more concrete highways. This strategy worked, and the federal government passed acts in 1916 and 1921 authorizing $75 million of matching funds for the states to build highways.

Between 1915 and 1925, the United States went from having one named highway, the Lincoln Highway, to having a confusing menagerie of highways marked by colored bands on telephone poles (where there were telephone poles!). A more organized system was proposed to keep drivers from getting confused and lost. This system

Figure 13-4. The old Callao hotel was used frequently when the Lincoln Highway, the first transcontinental automobile route, passed through Callao.

would use numbers rather than names for routes. With these newly numbered highways, interest in the Lincoln Highway dropped, and the Lincoln Highway Association faded away in 1927. People remembered it throughout the years, though, and in 1992 the association was restarted to preserve the highway. Today, people drive the route to get a taste of history, and Lincoln Highway signs are proudly displayed along the route (Lincoln Highway Association 2007).

Because the Lincoln Highway passed through Callao, it brought business to town. Clara Tripp, who ran the post office from 1915 to 1940, also operated the Callao Hotel from 1915 to 1928 (figure 13-4). It cost twenty-five cents for a meal and thirty-five cents for a place to sleep. In 1928, her husband died, and she stopped running the hotel but continued at the post office and also sold gas, candies, and more. In 1940, she retired from the post office and her son Gray continued until his death in 1955 (M. Bates 1994, 135–36).

Callao Adjusts to a Changing World

During this period, a few world events touched the lives of those in Callao. World War I pulled some men away. Early in 1918, the flu epidemic hit Utah, and by the fall the state health officer banned all public meetings. When the war ended in November 1918, many celebrations were held, which worsened the flu epidemic (P. Wilson 1999, 165).

It was during the Great Depression that Callao was at its peak, with over two hundred inhabitants in 1936, along with two service stations, a post office, a store, and a hotel. The nearby CCC camp probably helped to keep spirits up with regular dances, although drought years from 1931 to 1934, with 1931 the driest year on record in Juab County, did drive some farmers away (P. Wilson 1999, 188, 196).

With the start of World War II, a large change occurred to the north of Callao with the establishment of Dugway Proving Ground, a place for testing chemical and biological agents, among other things. Several residents from the Callao area went to work in Dugway, providing a welcome source of income to the community. However, several military accidents, including the accidental blowing up of the cattle chute and corral at Parker Ranch at Redden Springs, about 8 miles (13 km) from Callao, and fiery crashes out in the salt flats made locals a little nervous (Layland 2007).

Although most Callao residents ranched and farmed, a new employment opportunity came in 1959, when the US Fish and Wildlife Service opened Fish Springs National Wildlife Refuge to the east of Callao (chapter 14).

RaeJean Layland recalls how important the Callao Fair was. Every August, all the children exhibited their animals and 4-H projects. There were three days of sewing at the church, a modeling show, and demonstrations. One year, army officials from Dugway Proving Ground came and took blood samples from everyone to test them, claiming to be checking for tuberculosis. The locals never found out the results of the tests and were always left wondering if the army was really checking for something else.

When more national attention was directed toward aliens, inhabitants of Callao were able to look in their backyards. Residents recall seeing strange sights over the proving ground, like UFO sightings and lightning in the clouds that would last forty-five to sixty minutes. One time when RaeJean was driving south, she saw light shoot out across the valley in her rearview mirror. She thought Dugway had blown up and was deliberating whether to go back for her family or just drive as fast as possible because it was hopeless. The shifting lights that lit up the sky turned out to be a spectacular display of the northern lights (Layland 2007).

In 2004, a small, UFO-shaped metallic object fell from the sky and landed in Dugway Proving Ground. It turned out this object had collected extraterrestrial material, but the capsule originated on Earth. It was called Genesis. Launched in August 2001, Genesis's mission was to learn about the early solar system by collecting solar wind. Sampling began in December 2001 and continued until April 2004. Then it was time for Genesis to return to Earth. As planned, the sample return canister was coming in to land at Dugway Proving Ground in September 2004. However, due to faulty sensors, the parachutes did not deploy, and the canister crashed to the ground at a speed of 193 mph (311 kmph), lodging half of its round shape in the earth. Fortunately for the scientists, the samples remained intact, so the $264 million project was not a loss. The collected samples are being analyzed to determine the makeup of the solar wind atoms and ultimately the sun itself, because the sun contains 99 percent of the mass of the solar system (McKee 2004; NASA 2007).

Callao Today

Today, signs at either end of Callao show a map of the town and indicate where the residents live (figure 13-5). The Willow Springs Station is about 1 mile (1.6 km) from the west end of town, near the Pony Express monument. It was purchased in 1886 by Charles Bagley and has been used for over 120 years by generations of Bagleys. The station is a frame structure, in contrast to those built of rock in most of the rest of the state. An elementary school with one teacher educates students from kindergarten through eighth grade in the old LDS church building. The building came from the CCC camp in 1953 and served as the church for many years, until a new LDS church was built near Trout Creek. Children from Callao have been able to go to school in Callao or Partoun for nearly a century now (Garland 2007). A variety of houses line the main road, many of them built by the earliest families, in particular the Tripps. Several of the original homesteads remain and are carefully maintained. This is one of the most scenic communities in Snake Valley. The West Desert station of

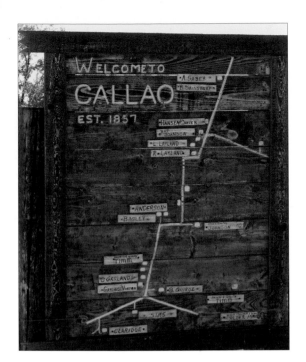

Figure 13-5. A Callao map sign graces each side of town.

the Juab County Road Department is located nearly in the middle of the strung out town. A rather unattractive addition to town is next to the road department: two large orange buildings, remnants of Cold War days when they contained missiles. The large "Do Not Hump" markings on them refer to railroad lingo but seem quite out of place in the quaint town. A bit farther west is the old hotel, with a red roof covering the original wood shingles.

The town has electricity, although it took some residents time to get used to it. RaeJean Layland recalls hating it when it came in, because she thought the power poles were ugly and messed up the view. They had lived just fine without it. In the past they needed power only on wash day, when they turned on a generator that powered the washing machine and the television. They were able to catch up on the world's happenings during wash day (Layland 2007). Telephones were much more welcome; previously, residents had to drive to Fish Springs or Ibapah to make a call.

Callao today is rather quiet. No public services are provided and mail comes only three times a week. Although Callao is no longer the hub of anything, it retains the charm of country life in a beautiful setting.

Figure 14-1. Wetlands at Fish Springs National Wildlife Refuge provide an oasis for over 200 bird species.

FISH SPRINGS NATIONAL
WILDLIFE REFUGE

An oasis in the desert, Fish Springs National Wildlife Refuge covers 17,992 acres (7,253 ha), of which more than half is water (figure 14-1). The national wildlife refuge was established in 1959 and named Fish Springs due to the numerous Utah chub found in the spring waters.

Fish Springs National Wildlife Refuge is a fun day trip from Baker, Nevada. Located 75 miles (120 km) to the northeast of Baker, it is not in Snake Valley proper but is adjacent to it and receives a great deal of water from there. Water emerges along a fault line at the base of the eastern front of the Fish Springs Range. Five regional springs produce 22 cfs (0.6 m³/s), with an additional 8 cfs (0.2 m³/s) coming in from other areas. The water temperature at the springheads averages about 74°F (23°C). Carbon-14 analysis shows that the water coming from the springs probably fell as precipitation fourteen thousand to nine thousand years ago. The precipitation in those days was most likely much greater than the 8 inches (20 cm) of average annual precipitation today (USFWS 2004). Note that nearby Wilson Health Hot Springs is not on the refuge but rather on army property. The 142°F (61°C) water is hot enough to kill pets that fall into it. Refuge personnel have had to assist enough people who get stuck on the way to these hot springs that they have a warning about them on their website directions page (http://www. fws.gov/fishsprings/Directions.html).

The wildlife refuge has become a major attraction for birders and hunters, encompassing both wetland and upland habitats. Of the nearly 18,000 acres (7,300 ha), 10,000 acres (4,000 ha) are a saline marsh that was divided in the 1960s into nine impoundments; 6,000 acres (2,300 ha) consist of mud and alkali flats; and 2,000 acres (800 ha) are semidesert upland. Over 275 species of birds have been observed at the refuge, with 61 nesting there. Spring migration in mid-April and fall migration in late September are peak bird-watching times. Migrating wetland birds stop to rest and feed before moving on, while other species stay to nest and rear their young. Some of the waterfowl species include tundra swans (*Cygnus columbianus*), Canada geese (*Branta canadensis*), mallards (*Anas platyrhynchos*), green-winged teal (*Anas carolinensis*), cinnamon teal (*Anas cyanoptera*), northern pintails (*Anas acuta*), American wigeons (*Anas americana*), gadwalls (*Anas strepera*), redheads (*Aythya americana*), canvasbacks (*Aythya valisineria*), buffleheads (*Bucephala albeola*), common goldeneyes (*Bucephala clangula*), ruddy ducks (*Oxyura jamaicensis*), and mergansers (*Mergus* spp.). Shore and wading birds include great blue herons, snowy egrets (*Egretta thula*), black-crowned night herons (*Nycticorax nycticorax*), white-faced ibis (*Plegadis chihi*), American avocets (*Recurvirostra americana*), black-necked stilts (*Himantopus mexicanus*), and eared grebes (*Podiceps nigricollis*). Additionally, forty-eight mammal, twelve reptile, four fish, and two amphibian species use the wildlife refuge (USFWS 2004).

An 11-mile (18 km) self-guided auto tour route is available at the refuge, along with picnic areas, bathrooms, a pay telephone, and drinking water. Nothing else is available—no gas, no food, no camping in the refuge (although there is plenty of BLM land surrounding it for primitive camping). The wildlife refuge is an amazing oasis surrounded by hundreds of miles of dry land. The auto tour (which can also be done by bicycle or on foot) is highly recommended. The different ponds often have different birds, so you might see a lot of egrets in one, ibises in another, avocets in a third, and pelicans in the last. The refuge has been designated an Important Bird Area due to its significance, especially during migration. It also has the only large open water areas and trees in a 25-mile (40 km) vicinity, which helps to attract birds. As for humans, the nearest neighbors are 25 miles (40 km) away in Callao, and the nearest post office is 60 miles (100 km) away in Dugway.

Managing the Refuge

In 2004, a Comprehensive Conservation Plan for Fish Springs National Wildlife Refuge was released, guiding the refuge for the next fifteen years. The overall goal of the refuge is to provide habitat for maximum wildlife diversity. One of the ways the refuge accomplishes this is by actively managing eight of the nine impoundments. They are on a five-year cycle to draw down the water to mimic the natural cycles of an undisturbed wetland. During a drawdown, plants decay more rapidly and release additional nutrients, which in turn support greater numbers of invertebrates, which the birds can then eat. Then a prescribed fire is used to help get some of the nutrients into the soil, where they are released more slowly and support vegetation. Studies have found that using drawdowns and prescribed fires increases the number of birds (USFWS 2004).

One goal of the refuge is to reintroduce the native least chub into several impoundments. This small fish is found in only a handful of places in Utah, and Fish Springs makes an ideal reintroduction location. One of the challenges with least chub reintroduction is that nonnative mosquito fish (*Gamusia affinis*) are extremely abundant in all of the ponds and impoundments. The refuge has tried to remove the mosquito fish by using the piscicide rotenone, but so far the mosquito fish have been able to resist total eradication and the populations bounce back. The mosquito fish aggressively displace the least chub and are also predators on the least chub's young-of-the-year. Least chub can reproduce very quickly; three hundred were reintroduced into Walter Spring several years ago and expanded into a population of several thousand within three years. Unfortunately, since then the least chub have disappeared, likely due to the mosquito fish. Fish Springs has over 2,000 acres (800 ha) of potential habitat available, which would add 50 percent to the total least chub habitat in Utah. However, until nonnative fish can be effectively eradicated from the complex interconnected system, least chub are unlikely to be part of the Fish Springs National Wildlife Refuge ecosystem (Brian Allen, personal communication, 2011).

The refuge actively tries to remove some of the invasive nonnative plants, such as saltcedar (tamarisk), spotted knapweed (*Centaurea stoebe*), whitetop, common reed, and Russian olive. Two-thirds of the seasonal staff's time is dedicated to weed control. More information is available at http://www.fishsprings.fws.gov.

Roughing It—Mark Twain's Recollections of the Overland Stage

Fish Springs has an interesting past. In 1859, George Chorpenning established a mail and water stop at the marshes for the Overland Stage and Freight Company. The overland stage carried passengers, freight, and news across the West from 1859 until 1869, when the transcontinental railroad replaced it. It passed through Fish Springs, one of the greener spots west of the Wasatch Front. Traveling the overland stage was not for the weak of heart—or body. One of the early travelers on it was Samuel Clemens, also known as Mark Twain.

The year was 1861, and Twain's brother had just been appointed secretary of Nevada Territory. Curious about that far-off place, Twain packed up and decided to go for an adventure, paying $150 to travel via the Overland Stage. He left Missouri with only a small amount of luggage, because travelers on the overland stage were allowed only 25 pounds (11 kg). The trip is documented in entertaining language in *Roughing It*, published in 1872. Below, Twain writes about traveling west from Salt Lake City, after leaving Camp Floyd:

> And now we entered upon one of that species of deserts whose concentrated hideousness shames the diffused and diluted horrors of Sahara—an "alkali" desert. For sixty-eight miles there was but one break in it . . .
>
> We plowed and dragged and groped along, the whole livelong night, and at the end of this uncomfortable twelve hours we finished the forty-five-mile part of the desert and got to the stage station where the imported water was. The sun was just rising. It was easy enough to cross a desert in the night while we were asleep; and it was pleasant to reflect, in the morning, that we in actual person *had* encountered an absolute desert and could always speak knowingly of deserts in presence of the ignorant thenceforward . . . All this was very well and very comfortable and satisfactory—but now we were to cross a desert in *daylight*. This was fine—novel—romantic—dramatically adventurous—*this*, indeed was worth living for, worth traveling for! We would write home all about it.
>
> This enthusiasm, this stern thirst for adventure, wilted under the sultry August sun and did not last above one hour. One poor little hour—and then we were ashamed that we

had "gushed" so. The poetry was all in the anticipation—
there is none in the reality. Imagine a vast, waveless ocean
stricken dead and turned to ashes; imagine this solemn
waste tufted with ash-dusted sage bushes; imagine the life-
less silence and solitude that belong to such a place; imagine a coach, creeping like a bug through the midst of this
shoreless level, and sending up tumbled volumes of dust
as if it were a bug that went by steam; imagine this aching
monotony of toiling and plowing kept up hour after hour,
and the shore still as far away as ever, apparently; imagine
team, driver, coach, and passengers so deeply coated with
ashes that they are all one colorless color; imagine ash drifts
roosting above mustaches and eyebrows like snow accu-
mulations on boughs and bushes. This is the reality of it.

The sun beats down with dead, blistering, relentless
malignity; the perspiration is welling from every pore in
man and beast, but scarcely a sign of it finds its way to the
surface—it is absorbed before it gets there; there is not the
faintest breath of air stirring; there is not a merciful shred
of cloud in all the brilliant firmament; there is not a living creature visible in any direction whither one searches
the blank level that stretches its monotonous miles on every
hand; there is not a sound—not a sigh—not a whisper—not
a buzz, or a whir of wings, or distant pipe of bird—not even a
sob from the lost souls that doubtless people that dead air . . .

At last we kept it up ten hours, which, I take it, is a
day, and a pretty honest one, in an alkali desert. It was
from four in the morning til two in the afternoon. And
it was so hot! And so close! And our water canteens went
dry in the middle of the day and we got so thirsty! It was
so stupid and tiresome and dull! . . . and truly and seri-
ously the romance all faded far away and disappeared,
and left the desert trip nothing but a harsh reality.

The Thomas Ranch

Not all felt the same about the desert as Mark Twain. In the 1890s,
John Thomas arrived at Fish Springs and decided to settle there. He
established a ranch on the edge of the marsh and raised horses and
cattle, which he sold to the nearby Utah and Galena Mines. He also

provided supplies to sheepherders, and lodging, meals, and hay to the stage service.

The first transcontinental highway, the Lincoln Highway, passed right through his ranch beginning in 1913, heading on toward Callao. At its peak, about 5,000 cars a year traveled the route, compared to an estimated 2,500 vehicles today. Thomas figured out a couple of ways to make money from some of these travelers. He built a stone house and a shed behind it, where he kept fifty-gallon barrels of whiskey under a huge padlock. When he saw people coming, he would get a jugful out of the barrel and set it on the table with cups. At that time it took six days to get across the mudflats, and when they arrived, the travelers asked if he had any water. He said that there was plenty out in the bulrushes as he poured whiskey and told them it was "two bits a drink." If they waited too long, he would say it was four bits and would keep increasing the price (Menzies 1981, 58–59; USFWS 2004).

Thomas found another way to make money. When people got stuck, he towed them out for a fee. To improve business, he diverted a spring across the road at a blind curve to make a nice mud trap. He erected a sign next to a pile of dry sagebrush that read "If in need of tow, light fire." At the sight of smoke, he brought a tape measure and his team of horses. He charged the stuck occupants one dollar per foot for towing. Some people argued, like aviator Eddie Rickenbacker. Eventually Mr. Rickenbacker realized the futility of quarreling and ended up paying three times the initial charge: to get pulled out, pulled back in, and pulled out again (Bluth 1978, 148–49).

Thomas died in 1917, and the ranch passed through a series of different owners until 1925, when Tass Claridge and James Harrison bought it and operated it as the Fish Springs Livestock and Fur Company for the next twenty-four years (USFWS 2004).

Trapper Jim

One of the inhabitants of Fish Springs who lived there the longest was James Harrison, better known as Trapper Jim. When he first arrived in the early 1920s, Indians were living in wickiups all over the hill. During the winter, they ate mud hen ducks, or American coots (*Fulica americana*), by cutting off only the wings and cooking them with everything else intact: feathers, guts, feet, neck, and head (Menzies 1981, 61). Lots of miners came in buckboard wagons and gambled all day and night. For supplies, Old Lady Laird's store by the Utah Mine had everything.

Jim made his living from trapping. To make it easier to trap close to home, he brought muskrats to Fish Springs from four different places to make sure he had a genetically viable population. Once they were established, he said he could easily get eleven thousand to twelve thousand rats from the swamp each year (Menzies 1981, 81–83.)

Although Jim was in an isolated place, he did not seem to want for company. The Green boys, notorious horse thieves, stayed with him off and on for twelve years. They collected colts, branded them, later broke them, and took them to horse buyers who paid thirty dollars a horse. At one point, one of the brothers became paralyzed from the hips down. His brother took him to Warm Creek near Gandy and had him soak in the water. After seven months of daily soaks, he was walking again. Later, the horse thieves met a dismal fate: they fell into wells near Delta and drowned (Menzies 1981, 65–67).

Jim married three times. His third wife, from Colorado, loved to trap and brought along her two daughters and a son by a previous marriage. Although they were between the ages of nine and twelve, they did not attend school but instead watched Jim's herd of five hundred cows. They also made a lot of money by catching and selling bullfrogs, which were introduced into Fish Springs. They caught them at night with a flashlight and a .22 rifle. On a poor night they caught only 5 to 20 frogs, but on a good night they could catch 150 frogs, which they sold for one dollar each in Wendover or for seventy-five cents a pound in Ely (Menzies 1981, 103–10, 125–27).

Jim remembers the winter of 1949 as fifty-six days and nights of snow. Cattle froze to death standing up, and the snow was 7 to 8 feet (2 m) deep. Jim was alone out at Fish Springs, and in order to save some of his livestock, he threw all the furniture out of the house and brought thirty-two cows and two horses inside and fed them a little barley each day. A couple of pigs survived in a cement house nearby, but everything else froze to death. Even the ducks and geese froze, with their mouths frozen solid. The spring holes became rock-hard ice, so no open water was available. The pigs could walk on the snow and every day brought back a couple of ducks. Jim could not walk on the snow for fear of falling through, and he later found where the pigs had nibbled on tree bark 17 feet (5 m) above the ground. Eventually the winter ended, and the sheriff came out in May or June to make sure he was okay (Menzies 1981, 131–33).

RaeJean Layland from Callao remembers that when she was a child, Trapper Jim seemed like Santa Claus. He came into their

Figure 14-2. The Utah mine in 1922.

house with a paper sack of candy bars, a real treat. You always knew he was coming because you could smell him before you could see him. One time when he was in his seventies, his vehicle broke down about 10 miles (16 km) out of Callao, and he hiked all that way in 2 to 3 feet (1 m) of snow to reach the Layland house, where he fell asleep on the couch. As the family returned from a Christmas party, RaeJean's brother said, "Mom, I think we've got a skunk." They walked into the house and found Trapper Jim. He eventually got stomach cancer and treated himself by eating a bunch of Epsom salts and then farting like a shotgun, which made him feel better (Layland 2007).

The Fish Springs Range

The long, narrow Fish Springs Range lies to the west of Fish Springs National Wildlife Refuge. George H. Hansen Peak tops the range at 8,353 feet (2,546 m) and was named for a geology professor at Brigham Young University. Much of the range is composed of volcanic rock and is under consideration as a Wilderness Study Area.

Photo courtesy Fish Springs National Wildlife Refuge
Figure 14-3. Freighters transported ore from the mine to the smelters.

There are no trails in the range, but the sparse vegetation makes it possible to hike cross-country.

Utah Mine and No-Nose Maggie

On the west side of the Fish Springs Range are mine tailings from the Utah and Galena Mines. C. C. Van Alstine located them and organized the Fish Springs Mining District in 1891 (figure 14-2). Although it cost $20 per ton to carry the ore by wagon to the nearest railroad, the ore was a higher grade, averaging $122 per ton. That made it worthwhile for the eight-horse teams to make the twelve- to fourteen-day trek (Bluth 1978, 131). A mining camp was set up, complete with a saloon. During the first year, the Utah Mine shipped $480,000 of silver bullion (figure 14-3). The mine contained about 80 percent lead and 150 ounces (4.3 kg) of silver per ton. The mining boom continued, with about 250 people living in the mining camp (M. Bates 1994, 158).

One of the more memorable—or lurid—stories about these tough times is that of Maggie Laird. Born in North Dakota as Mary Alice Ann Devitt, she moved west and quickly found that she could do quite well for herself as a dance hall girl and prostitute. She moved from mining town to mining town, eventually arriving in Fish Springs as the only prostitute. Things went well until Katie Kilkoski also moved into the mining camp. One night at the bar, the two women started fighting, rolling on the floor, kicking, and pulling hair. The gleeful miners made bets on which one would win. As blood started covering everything, the miners pulled them apart and helped them to their feet. Katie suddenly grabbed a beer bottle and smashed it into Maggie's face, cutting off her nose and leaving her with numerous scars. No-Nose Maggie realized that she now had few choices of what to do with her life, so she kept working the grimy mining camp, continuing her cheery, bawdy greeting to customers of the saloon. One morning after a boisterous evening, she felt herself pitching back and forth. When she gathered the strength to open her eyes, she found herself naked in the back of a wagon, being taken by an unknown miner to the Joy Mine in the nearby Drum Mountains. After threatening to walk back and having the driver tell her to go ahead, she reconsidered and made the best of a bad situation, talking and laughing with the driver. After a few years of working at the Joy Mine, she decided she was getting too old to move to the next boom town. She married Ardabold Laird and became postmaster and shopkeeper in Joy. Katie's demise was a little more sudden: she was thrown down one of the mine shafts just a couple of weeks after the fight in the bar (Spendlove 1967).

Eventually, the ore played out in the Fish Springs District, but from its inception until 1917, it yielded $2.5 million in gold, silver, and lead (Bluth 1978, 131). John Fritch worked the mine for the next fifty years, hiring a few men a year to help him (M. Bates 1994, 159). Today, the tailing piles are quite obvious, and there is one exposed mine shaft near the road. All mines are inherently dangerous due to their uncertain stability. Old abandoned mines are especially precarious, so stay out if you want to stay alive.

Getting to Fish Springs

One suggested way to get to Fish Springs is to go through Callao, with perhaps a side trip to the Deep Creek Range or Gold Hill. On the return from Fish Springs, head back around the north end of the Fish Springs Range. Then, near the Boyd Pony Express Station, take the road to the south that leads to Trout Creek in 18 miles (29 km), Partoun in 23 miles (37 km), and Highway 6/50 in 65 miles (105 km).

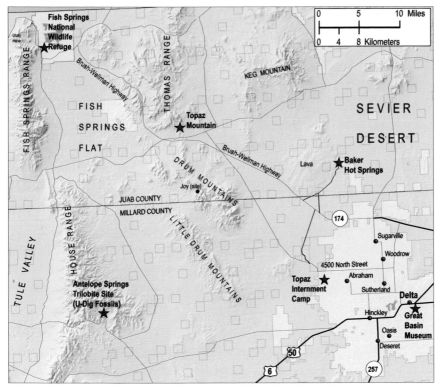

Figure 14-4. The scenic route to Delta, via Fish Springs, Topaz
Mountain, Baker Hot Springs, and the Topaz Internment Camp.

You can also combine a trip to Fish Springs with an alternative
route to Delta, especially if you like to travel remote back roads with
great scenery (figure 14-4). Topaz Mountain is 34 miles (55 km)
away via the Brush-Wellman Highway (gravel for this section). Topaz
Mountain is a popular rock hounding site for small topaz crystals.
Eighteen miles (29 km) farther down the now paved Brush-Wellman
Highway (Utah Highway 174), on the east side of a large volcanic
plateau, is the turnoff to Baker Hot Springs, about 7 miles (11 km)
north. To continue the scenic route to Delta, go back to the highway,
head west 0.5 miles (0.8 km), then turn south and follow the main
road about 10 miles (16 km) to go to the site of the Topaz Internment
Camp, where thousands of Japanese Americans were held during
World War II. It is just 15 miles (24 km) farther to Delta and the Great
Basin Museum, where you can learn more about the area.

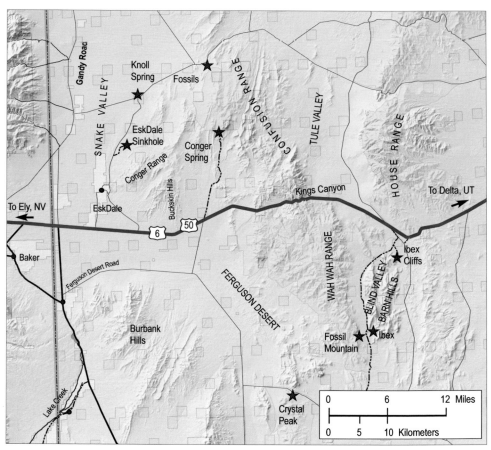

Figure 15-1. Map of eastern Snake Valley and environs, aka the Fossil & Geology Tour

CRYSTAL PEAK, CONFUSION RANGE, AND ESKDALE

If you would like to climb a strange mountain, look for fossils, observe interesting geology, find wild horses, ride OHV (off-highway vehicle) trails, or find some solitude, Crystal Peak and the Confusion Range are for you. The Confusion Range is named for its confusing geology, with numerous faults showing rocks at strange angles. The range extends almost the entire length of Snake Valley along its east side from east of Trout Creek to near Crystal Peak, although it is split into several named ridges (figure 15-1). Most of the range is sedimentary rock, but black volcanic rock of Tertiary age is seen in the Middle Range and in Smelter Knolls, a series of hills visible from Partoun. The extreme southern end of the range is also composed of volcanic rock, white Tunnel Spring Tuff. At the base of the Confusion Range is EskDale, the newest community in Snake Valley.

Due to the large amount of porous limestone and dolomite, no perennial streams and few springs exist in the Confusion Range. The vegetation consists primarily of Indian ricegrass, Mormon tea, and galleta (*Pleuraphis jamesii*) interspersed with cheatgrass, along with yellow rabbitbrush (*Chrysothamnus viscidiflorus*), winterfat, saltlover (halogeton), and fourwing saltbush (*Atriplex canescens*). Higher elevations support pinyon and juniper trees.

Figure 15-2. Aerial view of rodent burrows that dot the alluvial fans.
Cheatgrass has replaced the native vegetation.

Scattered on the alluvial fans are round patches of rodent burrows, where the yellow cheatgrass stands out from the surrounding vegetation (figure 15-2). The circles are 10–50 feet (3–16 m) in
diameter and can cover up to 10–15 percent of the landscape. Some
may have existed for an amazing fifteen thousand years. These burrow islands were created by pocket gophers (*Thomomys bottae*), kangaroo rats (*Dipodomys* spp.), and deer mice (*Peromyscus maniculatus*).
While the pocket gopher and kangaroo rat are solitary animals, and
only one adult of each species may inhabit a burrow site, it is common for other species to coexist. These include the American bad-
ger (*Taxidea taxus*), kit fox, burrowing owl (*Athene cunicularia*), and
reptiles and arthropods (Kitchen and Jorgenson 1999). Originally,
native winterfat covered the burrows. Winterfat, also called white
sage, can live more than fifty years and develops a taproot that can
penetrate up to 25 feet (8 m) deep. The silvery color of the winterfat contrasted greatly with the surrounding vegetation, leading

early researchers to nickname the rodent burrow clusters "silver dollars." Today, unfortunately, very few burrow sites are still covered with winterfat, which has experienced a sharp decline throughout the Great Basin (Kitchen and Jorgenson 1999). Winterfat provides food to grazing animals, particularly in the winter (hence its name), yet the newly arrived annuals do not provide any feed during the winter months.

Sheepherders use this land, and corrals are scattered throughout the range. During the winter, sheep camps can be found interspersed among the canyons and ridges. Generally, sheep camps are moved every three to five days so that the sheepherder can stay close to the sheep.

Very little mining has taken place in the Confusion Range, primarily because the rocks are mostly sedimentary, without the igneous intrusions that would bring minerals and metals from deeper in the earth to the surface. That fact did not stop author Louis L'Amour from basing his novel *The Empty Land* in the Confusion Range. The book refers to some of the geographic landmarks in Snake Valley and gives a sense of how rough-and-tumble some of the early mining camps were.

Crystal Peak

Crystal Peak is a beacon in the afternoon light, its white volcanic rock glowing in contrast to the tree-covered hills around it (figure 15-3). Made of mid-Tertiary Tunnel Springs Tuff about thirty-three million years old, it is a rather blunt-topped mountain and steep on three sides, rising about 800 feet (240 m) above its base. It is located at the southern end of the Confusion Range. You may be surprised to see how crumbly the volcanic tuff is. Some of the volcanic material has recesses, looking like pockets in the rock, with cavelike formations draped over them. The tuff has a large component of sand-sized quartz crystals that are rough on your hands.

The easiest way to get to Crystal Peak from Baker is go east on Highway 6/50 to about mile marker 16. Turn south and go about 5 miles (8 km) until the gravel road ends at a *T*-intersection. Turn east and follow the main road for 13 miles (21 km) as it turns to the south and climbs into Mormon tea and sagebrush country. Your views of Crystal Peak keep improving as you get closer. Turn at the sign that points east to Crystal Peak, and then it is just a few miles farther.

Figure 15-3. Crystal Peak was once known as White Mountain due to its light colored Tunnel Springs Tuff.

Ponderosa pines dot the lower slopes of Crystal Peak, taking advantage of small pockets in the tuff that trap water and nutrients. Surrounding the volcanic rock is Kanosh Shale, a member of the Ordovician Pogonip Group, a rock layer full of fossils, including trilobites and brachiopods.

It is fun to spend a morning or afternoon exploring this area or camping in one of the primitive campsites. Keep in mind that water is not available and that sometimes it can be days before someone else ventures out here. This area is part of the Wah Wah Mountains Wilderness Study Area, which covers 41,140 acres (16,650 ha).

To climb Crystal Peak, go around the base to the southeast side and follow the seam between the bare rock and the trees up to the ridge. Then ascend the ridge to the 7,108-foot (2,167 m) summit. Climbing the other sides can be dangerous due to the crumbly rock. This peak's lower elevation makes it a good choice in spring and fall.

Ferguson Desert

From Crystal Peak, you have an excellent view to the northwest of the Ferguson Desert, named after Bob Ferguson, who settled near present-day EskDale in the early 1870s (Quate 1993, 125). It contains virtually no water sources, which might be why the mapmakers called it a desert when in fact the whole area is a desert. It does contain several playas, or hardpans, and these lend it an even more desolate appearance, since no vegetation grows on the hardpans. The Ferguson Desert area was one of the largest winter ranges for sheep in Utah.

MX Missile Project

Many people appreciate the open spaces in Snake Valley and surrounding areas for the scenic views, quiet, and opportunity to escape from the rest of the world. When the US Air Force looked at the area in the 1970s, they saw a place where they could wage the Cold War. In 1979, the air force announced plans supported by President Jimmy Carter for a new intercontinental ballistic missile (ICBM) system that would be centered in western Utah and eastern Nevada. About two hundred missiles would be placed in the desert, each with its own "racetrack" of 10–15 miles (16–24 km), with twenty-three underground shelters. A 180-foot (55 m) TEL (transporter-erector-launcher) would haul the missile, or sometimes a dummy missile, from one shelter to another to confuse Soviet spy satellites. That would prevent the Soviets from taking out all the missiles unless they targeted all 4,600 shelters.

The tracks would have covered 45,000 square miles (116,500 km^2) of federal land, according to a map in the February 7, 1980, *Millard County Chronicle* (figure 15-4). Within the Snake Valley area, one loop was planned south of Fish Springs, one north of Callao, two between Trout Creek and Gandy, two more between Gandy and Highway 6/50, one near EskDale, three south of Big Springs, two south of Burbank Hills, and two in the Ferguson Desert, for a total of fourteen missiles to be located in Snake Valley, along with many more in the surrounding valleys.

The air force said that the project would have little impact on those who lived out in rural Great Basin areas and that the residents would be able to continue ranching and mining. To further prevent disrupting the region, the air force would forbid the twenty-five thousand to fifty thousand construction workers from bringing their families with them during the seven years of assembly necessary to get all the tracks and shelters built (*Time* 1980).

Snake Valley residents did not take this plan sitting down. They formed the MX Missile Alliance and spent a great deal of time spreading the word of how terrible this plan was. Cecil Garland in Callao was extremely vocal, as were Dean Baker, Sylvia Baker, Joe Griggs, and JoAnne Garrett of Baker. People put bumper stickers on their vehicles, contacted their state and federal representatives, and made frequent presentations to the media. Although the group against the project was initially small, it had great success in getting out its message and attracted important allies.

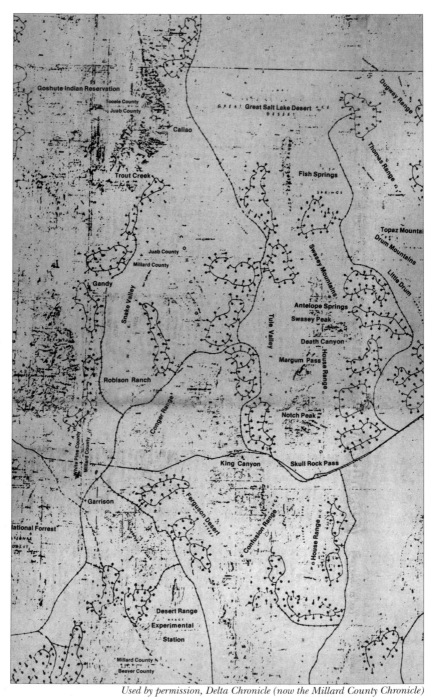

Used by permission, Delta Chronicle (now the Millard County Chronicle)

Figure 15-4. A map of the MX Missile plan shows several missile loops in Snake Valley, including two in the Ferguson Desert.

In 1980, Utah governor Scott Matheson and Nevada governor Robert List went to Capitol Hill to argue against the $34 billion system. They brought up concerns about the severe water shortage in the area and the way that this project would change a way of life forever. The Church of Jesus Christ of Latter-day Saints came out with a statement against the project. In addition, after the collapse of SALT II treaty negotiations, the Soviets could build as many missiles as they wanted—certainly enough to knock out the 4,600 missile shelters in the Great Basin, as well as the 1,054 sites for Minuteman and Titan ICBMs, and still have plenty of missiles left to bomb as many US cities as they wanted (*Time* 1980; Bradley 2007). Nevertheless, the air force continued to defend the MX project, claiming that it was cheaper to build more missile shelters than missiles. Brigadier General Guy Hecker, project boss of the MX project for the air force, said, "All of the solutions are ugly. None of them is pretty. But of all the uglies, the MX is the most attractive" (*Time* 1980).

When newly elected president Ronald Reagan looked at the project in 1981, Senator Paul Laxalt from Nevada recommended that he not support it. The president agreed. Instead, he had more grandiose ideas that included defending the country with the Strategic Defense Initiative (Star Wars), based in outer space. By the end of 1981, the MX Missile Project was left in the dust.

Fossil Mountain

From Crystal Peak, you can continue into the backcountry to the east side of the southern Confusion Range to the aptly named Fossil Mountain, about 15 miles (24 km) away in Blind Valley. Fossil Mountain is made of the Lower Ordovician Pogonip Group and has an extremely large number of fossils.

Following the Cambrian period, shallow seas continued during the Ordovician period, with many trilobites inhabiting the waters. The sediments that became the rocks of the Confusion Range and the Wah Wah Mountains were located along a shoreline that was continually rocked with waves, so many of the trilobite fossils are fragmented. Other sea creatures were becoming more common, including brachiopods, animals in seashells about the size of a dime; crinoids (feather stars), animals looking like a marine plant with a stem and a branching cap; corals, which have a free-swimming larval stage before developing an external skeleton and settling either singly or in a colony; ostracods, tiny bivalve crustaceans; ammonoid cephalopods, widely distributed animals similar to modern squid, with excellent eyesight and a sophisticated nervous system; gastropods (snails); conodonts, ancient jawless fish that left behind fossils of minuscule toothlike structures; and graptolites, mysterious invertebrates that left behind tiny fossils that resemble pieces of a hacksaw blade (Fiero 1986; DeCourten 2003; Hintze and Davis 2003).

From Fossil Mountain, Highway 6/50 is about 12 miles (19 km) north, with the road reaching it near mile marker 39.

Ibex

If you have some extra time, you might want to make a stop at Ibex, about 1 mile (1.6 km) east of Fossil Mountain. Some old corrals, dams, and building remnants are all that remain of one of the most remote sheepherder stores in the West Desert. Jack Watson settled at this unlikely spot back at the turn of the nineteenth century and lived there for a few decades, raising livestock, providing supplies to the sheepherders who came through, and welcoming travelers to his rustic hotel (Kelsey 1997).

On the other side of the Barn Hills is the Tule Hardpan, a large playa that is fun for bike riding, driving, and other pursuits where you want to go as fast as you can and not be constrained by a road. Every spring there is a fly-in, when pilots fly their small planes and land on the hardpan for a get-together.

Tall cliffs on the west side of the Tule Hardpan are known as the Ibex Cliffs (figure 15-5). They were "discovered" by rock climbers in the 1980s and have since become a world-renowned bouldering area. There are also many traditional climbing routes that go high up onto the cliffs (Garrett 2001).

OHV Trails and Conger Mountain Wilderness Study Area

The Confusion Range has 127 miles (204 km) of designated OHV trails. Signs with maps are located at the trailheads accessed from Highway 6/50 near mile markers 16 and 24. These routes follow existing roads in the Confusion Range, but some of them are extremely rough and not passable to normal four-wheel drive vehicles (http://www.millardcountytravel.com/maps/atvmaps.htm).

Figure 15-5. Ibex Cliffs are a world-renowned climbing area.

Conger Mountain Wilderness Study Area is a roadless area centered on Conger Mountain, with 20,400 acres (8,260 ha) under consideration as a wilderness area. No trails are maintained in the Wilderness Study Area, but it is possible to hike to Conger Peak, which is 8,144 feet (2,482 m) high, from several directions. One way to access it is to drive to Conger Spring (see directions below), then hike about 4 miles (6 km), gaining nearly 1,600 feet (490 m) of elevation. Having the Wilderness Study Area surrounded by OHV trails might present a conflict in some areas, but due to extremely low visitation, the two uses seem compatible here.

Conger Spring

Just south of Conger Mountain is Conger Spring, one of the few springs in the Confusion Range. It may be best known for its abundant crinoid fossils. One of the easier ways to reach Conger Spring is to take the gravel road off Highway 6/50 near mile marker 16 and head north. Follow the signs for 9 miles (14 km) until you reach the southwest side of Conger Mountain, the largest single mountain in the area. The spring has been developed, and the water is being piped away. A little patch of surface water is still available for wildlife. Nearby is a spot where some obvious digging has occurred. Look by your feet, and you will find what looks like little rock stems. These are crinoid stems, the remains of extinct animals, despite their plantlike appearance. The stems supported a round protuberance called a branching cap, but the fossilization process did not allow branching caps to be preserved. The crinoid stems have weathered out of the surrounding Mississippian Chainman Shale to become exposed. You may even find a brachiopod shell that has weathered out. Exploring the nearby ravines, you may find some scattered rocks that contain more fossils.

Herd Management Areas

The Confusion Range is one of the best places to find wild horses in Snake Valley. These highly controversial animals are now protected by law and managed by the BLM in three Herd Management Areas (HMAs) in this range: Confusion, Conger, and King Top. Combined, they are managed for up to 260 wild horses of various colors. These HMAs came about as part of the Wild Free-Roaming Horse and Burro Act of 1971, which made it illegal to chase, catch, or shoot at wild horses.

The wild horses are not native; they are descendants from runaway horses and ponies, beginning back in the early explorer and mining days. The wild horse populations can explode, stressing the desert ecosystem and ruining watering holes. When the populations become too large, the BLM conducts roundups and takes excess wild horses to town to be auctioned off, although there are usually many more horses than buyers. If you would like to see wild horses, keep a close eye out because they can be anywhere. However, because water supplies are limited, you might have the best chance of seeing them near a spring or guzzler. Some guzzlers are simply tin roofing laid on the ground at an angle. Any water that falls on one runs to the low end and into a holding tank. A float in the trough regulates the release of water from the holding tanks into the trough. Other guzzlers have water trucked in and stored in ten-thousand-gallon tanks in the hillside.

Horse bones were found in Crystal Ball Cave, but these belonged to at least two extinct species of horses, one large (*Equus* cf. *scotti*) and one small (*Equus conversidens*), and both native to North America.

These horses disappeared about ten thousand years ago along with the woolly mammoths (*Mammuthus primigenius*) and dire wolves that used to inhabit the Snake Valley area (Heaton 1985).

EskDale

EskDale is found at the base of the Conger Range, which is part of the Confusion Range. It is reached by turning off Highway 6/50 near mile markers 5 or 9. It is the newest community in Snake Valley, started in 1955 by members of the House of Aaron, also called the Aaronic Order (http://www.houseofaaron.org/). Community members consider themselves descendants of Levites, the musicians of the Bible, and music is extremely important in EskDale. The primary religious tenets follow the laws of the Old Testament. The House of Aaron is centered at EskDale, but there are also adherents in Partoun, in the Salt Lake City area, and in Missouri, along with others scattered throughout the country. Yearly meetings bring everyone together.

When the House of Aaron decided to make their new communal home at EskDale (figure 15-6), claiming land under the Desert Land Entry Act, nothing except the native vegetation existed there. They had to clear the land and plan a community. A semicircle was laid out as the living plan, with the church, school, and large dining room along the straight side and houses on the circle side.

Dr. Bob Conrad remembers the early days, when they lived in tarpaper shacks with no indoor plumbing or electricity. When they got indoor plumbing, the school kids decided they needed a celebration and got permission to burn down the outhouses. The houses were built without kitchens or with very small ones, because all meals were eaten together. Because they were a communal order, members gave everything to the community. The land, houses, and vehicles all belonged to the community. About 95 percent of communal efforts fail, and although the Mormons tried in several places in Utah, none of them worked (Conrad 1996). The EskDale communal order has survived over fifty years, which Dr. Conrad attributes to the tenacity of its founder, Dr. Glendenning, who helped greatly in getting the group through the first fifteen years.

The combination of shared challenges to make a living helped the group work well together, and they kept building the community. Many people in the valley did not understand what was going on there, and rumors started flying, in particular that it was a polygamist

Figure 15-6. An aerial photo of EskDale showing its planned layout, with the pivot fields at the top, the residential area in the semi-circle in the middle, and the dairy at the bottom.

community. One day, when directly asked if there was polygamy at EskDale, Dr. Glendenning, with a sparkle in his eye, said, "You bet. We have hundreds of chickens and just a handful of roosters, and lots of sheep and only a few rams" (Conrad 1996).

During the early years, about half of the people who came to EskDale left. For some it was extremely difficult to lose some of their privacy and have no secrets. For those who stayed, it was tough when people left whom they had grown close to. Over the years, the EskDale community has learned how to help people leave if they so desire (Conrad 1996).

Because everyone ate together, meal preparation required large quantities of food. Arlene Hanks recalls what it was like to feed eighty people a day in the beginning. In order to make enough cake to feed everyone, five cakes were needed. The first step was to go to the flour mill to get the flour. Then she had to get a five-gallon milk can to get some milk from the dairy cows, which the boys milked. Then she went to the chicken pen to get some eggs. By the time she finished baking the cakes, she was worn out, but then it might be time to make forty loaves of bread (Hanks 2007). The kitchen and dining room had no running water at first, but they had fifty-gallon drums installed on the roof. Each evening it was one man's chore to pump the drums full, and the sun warmed the water during the day (Childs 2007).

The nearest telephone was at the Border Place and the next closest in Garrison. Needless to say, neither was used much. When they saw Bud Richardson, the deputy sheriff, coming, they knew he had bad news, because he had a telephone and delivered messages (Hanks 2007).

The community started an elementary school early on. Junior and high school education were also provided, and an excellent orchestra and choir developed. The school educated not only the children in the community but also children who came to the school as boarders. Dorms housed the boarding students, and many of the students in the community also moved into the dorms because that was where all the activity was. Dorm parents monitored activities. Boarding continued until 1999, and the school stayed private until 2004.

Doug Childs was the principal of the school for twenty years and during that time taught all subjects, including driver's education. He always prayed before driving lessons and never had an accident, although a couple of close calls stick in his mind. He said the instructor brake was invaluable several times (Childs 2007).

With the school now public, the students in Baker and Garrison no longer have to go to Ely or Delta for high school but can stay in Snake Valley. Many of the students continue to do well academically and go on to college.

Those who call EskDale their home today live in peaceful, beautiful surroundings. An amphitheater that doubles as a basketball court is located in the middle of the community, along with beautifully landscaped grounds. Everyone is assigned a task, whether it is helping with the dairy farm, raising hay, running a mechanic shop, cooking meals, cleaning community buildings, or teaching school.

The dairy milks 260 cows and has plans to expand to up to 500 cows. Every other day, milk is shipped to Logan, Utah to make cheese. In addition, the dairy develops genetically superior embryos and sells them via their website (http://www.eskdaledairy.com). The farm began as 40 acres (16 ha) but now includes 1,600 acres (650 ha), with thirteen pivots. Hay is used for the dairy in EskDale and also sold to a dairy in Delta. The mechanic shop began as a small building, but in the 1970s a larger one was built to service vehicles throughout the valley. The shop can mill out parts, repair anything, and conduct Utah vehicle inspections.

Until the last fifteen years, EskDale was mostly a closed community, eschewing television, wearing uniforms, and trying to be totally self-sufficient in raising all the food they needed. Gradually, the community opened up, and today the teenagers seem like teenagers anywhere—learning to drive, listening to music, chatting on the Internet, and going to school with other students in the valley.

Today, EskDale hosts a fantastic Fourth of July celebration open to all. A musical program is followed by fireworks that would be expected from a much larger community. A full-course Christmas dinner, accompanied by the orchestra and choir and followed by a Christmas play, is an annual fund-raiser for the school. In addition to running the school, dairy, and farming operations, EskDale residents also work at a variety of places in the valley, including Great Basin National Park and the Border Inn.

Hole-in-the-Ground Sinkhole

If you are interested in an easy-to-reach geologic wonder, look 5 miles (8 km) northeast of EskDale for Hole-in-the-Ground Sinkhole. This large sinkhole was caused by the collapse of a limestone cavern and the overlying sediments (figure 15-7). The sinkhole is roughly 150 feet (50 m) deep and 210 feet (60 m) wide at the top. The sinkhole probably formed during the Pleistocene era and is located about 650 feet (200 m) east of the Lake Bonneville shoreline and about 14 feet (5 m) above it (Hintze and Davis 2003). This is an impressive sight, and if it were in the eastern United States, it would garner a lot of attention. Here it has escaped the notice of even most locals. An additional attraction of the sinkhole is that it is a great place to observe wildlife, such as breeding raptors and rattlesnakes. Close to the sinkhole is a playa, also called a hardpan. Void of any vegetation, this area is a hangout for teenagers.

Fossils in the Northern Confusion Range

The Confusion Range is one of the best places in Snake Valley to look for fossils (figure 15-8). It would be easy to spend days in this range,

Figure 15-7. Sinkhole north of EskDale.

with its wide array of rock types, including a lot of the heavily fossil-iferous Mississippian Chainman Shale. A good geologic map is certainly helpful for finding the fossiliferous strata.

In addition to Conger Spring, Cowboy Pass is another area to look for fossils. Look for ammonites in the Triassic Thaynes Formation at the northeast end of Cowboy Pass. Take the road south at the east end of Cowboy Pass for 1.2 miles (1.9 km) and then walk to the right of the road across a wash (J. Wilson 1995). These fossils are from the Mesozoic era—nicknamed the Age of Reptiles, when it was likely that dinosaurs roamed the Great Basin—but no fossils have ever been found. This was a time of massive erosion, so little fossil-bearing rock of this age has been found in Snake Valley. One exception is the Thaynes Formation, created during the Triassic, when turbid seas persisted. Filter feeders did not flourish, but mollusks succeeded, along with ammonites, which preyed on other swimming creatures (DeCourten 2003).

Figure 15-8. One of many fossils found in the rocks of the Confusion Range.

Help for Finding Fossils

If you are not comfortable reading geologic maps and want some help finding fossils, a great place to start is U-Dig Fossils, 30 miles (48 km) east of Snake Valley. This commercial operation allows visitors to dig on their land in the Wheeler Shale (http://www.u-digfossils. com). Excellent trilobites from the Cambrian period are here, preserved under near-perfect conditions (figure 15-9). Trilobites from western Utah are the ones you are most likely to buy in souvenir shops across the United States. Trilobites, three-lobed creatures that had hard exoskeletons, excellent eyes, and a long tail, looked like today's crabs or sow bugs. They dominated the shallow seas that covered the area. Because trilobites shed their exoskeletons many times during their life in order to grow, up to 90 percent of the fossils in the Cambrian period consist of trilobites. Some public land near U-Dig Fossils is also available for recreational searching and contains the same trilobites. To get there, you can go across Cowboy Pass, across

Figure 15-9. A trilobite fossil from Wheeler shale.

Tule Valley, and up Marjum Pass. Shortly after exiting the canyon, take the Death Canyon road north about 8 miles (13 km) to the quarry. Another route is to go toward Delta on Highway 6/50 and at the sign between mile markers 56 and 57 turn north and continue on gravel roads for 20 miles (32 km).

Figure 16-1. View of Burbank Hills from a small cave. The abundance of limestone and dolomite allows water to filter into the rock, and no streams or springs are found in the hills.

Burbank Hills and Garrison

Prominent in the view to the south from Great Basin National Park and Baker are the Burbank Hills, a small mountain range that is infrequently traveled (figure 16-1). Its proximity allows quick trips for desert exploration. At the base is the small town of Garrison, which was more vivacious in past eras than now (figure 16-2). Today Garrison is traversed by the coast-to-coast American Discovery Trail.

Burbank Hills

In many other places, the Burbank Hills would be called mountains, but with nearby ranges containing peaks over 1 mile (1.6 km) higher than the valley bottom, the Burbank Hills are diminutive by comparison; the highest peak reaches to only 7,822 feet (2,384 m). This is a good place to enjoy desert scenery with easy access. Almost 100 miles (160 km) of OHV routes wind their way through the Burbank Hills, and most are accessible to four-wheel drive vehicles, some even to passenger cars. Maps are available from the BLM in Fillmore, Utah, or online at http://www.stateparks.utah.gov/ohv/maps-publications. There are trailheads at Pruess Lake and Mormon Gap (mile markers 3 and 16 on Utah Highway 21).

Figure 16-2. Aerial photo of Garrison. The addition of pivots in the last decade has changed the shape of the fields surrounding Garrison.

The geology of the Burbank Hills is similar to that of the Confusion Range, although the rock layers are more predictable. The majority are limestone and dolomite of Devonian to Permian age located in a massive syncline. No streams or springs are present, but in a few areas greasewood grows, indicating that groundwater is not far below the surface.

Although there are only a couple of vegetation zones—sagebrush and pinyon/juniper—the drying winds and more intense solar radiation on south- and west-facing slopes lead to different vegetation than that on north- and east-facing slopes. In narrow canyons that are more protected, you might find extensive stands of tall Basin wildrye, which early settlers said was so tall when they arrived that it reached their horses' bellies.

Garrison

Garrison is one of the oldest existing towns in Snake Valley, founded in 1870. Named for its postmaster and early teacher, Mrs. Emma Garrison, it has gone through several cycles of ups and downs. Currently, the town is home to about forty residents. Lorene Wheeler, who has lived her whole life in Snake Valley, is proud mother to four children, twenty-three grandchildren, and thirty-plus

Photo courtesy Russ Robison

Figure 16-3. Tom Dearden's Rancher's Store in Garrison was a popular resupply spot for sheepherders. This photo was taken about 1905. Left to right: Eva and Lola Heckethorn, Bert Ashman, and Mattie Heckethorn with child.

great-grandchildren. Despite this impressive progeny, only one child and one grandchild still live in Garrison. This helps to explain the look of the town, with its numerous abandoned buildings and memories of more vibrant times.

Early Years in Garrison

Robert and Nick Dowling are remembered as the first settlers in Garrison, claiming squatters' rights on a piece of land for a few years. In 1898, the first store was established in Garrison by Mr. James and Mr. Clay. Tom Dearden bought it from them in 1905, expanding his operation from the store he had established in Baker in 1892. A hotel was built next door, and soon after a dance hall/community building. There were enough people in the area to support a second store, the Heckethorn store (Quate 1993; figure 16-3).

The following poem by Graham Quate, prepared for a school play in honor of Vivian Dearden, gives a taste of life in 1918:

I live in a place of some renown
And Garrison is the name of the town.
There is sagebrush there and cactus too
And it is ten miles north of the Burbank Slew.
Garrison as you have heard before
Has no saloon but a General Store.
All is still and quiet there
With never a stir in the peaceful air.
It's the home of some ranchers good and true
Some I think may be known to you.
There's Smith, Dearden, Gonder, and Clay
Who run a few cattle out this way.
Smith brands with a big ME
While Dearden uses the swinging V.
Gonder's iron is Bar G Bar
And his cattle wander near and far.
Steers that wear the 7 K
Belong as I said before to Clay
Joe Dearden runs the Newhouse Mail
And Heckethorn has things for sale.
With the hay they raise and the grain they sell
The people there do mighty well.
Each one owns a fine machine
And likes to burn the gasoline.
As far as it is from the city roar
You'll like old Garrison more and more.

During the Depression, making a living was difficult in Garrison, as it was throughout the country. Most people paid with credit, and one sheepherder offered two thousand sheep to settle his bill at one of the stores, now called the Snake Valley Trading Company. The sheepherder had probably bought the sheep for thirty to forty dollars a head, but they were now worth only one dollar a head, if a buyer could be found. To help make ends meet, the store owner, Graham Quate, taught himself surveying and became a county surveyor. When the CCC camps started, he got a job surveying roads they were building. His wife, Margie Elise Lake Quate, taught school. In those days, if five children lived near the same spot, that was enough for a school. Because they had several children, she would find another family that had some and then pack up her kids and make a new school, earning twenty-five dollars a month (Quate 1993, 206–9).

School

At first, school was in the homes of the settlers, with enough money to pay the schoolteacher for only two to five months a year. Emma D. Garrison was one of the first recorded schoolteachers in the valley (Richardson 2006). In 1899, Louisa Sorenson came to Snake Valley as the schoolteacher, having mastered part of a year of high school. Her twenty-eight pupils ranged in age from five to eighteen, and she said she learned more in that first year of teaching than in all her previous years of being taught (Quate 1993, 60). Reading, writing, and arithmetic were the main subjects, with considerable time spent on penmanship.

Before vaccinations were available, the school was also a place where disease spread quickly. Lorene Wheeler remembers a measles outbreak when she was a child in the Garrison school. Even more memorable was the whooping cough epidemic. For months after a child had survived the worst part of the disease, each time he or she began to cough it would come out in whoops. If one student started, the whole class would join in (L. Wheeler 2007).

A brick two-room school building was built in about 1958, but because there was just one teacher, the first through the eighth grades were taught in just one room, with a class size varying from seven to twenty. The same school building is still in use today, with one teacher instructing kindergarten through second grade.

Church

Garrison has had a strong Mormon influence for much of its history, although many of its first settlers were of mixed religious backgrounds. In 1925, the LDS Church organized a branch of the Deseret Stake (Warner 1951, 530). Early church meetings were held in a small building in Garrison. A couple of years after Baker High School closed in 1945, the LDS Church bought the property and held services there for many years. Eventually, the church became part of the Nevada Stake, East Ely. About 1976, a new LDS church was built in Garrison, and half the funds came from the locals. After investing so much in their church, attendance increased (Dearden 2007). Behind it is the Garrison Cemetery, one of the oldest and largest in Snake Valley, established in 1876, when the six-month-old daughter of Charles Rowland was interred. Many early settlers are buried here.

Modern Buildings

One of the first buildings you will see upon entering town from the north is the fire station on the west side of the road, which is also used for a variety of community gatherings. The story of the fire station is more interesting than one might imagine. For most of its history, Garrison had no fire department and got along fine. Then one spring day in 1960, some ranchers were burning ditches. When they went in for lunch, they thought the fire was under control, and as this particular family often did, they took a siesta. However, all was not well. When they got up, they found that fields were on fire, along with several lines of fifty-year-old poplar trees. The fire was spreading fast, and the call for help went out to Delta, Ely, and Fillmore. Eventually a fire truck from Delta showed up, and in the meantime residents used buckets and garden hoses to try to put out the fire. The feedlot, shops, haystacks, and fences burned, but they were able to save all the houses. Bill Dearden recalls that when he was finally released from school that day, it seemed like the whole world was on fire (Dearden 2007).

The residents of Garrison did not want to feel so helpless if another fire broke out, so they found a 1941 fire engine. Vivian Dearden built a root cellar on his property, and the fire engine was stored there. Because it was so old, only a couple of people could start it in extreme weather, and sometimes it had to be towed out of the root cellar with a tractor. Nevertheless, it was of great help and was used on several fires (Dearden 2007).

When the Intermountain Power Plant came to Millard County in the mid-1980s, funds became available for fire departments. Garrison received enough to build its own fire station, built by prisoners from Millard County and overseen by Clay Iverson from farther north in Snake Valley. The department received more funds in 2003 and got a sparkling brand-new fire truck. What the fire department needs now is more people willing to fight fires; only about three people are on its rosters as trained firefighters—not enough to send into a burning building (Dearden 2007).

Just beyond the fire station is the new town park, where trees were planted in 2004. Across the street is the Millard County Road Department, in a dilapidated white shed. They take care of about 400 miles (600 km) of roads in western Millard County. Next to the park is a fence that surrounds a large lot and a brick building that houses the Garrison station of the Utah Department of Transportation. The station ensures that west-central Utah highways are kept in tip-top shape, including Kings Canyon on Highway 6/50.

The Garrison Site

Near the present-day town of Garrison, the Fremont Indians constructed a village about one thousand years ago. Excavations in 1954 by the University of Utah revealed a village site between two former stream channels of Snake Creek. Nine buildings with a total of eighteen rooms were excavated, consisting of a community area and a peripheral area. The houses were clustered, but each family had a separate unit. It appears that the village was a sedentary gardening community, most likely growing maize, squash, and beans. Hunting was probably a communal effort, and additional food would have come from pinyon pine nuts. The Fremonts made pottery and wove baskets. Recreation may have consisted of singing, dancing, and games with bone dice and stone balls. The village appears to have been inhabited for one short period, probably after AD 1000 and before the Fremonts disappeared in AD 1276 (D. Taylor 1954, 3–9).

One story relates that some Indians took their dead to nearby Indian Burial Cave (also called Snake Creek Burial Cave) and lowered them partly into the abyss before plunging them over a boulder along with their possessions, blankets, baskets, and sometimes a horse (Read 1965, 133–34). Archaeological excavations of this cave in the 1980s found human remains and an estimated thirty thousand bones from fish, amphibians, reptiles, birds, and mammals. These included some species that no longer inhabit the area, such as black-footed ferrets (*Mustela nigripes*), least weasels (*Mustela nivalis*), wolverines (*Gulo gulo*), American martens (*Martes americana*), extinct noble martens (*Martes nobilis*), extinct short-faced skunks (*Brachyprotoma brevimala*), and more (Mead and Mead 1989).

Winter of 1948–49

Old-timers remember the winter of 1948–49 clearly. Many thought they were going to lose all their cattle or sheep in the worst winter of the century and not be able to feed their families. Throughout the area, millions of sheep and cattle were stranded in deep snowdrifts, and sometimes herders were stuck out with them.

Fortunately, most survived and are proud to be able to tell the story. Lorene Wheeler was living in Burbank at the time and recalled that the temperature dropped to -30°F (-1°C). One day the wind blew out of the north, causing drifts. The next day it blew out of the south. Every day the wind reversed, so that the snow was always moving, covering roads and tracks. The cold temperatures prevented the snow from melting. Lorene was pregnant, expecting her first son in the middle of winter. Afraid that she would not be able to get to medical help in time, she made it to Ely and stayed in the Hotel Nevada for six weeks. Her mother was able to come just in time for the birth. After Lorene recovered, they drove back through Spring Valley, which she said was like driving through a tunnel because the snow was so high on either side of the road. They made it to Garrison but could not get to Burbank. In fact, they could not even get the car to her parent's house, so she had to walk across the field with her newborn son (L. Wheeler 2007). Garrison was isolated from the outside world long enough that a pilot from Milford flew the mail in and dropped it so that the town could still hear about the outside world (Richardson 2006).

Meanwhile, Lorene's father took a Caterpillar out on the desert to try to reach the cattle and get feed to them. The tracks filled up with snow in a matter of hours. Sheepherder Carl Nielsen described the wind as a "lazy wind, it would rather go thru you than go around you" (Nielsen 1947). The US Air Force began Operation Haylift to keep the cattle and sheep from starving. The haylifts were organized mainly by George Swallow, who had grown up on Shoshone Ranch in Spring Valley and knew firsthand what the sheepherders were facing. Despite these efforts, many cattle and sheep did not survive the harsh conditions, but without the airlifts, the losses would have been much greater. The 1950 movie *Operation Haylift* was filmed near Ely and contains actual footage of the airdrops.

American Discovery Trail

Want to hike across the United States? The Appalachian Trail, Pacific Crest Trail, and Continental Divide Trail will get you from north to south across the country, but only one nonmotorized trail exists to take you from coast to coast, the American Discovery Trail (ADT).

This trail is much longer than the others, covering 6,800 miles (10,900 km) through fifteen states. The trail splits in the middle of the country, with a northern route through Chicago that goes a total of 4,834 miles (7,780 km) and a southern route through Saint Louis that is 5,057 miles (8,100 km). The National Park Service conducted a feasibility study in 1995 and recommended that the ADT be added to a new category of long-distance trails to be known as National Discovery Trails.

The route was first laid out in 1990–91 and passes through fourteen national parks and sixteen national forests. It connects five national scenic trails, ten national historic trails, twenty-three national recreation trails, and many local and regional trails. The first through-hike was completed in 2003 by a couple in their fifties who had taken up hiking just a decade earlier. The trail is also possible to do on bicycle or horseback; the first equestrian through-trip (using alternate routes for portions of the trail) was done from 2003 to 2005.

At present, no signs marking the trail exist in Snake Valley, so it is not widely known, even by locals. State-by-state guides are available from the ADT website (http://www.discoverytrail.org), along with tips for hiking and additional information. Many through-hikers also keep diaries of their trips, and it is interesting to read what they have to say about traversing Snake Valley. They get to see a variety of features. The trail passes by Crystal Peak, then through the Ferguson Desert to Garrison, Utah, and up to Baker, Nevada, then out along Highway 6/50 to Weaver Creek, and then via back roads to Osceola. Little water is available on this section of trail, particularly from Milford to Garrison. The ADT website recommends caching food and water along the way.

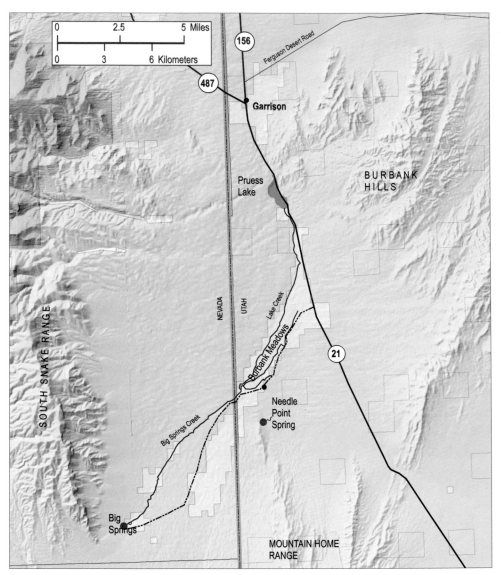

Figure 17-1. Map of southern Snake Valley.

PRUESS LAKE AND
FARTHER SOUTH

S outh of Garrison there are a variety of places to visit. Pruess Lake is a good place for a summertime swim or kayak. Farther south are wet meadows that made early travelers decide to settle instead of continuing on to California. The aquatic habitats in the area support an interesting biota and have a history of inspiring ambitious (but not necessarily well-planned) water projects and developments.

Pruess Lake

Pruess Lake, about 3 miles (5 km) south of Garrison, is the largest perennial body of water in Snake Valley (figure 17-1). It was named after Major Preuss of General Frémont's party, but a typographical error changed Major Preuss's name slightly. The same water body has also been called Lake Creek Reservoir, Garrison Reservoir, and Burbank Reservoir. Technically, it is a reservoir when the dam holds back water, but usually it is a lake for several months each year when the water level drops and does not reach the dam.

Pruess Lake is fed year-round from Lake Creek, a perennial creek that rises from a series of springs beginning in Nevada at Big Springs and continuing through Burbank Meadows, a green swath that was one of the first settled places in the valley. During high-water years, the lake receives inputs from two other streams, Lexington Creek at the south end and Big Wash on the north end. During most years, these two creeks are dry at lower elevations year-round, but during the wet year of 2005, both flowed into the lake from May to November. The lake is large enough for sailing and kayaking, along with swimming, if you do not mind the extremely turbid water.

Water Speculation

Pruess Lake started as a shallow lake at the end of Lake Creek, but some early developers devised a plan to deepen the lake and make money. In the 1890s, the developers thought if they built a dam at the north end of the lake, enough water would be available to water the area between the lake and Conger Ranch, near today's EskDale. Clients of the water company filed upon this large area of land under the 1877 Desert Land Act, and shares were sold to many people. A ditch was built to take the water north past Garrison, and remnants of it can still be seen today along the highway and where it crosses it near the state line. Willard Burbank surveyed and planned the dam. William Atkinson had homesteaded land at the south end of the lake in 1878, and the water company bought him out because they antici-pated his land being flooded. Bricks from Tom Matthews's lime kiln in Snake Creek were brought in to build the dam, a tunnel was cut by Mr. Perry Imas, and a headgate and wheelhouse were installed. By 1898, they were ready to sell off lots and farm sites but had a slight problem—the reservoir would not fill up. It turned out that some of the rock on the southeast side of the reservoir was too porous, and water would simply soak through it instead of accumulating. By this time, several people had made their way to Snake Valley to help with the irrigation company or settle on the land, including Albert Quate and the Woodward family. The Quates settled in Garrison for a number of years, while the Woodward family eked out an existence in Lexington Canyon for about six years before moving on (Quate 1993, 204–5, 213).

The Covered Wagon

Although the first idea for using the lake to make money was not that successful, other ideas were brewing. One of these belonged to Otto Meek, who bought Baker Ranch in 1921. He had links to Hollywood and convinced director James Cruze to come out to make one of the

Photo from Meek's Dude Ranch brochure, courtesy of Dean Baker

Figure 17-2. Scene from the 1923 movie *The Covered Wagon*: wagon trail after crossing the reservoir.

first epic Western movies. Mr. Cruze agreed and used Pruess Lake as the principal setting for the 1923 silent movie *The Covered Wagon*.

The lake was the setting for crossing the Missouri River (figures 17-2 and 17-3). The basic plot of the movie involved two wagon trains heading west and converging at Kansas City. Dealing with intense heat, wildfires, and Indian attacks, the wagon trains also had one other important twist: a love triangle.

The film was extremely important to the local economy. Several thousand people were hired as extras, and local people furnished wagons and horses and helped build the city on the hill that came to be called Kansas City Hill. In one scene, they wanted to film oxen crossing the river. In order to keep them in a straight line, cables were run under the water. Unfortunately, as the first group of oxen entered the water, the cable pulled them under and they drowned. They did not attempt that again. It took six weeks to do the movie, and memories linger of music and square dancing every night (Quate 1993, 177).

Photo from Meek's Dude Ranch brochure, courtesy of Dean Baker
Figure 17-3. Scene from *Covered Wagon* of the Indian battle.

Warm-Water Fishery

Pruess Lake is the only warm-water fishery in southern Snake Valley. Native fish include Utah chub and Utah sucker. Introduced fish consist of Sacramento perch (*Archoplites interruptus*), brought from California in the 1890s by miners and later by Spring Valley ranchers (Brent Eldridge, personal communication, 2008), channel catfish (*Ictalurus punctatus*), and carp (*Cyprinus carpio*). Pruess Lake holds the record for the largest Sacramento perch caught in Utah, primarily because the fish did not survive well in the other places they were introduced in Utah.

Besides fish, the lake supports other aquatic organisms, including a large freshwater mollusk called a California floater (figure 17-4). The name *floater* is derived from the fact that when the mussel dies, it floats to the surface of the lake as a result of gas buildup in its thin, reddish-brown shell. California floaters like to burrow into soft, silty substrate, of which there is plenty in Pruess Lake. The California floaters in Pruess Lake most likely got there via Lake Bonneville and a connecting stream. A recent study found that the Pruess Lake population is genetically different from others in the Bonneville Basin, and the researchers hypothesized that the introduced Sacramento perch in the lake may have been carrying glochidia (larvae) of a different population of floaters and that the DNA between the two has been mixed as they hybridized (Mock et al. 2004).

Figure 17-4. A California floater from Pruess Lake.

Burbank

From south of Pruess Lake, in a generally southwest direction to the last house, is an area 20 miles (30 km) long that is considered Burbank (figure 17-5). There has never been a town center, but the proximity of the ranches, along with an early post office and school, made this a distinct community from Garrison until transportation improved in the early twentieth century.

After a bend in Highway 21, you come upon an old homestead with beautiful cottonwoods shading some log cabins. This is known as the Clay place and was the home of the Clay and Burbank families,

Figure 17-5. Burbank Meadows were the first place in southern Snake Valley to be settled due to the plentiful water.

some of the first settlers in the valley (figure 17-6). Willard Burbank settled near a spring in 1867. The spring was ditched down to the cabin, and a fifty-gallon barrel was placed by the road, along with a hose. When a thirsty cowboy arrived, the horse could drink from the barrel, and the cowboy drank from the hose. Mr. Burbank planted trees that still stand today (Quate 1993, 34–35).

In 1875, several families settled in the southern end of Snake Valley. We hear about them via the story of the eastern Nevada Indian war panic. One version of the story states that a Goshute Indian named Toby told two prospectors, James Tollard and Al Leathers, that he knew where some silver ore was in the North Snake Range (up what is called Deadman Creek, a tributary to Smith Creek). Toby guided the prospectors to the supposed ore, but they did not find any, so they did not pay him. Toby became angry and shot and killed Tollard. Leathers ran over the mountain to Cleveland Ranch, where Mr. Cleveland, having seen a large number of Indians gathered, had

Figure 17-6. A view of the Clay Place, the northernmost end of the Burbank Meadows.

sent a runner to Burbank with a letter telling the settlers to gather and fortify themselves. Lizzie Burbank donned men's clothing and rode at night to the ranches in the area to spread the news. The settlers gathered at Ben Lehman's ranch in Baker and erected a moat fort 6 feet (2 m) wide (Quate 1993, 42). From a different account, settlers in the early 1860s had dug a fort by hand in Burbank for protection from the Indians. The fort was 150 square feet (14 m²), 7 feet (2 m) deep, and close to a good spring (Day and Ekins 1951, 180–81). Neither site can be located today. A third account adds that someone sent a telegram to General John M. Schofield, commander of the far western US military forces, headquartered in San Francisco. The military expeditiously arrived a few days later and investigated. They captured Toby, and the local ranchers demanded that he be turned over to them. When he was, they hung him near the present-day Baker Ranch feedlot. The fright was apparently for nothing, because the Indians were simply gathered to collect pine nuts (Crum

1994, 27–28). Crum mentions that three other people died in this incident: Solomon, an innocent Shoshone who wanted to help the whites but was shot and killed by ranchers who thought he was the enemy, and two other innocent Indians (28).

Lizzie Burbank was apparently quite good on a horse. In order to get the mail, she met the wagons that traveled from Pioche to the salt marsh in northern Snake Valley to get salt. After picking up the mail, she delivered it to the recipients. When the stage line began running from Frisco, Utah, to Ely, Nevada, the Burbank family established a post office in 1881, the first one in southern Snake Valley, called Burbank. Lizzie was the first postmaster. The post office remained until the rural delivery system was established, in about 1900 (Quate 1993, 41).

Burbank Grows

After the Burbanks arrived in the late 1860s, Samuel Hockman, his wife, Jane Elizabeth, two children, and eight hundred head of cattle made the trip from Iowa to Burbank Meadows in May 1869 or 1870 (Day and Ekins 1951, 180; Quate 1993, 49). They were so impressed with the abundant water, which they estimated to be flowing at 22 cfs (0.62 m3/s) and watering 5,000 acres (2,000 ha) of meadow pasture, that they decided to settle there. Sam and Jane had four more children, including Brick, the first white child born in the valley.

Brick Hockman became Snake Valley's dentist, making his own forceps in his blacksmith shop. He treated both whites and Indians and was known for giving a shot of whiskey "for sanitation." One Indian woman returned repeatedly to have perfectly good teeth pulled just so she could get her "firewater sanitation." Brick's wife was in a wheelchair for years and was referred to by the Indians as his "automobile wife" (Read 1965, 136).

CCC Camp

The Clay place was the site for a CCC camp that was built around 1933. About 150 men lived here, many from Alabama (Sims 2006). Several buildings were constructed, although photos of them are scarce or nonexistent. The camp was situated next to a large, deep spring that provided both drinking and bathing water.

One of the CCC projects was making reservoirs in the desert to catch floodwater, including one about 10 miles (16 km) south near

Mormon Gap and one in the Burbank Hills, on the way to Cedar Pass. They also helped build roads and stock trails and may have assisted with some projects at Lehman Caves National Monument.

For fun, they held dances, which the local girls attended, providing a welcome diversion during the Depression years (Sims 2006). In addition, they had movies, and Lorene Wheeler remembers going down to the camp on Monday evenings to watch her first movies (L. Wheeler 2007). Some of the locals ended up marrying CCC men and moving away, but at least one CCC man, Merlin Terry, stayed in Snake Valley, marrying a local girl, Rhonda Jettson. They operated a very successful general store in Baker.

One of the few times in the history of Snake Valley that a doctor was present was during the CCC days. Tom Sims recalls that Dr. Martin treated his black widow bite (Sims 2006). When the CCC camp closed, the buildings were moved to new locations.

Outlaws

Ladd Davies remembers that his neighbor 1 mile (1.6 km) to the north, Fred Loper, was an outlaw. He shot a man in a poker game in Wyoming, then returned to Snake Valley and built a cabin way back in the Mountain Home Range, located at the southern end of Snake Valley. He spent two years living off the land in the isolated area but finally decided he should go back and face up to the murder charges. He went back to Wyoming and found out he had hardly hurt the man, and there were no charges against him. Then he came back to Snake Valley and married Stella Richardson, and they had nine boys and two girls (Davies 1999).

Burbank also saw some more-famous outlaws and was supposedly the headquarters for the Butch Cassidy gang at one time. They brought the cattle they stole and let them graze there until they could find a buyer (Davies 1999).

Cattle Rustling

Cattle rustling, or cattle stealing, has long been a part of western culture. In the very old days, cattle rustlers who were caught were simply hung from the nearest tree. Over time, a position was created to help ranchers protect themselves: the brand inspector. Both Utah and Nevada employ brand inspectors, and they are present whenever cattle are moved out of district or out of state or if the ownership changes.

A brand is a unique mark registered by an individual or a corporation with the state (table 17-1). In Nevada, the first law addressing brands originated in 1873 and required individuals with brands to register them with their county recorder. As might be expected, people in adjacent counties sometimes had very similar brands, so it was decided to make brands a state function, and in 1923 the Nevada state legislature created the Board of Livestock Commissioners, now the State Board of Agriculture. The next year, they issued the first official Nevada brand book, listing all the registered brands. In Utah, the first territorial legislature regulated the printing of brand books in 1851.

On the Utah side of Snake Valley, there are five brand inspectors in Millard County, including one in Garrison, and one in Juab County. On the Nevada side, a brand inspector is based in Ely, and thirteen part-time deputies help cover White Pine, Nye, and Lincoln Counties. Because there is a lot of space for cattle to roam in this area the size of the state of New York, the brand inspector is assisted by the Secret Witness Program, which provides $1,500 for information leading to the arrest and conviction of cattle rustlers (McPhee 1997).

The Nevada brand inspector knows the brands registered in his state well, even though there are over 3,500 brands listed in the *Nevada Livestock Brand Book*. Each ranch is required to submit its brand to the Livestock Identification Bureau in Reno for approval, and the brand inspector makes sure that the brand is not too similar to any neighbor's. Although many brands are letters or numbers, some are simple drawings. Generally a simple brand works best so that it does not leave a blotch on the animal (McPhee 1997).

A long-time brand inspector in White Pine County was Shirley Robison, who grew up at the sinks east of Baker, where the creeks sink into the basin fill. The first cattle rustler that Robison caught was the one-eyed deputy sheriff of Millard County, Art Loper from Snake Valley, son of outlaw Fred Loper. Robison went on to have a long and successful career, retiring in 1979. An excellent account about brand inspectors is featured in John McPhee's book *Irons in the Fire*.

Table 17-1. Some brands used in Snake Valley

BRAND	Name	Owners	Home	Location
Rafter Lazy C (symbol)	Rafter Lazy C	Cecil C. Garland	Wendover	LS (horse); RR (cow)
3X	Three X	William Henriod	Via Wendover	RH (cow)
ΛJ	Inverted V J	Alan D. Johnson Shelley C. Johnson	Callao	RH (cow); LH (horse)
Ω	Omega	Red Cedar Corp	Trout Creek	RS (cow)
2C	Two C	Gonder Ranch	Garrison	LH
B6	B Six	Baker Ranches Inc. (originally Bellander)	Baker	RH and RR (cow)
ꓶL	Crazy F L (Backwards F L Combined)	Baker Ranches Inc.	Baker	RH (cow); CB (sheep)
X–X	X Bar X	Moriah Ranches Inc. David Eldridge	Baker	LR (cow)
ƆG	Inverted G G.	Philipp G Heckethorn Annemarie Heckethorn	Baker; Ely	RR (cow)
VD	V D	Ray and Brian Okelberry	Goshen	RH, RR (cow)

BRAND	Name	Owners	Home	Location
Ⱦ (Seven K Combined Over Bar symbol)	Seven K Combined Over Bar	Dearden Livestock; Carl J. Dearden; Aleeda B. Dearden; Thomas C. Dearden; Glen G. Dearden	Burbank	RH (cow)
△ (Triangle Over Bar symbol)	Triangle Over Bar	Dearden Livestock; Carl J Dearden; Aleeda B Dearden; Thomas C Dearden	Burbank	RH
Ⱦ (Seven K Combined Over Bar symbol)	Seven K Combined Over Bar	Deardon Brothers; Glen J Deardon; Thomas C Deardon	Burbank	CB (sheep)
C (Rocking C symbol)	Rocking C (C Over Quartercircle)	Anderson Brothers Livestock	Fairview	Rump (sheep)
⊙ (Bullseye symbol)	Bullseye	Clark F Fitzgerald; Ben Fitzgerald	Heber City	CB, Rump, Withers (sheep); RS (cow)
6	Six	Ray Okelberry; Brian Okelberry; Eric Okelberry	Goshen	CB, Rump, Withers (sheep); RR (cow)
♡ (Heart symbol)	Heart	Ray and Brian Okelberry	Goshen	Rump (sheep)

CB=center back; LS=left shoulder; LR=left ribs; LH=left hip; RS= right shoulder; RR=right ribs; RH= right hip

Other Sights

A four-way intersection 5.5 miles (8.9 km) from Utah Highway 21 leads to several interesting points. Heading north, you can drive through the long-standing Dearden Ranch to get to the Burbank/Hockman Cemetery. Heading south, you can go to Needle Point Mountain, the lone low mountain, or farther south to the Mountain Home Range. On the east side of Needle Point Mountain is (was) Needle Point Spring. In 2001, a nearby rancher drilled a new irrigation well. Within months of pumping, the spring dried up and has never had water at the surface since then. Each year the water table drops farther (Summers 2001), which is of great concern because the Southern Nevada Water Authority has proposed to put in a well field in this same area to pump much more water—over 50,000 acre-feet (62 million m^3) a year.

Lake Creek

Past Needle Point Mountain, the valley is considered to be Hamlin Valley. The road crosses from Utah into Nevada; the state line is marked by a cattle guard and fence. On the north side of the road you may spot Russian olive trees from time to time. They are growing along Lake Creek, called Big Springs Creek on the Nevada side by some maps. Lake Creek is unique in the valley; it is the only valley-bottom creek in the south end (figure 17-7). It arises from a series of springs at Big Springs Ranch and is supplemented by a number of springs that rise near the state line. Despite attempts by both Nevada and Utah to introduce "valuable" fish like rainbow trout, brown trout, largemouth bass (*Micropterus salmoides*), and smallmouth bass (*Micropterus dolomieu*), the creek has persisted in supporting a native fishery. Five of the seven native fish in the valley live here: redside shiner, mottled sculpin, Utah chub, Utah sucker, and speckled dace. Most of these are small fish, but the Utah sucker can grow up to 12 inches (30 cm) long. At one point it was an extremely important food source for the Indians and Mormon pioneers because it is so readily caught, especially during spring spawning (Sigler and Sigler 1987). These native fish are joined by an occasional rainbow trout (they do not appear to be able to reproduce in the creek) and many crayfish, which were introduced within the last fifty years (Glen Dearden, personal communication, 2004) and

Figure 17-7. Lake (Big Springs) Creek contains five of the seven native fish species in Snake Valley. It supplies much of the water for the Burbank Meadows.

have unknown effects on the native fish. Lake Creek feeds Burbank Meadows and eventually empties into Pruess Lake. This ecosystem is delicate. Thousands of birds rely on the wetlands, and fish species that have survived since Lake Bonneville days depend on specific water conditions.

Big Springs

The last group of trees, found 13 miles (21 km) from the highway, marks the location of Big Springs Ranch, for several decades the headquarters for the Murray Sheep Company, and today part of the Okelberry holdings. This ranch really feels like the last frontier. With a dependable supply of water from Big Springs, the ranch raises sheep and cattle. The constant flow, temperature, and chemical properties of the springs in the area make them home to springsnails, including one species, *Pyrgulopsis anguina*, that is endemic to Snake Valley. The water from Big Springs is divided among the Big Springs Irrigation District members and heads down through Burbank Meadows.

From Big Springs, you can take off to distant places in Nevada: Atlanta is 21 miles (34 km) away, Shoshone is 30 miles (48 km) away, and Ursine is 57 miles (92 km) distant.

Farther South on Utah Highway 21

The southern end of Snake Valley is pinched together by low hills, forming what is called Mormon Gap. Utah Highway 21 passes right through the gap into Antelope Valley. A Civilian Conservation Corps (CCC) dam built to collect spring runoff is visible on the east just after passing through the gap. A corral is next to the dam.

The Desert Range Experimental Station lies just 8 miles (13 km) to the southeast of Snake Valley in Pine Valley. It was established in 1933 when President Herbert Hoover withdrew 87 square miles (225 km²) from the public domain "as an agricultural range experiment station." In 1935, the CCC built an office, living quarters, support buildings, a 500-foot (152 m) well, a tennis court, major roads, and over 118 miles (190 km) of fence.

Sheep grazing studies began during the winter of 1934–35 in order to study the economic and ecological effects of different grazing regimes, including intensity, timing, and diet. These studies have continued for over six decades. Cattle grazing studies have also been conducted and research later broadened to include insects, birds, rodents, pronghorn, soil crusts, soils, and weather. Permanent exclosures ranging from 1 to 1,828 acres (0.4–740 ha) are present in all plant community types.

About 75 percent of the station is in the salt-desert community. The dominant shrubs are shadscale, winterfat, bud sagebrush (*Artemisia spinescens*), and yellow rabbitbrush. Cool-season grasses include Indian ricegrass and bottlebrush squirreltail (*Elymus elymoides*), while warm-season grasses are galleta, sand dropseed (*Sporobolus cryptandrus*), purple threeawn (*Aristida purpurea*), and blue grama (*Bouteloua gracilis*). Exotic annuals including cheatgrass, saltlover (halogeton), and Russian thistle have made an appearance at the station.

Recognition of this protected biome, along with the research being conducted there, came in 1976 when the Desert Experimental

The charcoal ovens at Frisco stand as monuments to the rough-and-tumble mining town that was the starting point for many sojourners to Snake Valley.

Range was designated as a Biosphere Reserve by the United Nations Educational, Scientific, and Cultural Organization (UNESCO) under the Man and the Biosphere program (Kitchen and McArthur n.d.).

The station is open periodically for researchers who make arrangements in advance with the US Forest Service Shrub Sciences Lab in Provo, Utah. A piece of the range extends across the highway, so you actually travel through part of it on Highway 21.

Look on the Internet for "UFO Sightings in Utah," and one that will appear is the 1953 sighting near Garrison, Utah. Supposedly, a large spaceship crashed into the ground near the Desert Range Experimental Station, leaving a large, triangular scar on the land. According to the website, aliens fled into the nearby hills and have assimilated into the local population. Perhaps that is why some consider visiting Snake Valley an otherworldly experience.

When you ascend the Wah Wah Mountains at about mile marker 60, look for mining remains. This is Frisco, where the railroad from the Wasatch Front extended and many people from Snake Valley began the wagon portion of their journey. Old charcoal ovens along with many building foundations and tailing piles remain.

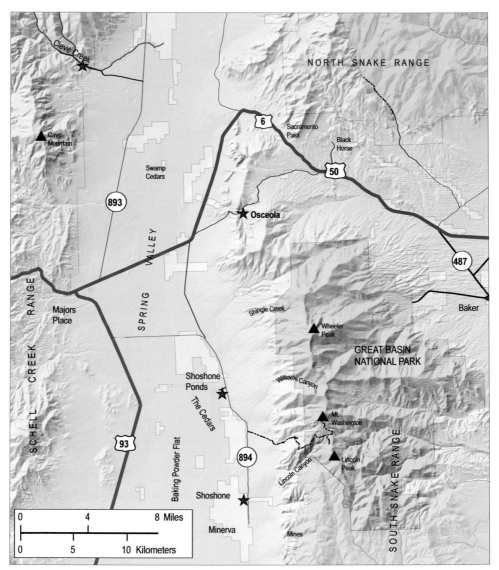

Figure 18-1. Map of central Spring Valley.

OSCEOLA AND SPRING VALLEY

Spring Valley, on the west side of Great Basin National Park, was named for the numerous springs that emerge in many places in the valley bottom (figure 18-1). The Native Americans called it the "Valley of One Thousand Springs" (Read 1965, 175). Despite this relatively large amount of water for the driest state in the nation, the valley has remained comparatively pristine. Settlers made their homes and ranches near these water sources, but much of it, flowing out into wetlands and wet meadows, has created a rare habitat in the valley.

Spring Valley is home to many mining districts, some still active. It also has a recreation area, unique swamp cedars, a refuge for endangered fish, and beautiful scenery. Although most people just drive across the valley en route to Ely or Great Basin National Park, it certainly deserves more attention.

Spring Valley has been getting more attention recently, but unfortunately for some reasons that threaten to change its character forever. The first is a proposal by the Southern Nevada Water Authority to put in nearly one hundred wells to pump water out of Spring Valley to the Las Vegas area. The second is a new wind farm in the middle of the valley.

Black Horse Mining District

Heading from Baker to Spring Valley on Highway 6/50, you cross the Snake Range at Sacramento Pass, 7,154 feet (2,181 m) in elevation. Near mile marker 88, as you approach the pass, is a spring area called the Willow Patch. Numerous willows are visible on the south side of the road. In 1908 a mill was constructed here, followed in 1909 by a more elaborate 20-stamp mill (Hall 1994). Ore was brought from the nearby mining community of Black Horse, about 2 miles (3 km) north of the highway, and a post office operated for a number of years (Read 1965, 171).

Tommy Watkins from Osceola discovered the Black Horse lode by accident in March 1906 when he was riding a black horse and found some gold under a ledge while taking refuge from a storm. He and ninety-five others staked claims, and by April, four hundred people, three stores, three saloons (including the ominously named Bucket of Blood), two boardinghouses, a blacksmith shop, and a barbershop opened. A school was built, and a post office opened in September 1906. The ore was very rich, with one sample returning more than $100,000 per ton. Yet the veins were quite small and ran out in 1913, after producing close to $1 million. The post office closed in March 1914, but Black Horse was not finished yet. Beginning in 1933, miners returned to the mine and removed ore again. In 1943 a 25-ton cyanide plant was built to treat tungsten ore from the newly discovered Gold King Mine but ceased operations in 1954 (Hall 1994). If you take the road to the north marked by a Forest Service access sign, you will be hard-pressed to find remnants of Black Horse. Some rubble, faint foundations, and open shafts are all that are left, along with a network of roads that make good bicycle routes.

Sacramento Pass Recreation Area

The marked Sacramento Pass Recreation Area is near mile marker 87 on Highway 6/50 (figure 18-2). Administered by the BLM, the area has an information kiosk, fishing pond stocked with rainbow trout, and ten covered picnic/camping sites with no fees charged. It has some new single-track mountain biking trails, which are also available for hiking and horse riding. A trailhead near the entrance is the starting point for the 2-mile (3 km) Sac Pass Loop, with an optional 0.5-mile (1 km) extension on the Lucky Boy Loop. From the Lucky

Figure 18-2. Sacramento Pass Recreation
Area offers camping, picnicking, fishing,
and several miles of trails for hikers,
mountain bikers, and equine enthusiasts.

Boy Loop, a 0.5-mile (1 km) connector trail extends south to the
4-mile (6 km) Mine Shaft Loop. A second trailhead, reached by driving on the gravel road southeast from the picnic/camping area, also
accesses these loops. This is one of the least-used single-track areas
in the state, so you are likely to have it to yourself. Located at 6,810
feet (2,076 m), it is a great spring and fall destination. Restrooms are
available, but there is no running water.

Osceola

The turnoff to the Sacramento Pass Recreation Area is also the
starting point to Osceola. Osceola played an important part in the

Photo courtesy Russ Robison

Figure 18-3. Historic photo of Osceola, circa 1900.

development of Snake and Spring Valleys. Gold attracted miners to the area, making it the largest community for some time. It also attracted a number of businesses that depended on produce grown in the adjacent fertile valleys. For many years Osceola was the gathering spot for young people, and some of those who met there married and lived for decades in Snake and Spring Valleys. Due to fires, few buildings remain in Osceola to mark the "good old days," but those who do some searching can find building foundations and trash piles.

Gold Discovered

In August 1872, Joseph Watson and Frank Hicks discovered gold in what came to be known as Osceola, named for a Seminole chief. A mining district was organized in October and grew quickly due to many mine claims (figure 18-3). During the first two years, about $300,000 of gold was found, including the largest nugget in the state of Nevada, worth $3,000 (McDonald 1913, 1046).

In early 1877, placer fields (gold flakes in the surrounding gravel as opposed to gold found in rock veins) were discovered in Dry

Gulch and Grub (Wet) Gulch. By 1878 over three hundred placer claims were staked, a five-stamp mill was operating, and a tent camp of about four hundred to six hundred people sprang up (Smith 1976, 61). A. J. Millich opened the first restaurant and started building a feed corral and stockade stable, and a post office was established (Miller 1924, 360). By 1881 Osceola consisted of two stores, a hotel, a restaurant, a livery stable, and a blacksmith shop. Most supplies came from San Francisco to Eureka, Nevada, by railroad and then by stage for the last 100 miles (160 km). A 12' x 20' (3.7 x 6.1 m) frame schoolhouse with a capacity of thirty students was built (Angel [1881] 1958, 662). The Osceola Placer Mining Company built an electric light plant, and office buildings and homes were constructed on Cemetery Hill. Telephone service arrived shortly thereafter, making Osceola the first White Pine County town to have that amenity (Hall 1994, 170–71).

As Osceola continued to expand, it was clear that more water was needed. Small springs in Wet Canyon provided one miner's inch of water (fifty miner's inches equal one cubic foot per second). The miners and mining companies devised a plan to get more water to Osceola.

The Osceola Ditch

Osceola is located on the northwest side of the South Snake Range, which has more than fifteen perennial streams flowing off its slopes into the adjacent valleys. The Osceola Gravel Mining Company employed Ben Hampton to oversee the construction of a ditch in 1884–85 to bring water from the west side of the mountain to Osceola. This ditch began at Williams Creek and then followed the contours of the mountain to pick up water from Ridge, Pine, Shingle, Board, and Willard Creeks. The 16-mile (26 km) ditch ended just below the townsite of Osceola and provided 356 miner's inches (about 7 cfs, or 0.2 m³/s) of water for six to eight hours a day. This was still not enough water, so an 18-mile (29 km) ditch was constructed in 1889–90 along the east side of the mountain (figure 18-4) extending from Lehman Creek around to Mill Creek and Strawberry Creek and ending at the same location. In some places a simple ditch was made by digging a trench in the ground, but in other places wooden trestles and flumes were needed to carry the water over talus slopes and debris fields. Many Chinese, Shoshones, and Paiute Indians were reportedly involved in the

Figure 18-4. The Osceola Ditch was constructed in 1889-90 to transport water around the Snake Range to the mining town of Osceola. The ditch was used for a scant period of time, but in 2005 part of the ditch held water for a short distance, bringing back memories of earlier days.

ditch construction. Wood came largely from Hendrie's (Hendry's) sawmill in the North Snake Range. William Hendrie had a house in Osceola and served as the first justice of the peace. The combined flow of both ditches was about 2,000 miner's inches (about 40 cfs, or 1.1 m³/s). This provided enough water for hydraulic mining and ground sluicing (Unrau 1990).

The ditches were not the panacea they were expected to be, however. By 1890, light snowfall, leaky flumes, and water theft made the ditches unprofitable. Despite their cost of $200,000, they were abandoned as placer deposits slowly ran out (Smith 1976, 61). Many parts of the Osceola Ditch can still be seen as a distinct line around the mountain, and a section between Wheeler Peak Scenic Drive and Strawberry Creek within Great Basin National Park has been converted to a hiking trail (see chapter 5).

Osceola Slows Down

At its peak, Osceola was an exciting place that offered many services and a variety of entertainment. Dances were held on a regular basis and some of the early pioneers met their spouses at these dances. One of the names that holds a place in local history is that of the Marriott family. By 1890, James H. Marriott was listed in the assessment roll book as owning the Felsensthal Store, stable and dwelling house, three lots, and the Fussy Saloon on Main Street, along with goods and wares (Shaputis 1999). He later became the justice of the peace and served for many years until his death in 1912. Out-of-towners often stayed with the Marriotts, who at one point were said to own almost every business in town. The little cemetery to the west of Osceola holds several members of the Marriott family.

Osceola was not destined to be a mining town that persisted. Placer deposits slowly ran out, fires burned the stables and buildings on the north side of Main Street, water ditches deteriorated, and the Osceola Placer Mining Company folded in 1900. About one hundred people stayed in town, keeping the post office open until December 1920. A store and two saloons stayed open a while longer.

A second spate of mining occurred from 1925 to 1932 by Nicholson Mining and Milling Company, which filed seventeen claims and built a 3,500-foot (1,067 m) water pipeline to an eighty-ton mill. Activity occurred in the mining district until the late 1950s, when a fire destroyed all the remaining buildings. Some stone ruins and the Nicholson Mill mark the site, along with the Osceola Cemetery. All told, a total of $3.3 million was made from the Osceola Mining District, including $1.9 million in placer mining (Hall 1994, 170–73). Today a couple of residences in Osceola are occupied. Mining occurs on a very small scale, as it does at the nearby Hogum mining site.

Rose Guano Cave

One of the most important caves in Spring Valley is Rose Guano Cave, located in the Snake Range (figure 18-5). It is not a cave you want to enter, because as its name suggests, it is known for its guano. The guano has been deposited by bats using the caves for thousands of years. Guano is rich in phosphate and was mined in the 1920s. In 1926 a tunnel was built into the cave under the high entrance to access the guano more easily. This upset the delicate ecosystem in the cave and the tunnel was sealed in 1995. The most impressive part

Figure 18-5. Rose Guano Cave is an important migratory stop for over a million Mexican free-tailed bats each year.

of Rose Guano Cave is not the cave itself, but witnessing thousands of Mexican free-tailed bats (*Tadarida brasiliensis*) exiting it at sunset on summer evenings (usually July to September). The bats, the same species that is found in Carlsbad Caverns, start leaving the cave en masse about two hours before sundown. The majority fly south, between 800 and 2,500 feet (240–760 m) above ground level, toward agricultural fields, where they forage for insects and water. A recent study found that over a million Mexican free-tailed bats use this cave as a migration stop, usually staying one to three days (Sherwin 2009).

Shoshone Ponds

Although Spring Valley was originally fishless, today it is home to Shoshone Ponds, an important refuge for the Pahrump poolfish and relict dace, the first a federally endangered fish. In 1970, the BLM designated the surrounding 1,240 acres (500 ha) as the Shoshone Ponds

Natural Area. This included a pond that the CCC built in 1937 near its camp, which was at the same location. In 1972 the BLM built additional ponds and brought the first Pahrump poolfish to them. These fish are native to the Pahrump, Nevada, area, but due to groundwater pumping, their habitat dried up. Relict dace are endemic to Nevada and were transported to four locations in Spring Valley, including Shoshone Ponds, to expand their habitat. Additional wildlife found at Shoshone Ponds includes northern leopard frogs, breeding birds, and bats.

The Nevada Department of Wildlife conducts annual population surveys at Shoshone Ponds and estimates an average of about three thousand Pahrump poolfish and a few hundred relict dace (NDOW 2004). Ironically, this habitat is also threatened due to groundwater pumping. The Southern Nevada Water Authority has applied to pump almost 100,000 acre-feet (123 million m^3) a year from Spring Valley and pipe it over 200 miles (300 km) to the Las Vegas area. Hydrologic models show that this will substantially lower the water table, which could dry up the artesian wells that feed Shoshone Ponds.

Swamp Cedars Area of Critical Environmental Concern

Looking out from a high vantage point over Spring Valley, you might notice something unique about it: there are two places on the valley floor where evergreen trees grow. These are populations of Rocky Mountain junipers, which are normally found growing higher on the mountain slopes. Additional water probably allows these junipers, called swamp cedars, to persist on the valley bottom.

The swamp cedars have been recognized as an Area of Critical Environmental Concern by the BLM. These swamp cedars provide additional diversity to the valley bottom not only for vegetation but also for wildlife, especially birds and invertebrates. The northern population covers about 3.5 square miles (9 km^2), while the southern population covers about 1.5 square miles (2.6 km^2; BWG 2009). Native Americans consider the swamp cedars to be an extremely important cultural area. At least one massacre occurred in the swamp cedars in the late 1800s. Angel relates that in 1863, "the cavalry charged down... but were brought to a halt by the swamp character of the land." Twenty-three Indians were killed ([1881] 1958, 181).

Mount Washington

Mining occurred in a variety of places in the area, but perhaps one of the most remote was up on the shoulder of Mount Washington. Claims were made as early as July 1869, some nearly 11,000 feet (3,350 m) high, but due to the inaccessibility, little work was done. In 1899, William Bacon located claims that would later become part of the St. Lawrence Mine. He mined several tons of lead and silver ore and took it by mule down the mountain. During World War I, the ore was tobogganed off the mountain on rock sleds. Although operations ceased after the war, they recommenced in 1928. The ore ran in a vein across the North Fork of Lincoln Canyon, with structures built on both sides of the canyon and also down in the canyon itself. In 1948, three men from Ely and Pioche constructed a jeep road to the top of the St. Lawrence claims. They mined for two years and shipped four railcar loads of lead-silver ore. In 1950, the Combined Metals Reduction Company and the American Zinc, Lead and Smelting Company made a long adit tunnel in Lincoln Canyon. They found large amounts of tungsten in the tunnel, and beryllium was also found there in 1951 (Unrau 1990, 98–104).

Beryllium was not known in many other locations at the time. Because it is lighter than aluminum and stronger than steel, it was in demand for use in missiles, rockets, and other facets of the space industry, and several companies started more exploratory work. In 1958 Kennecott Copper Corporation, based in Salt Lake City, conducted a spectrographic analysis of the tungsten ore samples and found the beryllium-bearing minerals phenakite and bertrandite. At the time, it was the only known deposit of phenakite in the world. Beryllium Resources paid Mount Wheeler Mines $1.9 million to explore and develop the mines. Although they found plenty of beryllium, an even larger and more accessible deposit had been found at Spor Mountain, 70 miles (110 km) northwest of Delta, Utah. Interest in the area waxed and waned over the years (Unrau 1990, 104–13). When the boundaries for Great Basin National Park were drawn, it was decided to exclude this mining area, creating a keyhole shape in the western side of the park. In 1999, National Treasure Mines sold 180 acres (73 ha) to the Long Now Foundation, which is interested in installing a ten-thousand-year clock in the limestone cliffs (http://www.longnow.org).

To explore this area, take the Mount Washington road, which begins between mile markers 5 and 6 on the paved Nevada Highway 894, opposite a ranch driveway. The road is passable to cars up to the Pole Canyon adit of the Mount Wheeler Mine, at about 7,850 feet (2,390 m). This adit is 8,318 feet (2,535 m) long (Unrau 1990, 105) and has water flowing out of it. This is not recommended as a water source, as it may contain heavy metals. Several structures still exist. The jeep road that ascends via steep switchbacks to the shoulder of Mount Washington begins just to the south. More information about the jeep road and trails in this area are in chapter 6.

Shoshone

Although there are no communities in Spring Valley today, between 1896 and 1959, Shoshone, in southern Spring Valley, was large enough to warrant a post office and a spot on the map. The area first attracted attention in 1869, when an Indian led some miners to an outcrop containing silver chloride. Ten claims were staked that day, and the Shoshone District was organized. Alas, the amount of silver in the vein was not worth the expense of mining it. However, tungsten and scheelite were later found to the south in what was called Minerva (Smith 1976, 76).

In addition to mining, ranching also became important at Shoshone. Benjamin Kimball settled in 1869, and when George Swallow traveled through in 1872, Mr. Kimball asked if he would stay and help. He did, and they formed a partnership that lasted until Mr. Swallow bought the ranch in 1880 (Read 1965). His descendants continued ranching in this remote location, going to Osceola and later Ely for supplies and socializing (Robison 2006a and 2006b).

Cleve Creek Recreation Area

North of Highway 6/50 is Nevada Highway 893, which runs up the length of northern Spring Valley, passing many ranches. About 12 miles (19 km) north is the turnoff to Cleve Creek Recreation Area. A decent 2-mile (3 km) gravel road leads to several campsites, shaded by cottonwood trees and picnic shelters. Nearby Cleve Creek is home to wild trout and its flow is monitored by a USGS gauge. Some gold and tungsten were mined from the Cleve Creek area, but today the canyon is known for its peaceful setting.

Cleve Creek is named for A. C. Cleveland, who bought the ranch in the valley bottom in 1882, which is still known today as Cleveland Ranch and is owned by the LDS Church. Mr. Cleveland was active in politics, serving as a state assemblyman and senator. In addition to his cattle and horses, his ranch was known for the post office, a line of poplars that still grows there, and the first strawberry patch in the county (Read 1965, 180–81; Healy 2005).

Fourmile and Eightmile Canyons

Access to the North Snake Range from the Spring Valley side is possible on several roads. The main road along the east side of Spring Valley, White Pine County Road 37, is gravel and starts north from Highway 6/50 near mile marker 81. In about 8 miles (13 km) you reach meadows fed by water from Negro Creek. Negro Creek Ranch, near the mouth of the canyon, was established in the late 1860s by a slave owner who moved West and brought his slaves with him. These were perhaps the first black people in White Pine County (Georgetta 1972, 320).

The road crosses old lake terraces and continues north about 4 miles (6 km) more to Fourmile Canyon Road (FS Road 469). The four-wheel drive road to the east is the main route up to the trailhead that accesses the Table and Mount Moriah. The trailhead is about 10 miles (16 km) away. More information about hiking in these areas is in chapter 10. To the west is Yelland Dry Lake, named for early settlers. Yelland Air Field in Ely is named for Louis Yelland, the first White Pine County boy to lose his life in World War I.

About 5 miles (8 km) farther north is Eightmile Canyon Road, which crosses the North Snake Range. This four-wheel drive route is a scenic 30-mile (50 km) back way to Gandy, Utah. Plan on several hours. If you would like to reach Gandy via a flatter route, continue north on the dirt road for about 18 miles (29 km). You will come to an intersection. Head east for 20 miles (30 km); it will still take at least a couple of hours. Or continue farther north to investigate more of Spring Valley. This area is fascinating, with lots of places to explore. Happy trails!

Appendices

Contact Information

Agencies

Bureau of Land Management, Ely
District Office
702 N. Industrial Way
HC 33 Box 33500
Ely, Nevada 89301
775-289-1800
http://www.blm.gov/nv

Fish Springs National Wildlife Refuge
PO Box 568
Dugway, Utah 84022
435-831-5353
http://www.fws.gov/fishsprings

Great Basin National Heritage Route
PO Box 78
Baker, Nevada 89311
775-234-7171
http://www.greatbasinheritage.org

Great Basin National Park
100 Great Basin National Park
Baker, Nevada 89311
775-234-7331
http://www.nps.gov/grba

Humboldt-Toiyabe National Forest
US Forest Service
Ely Ranger District
825 Avenue E
Ely, Nevada 89311
775-289-3031
http://www.fs.fed.us/r4/htnf

Spring Creek Rearing Station
Nevada Department of Wildlife
Baker, Nevada 89311
775-234-7319

Useful Websites

Great Basin Business and Tourism Council ..... http://www.greatbasinpark.com
Millard County Tourism .... http://www.millardcounty.com
White Pine Tourism and Recreation Board ..... http://www.elynevada.net
Information about Snake Valley........................ http://www.protectsnakevalley.org

Local Businesses
(all telephone numbers have a 775 prefix)

Lodging

Border Inn	234-7300	29 rooms, RV and tent spaces
End of the Trail...er	234-7272	sleeps 3
Getaway Cabin	234-7272	sleeps 7
Hidden Canyon B&B	234-7172	6 rooms
Silver Jack Inn	234-7323	9 rooms, tent spaces
Sinclair Gas Station	no phone	RV spaces
Whispering Elms	234-9900	6 rooms, RV and tent spaces

Food

Border Inn	234-7300	breakfast, lunch, and dinner; convenience store open 24 hours
LectroLux Café	234-7323	open seasonally, breakfast and dinner, and bag lunches
Lehman Caves Café	234-7221	open seasonally, breakfast and lunch
T & D's	234-7264	breakfast, lunch, and dinner; convenience store

Other

Border Inn	234-7300	fuel, laundry, showers
Happy Burro Trad'n Post	234-7115	gift shop
Icehouse	234-7323	local arts and crafts
Lehman Caves Café	234-7221	gift shop
Sinclair Gas Station	no phone	fuel, laundry, showers

SNAKE VALLEY PLACE NAMES

Baker, Nevada: Community in southern Snake Valley; named after early settler George W. Baker, who arrived in 1876 (Carlson 1974, 45).

Baker Creek, Baker Lake, Baker Peak: Located in the South Snake Range; named after early settler George W. Baker (Carlson 1974, 45).

Big Springs: Largest spring in southern Snake Valley; descriptive name.

Big Wash: Located in the South Snake Range; descriptive name.

Birch Creek: Stream in the Deep Creek Range; stream banks have many water birches.

Bishop Spring: Spring east of Gandy, now surrounded by Foote Reservoir; named for George Bishop, who settled nearby in 1887 or 1888 (M. Bates 1994, 8).

Black Horse: Mining area near Sacramento Pass area; gold was found on the underside of an overhanging ledge by a rider on a black horse taking refuge from a rainstorm (Smith 1976, 46).

Blue Canyon Creek: Tributary to Strawberry Creek in the South Snake Range; descriptive name.

Blue Mass Scenic Area: Area at the western end of Pleasant Valley; named for numerous rocks that have a bluish tinge in certain lighting conditions.

Boyd Station: Pony Express station between Callao and Fish Springs; named for George Washington Boyd, who accompanied Major Howard Egan to find stations along the route.

Brown Lake: Subalpine lake in the South Snake Range; descriptive name.

Burbank: Community in southern Snake Valley, now mostly abandoned; named after one of the first settlers, Willard Burbank, who was a surveyor (Quate 1993).

Burbank Hills: Located in southern Snake Valley; named after early settler Willard Burbank.

Burnt Mill: Canyon in the South Snake Range; likely named for a sawmill that burned.

Callao: Community in northern Snake Valley first known as Willow Springs; named after Callao, Peru, by early residents, who had to choose a different name for the post office since Willow Springs was already taken. One story states that sheepherders saw the Deep Creek Range and were reminded of Callao, Peru; another story says that someone had been to Callao, Peru, and liked the name (Bateman 1984, 84).

Can Young Canyon: Canyon in the South Snake Range; reportedly named after outlaw Canfield Young (Quate 1993).

Cedar Cabin Spring: Spring at south end of the South Snake Range; likely named for a cabin surrounded by or made from juniper (cedar) trees.

Clay Spring: Located in southern Snake Valley; named after early settler Elwin William Clay (Quate 1993).

Clifton, Clifton Flat: Mining town and area south of Gold Hill; named for rugged terrain (Van Cott 1990, 84).

Confusion Range: Mountains bordering the east side of Snake Valley; named for the confusing topography (Van Cott 1990, 88).

Conger Ranch, Conger Range: Located near present-day EskDale; named after homesteader Horace Conger, who arrived in the 1870s (Quate 1993, 125).

Cowboy Pass: Pass through the Confusion Range; during a dry year in the 1880s, word came that as many as thirty-three herds of hungry sheep were headed toward Snake Valley. Billy Meecham led local ranchers with guns to the pass and told the sheepherders, "No farther or we'll shoot" (Lambert 1991, 54).

Crystal Ball Cave: Located near Gandy; named by George Sims to describe numerous crystals within the cave (Sims 2007).

Crystal Peak: Mountain at south end of the Confusion Range; named for small quartz crystals embedded in volcanic tuff rock.

Dead Lake: Lake in a moraine in the Snake Creek drainage; named due to the apparent lack of life in lake.

Deadman Canyon: Located in the North Snake Range; named after the story of Tollard and Leathers being led there by an Indian and Tollard subsequently being killed (Quate 1993, 18).

Decathon Canyon: Canyon in the South Snake Range; origin unknown.

Deep Canyon: Located in the North Snake Range; descriptive name.

Deep Creek Range: Mountains that form the northwest boundary of Snake Valley; Major Egan penned the name Deep Creek (Bateman 1984, 442). Formerly known as the Goshoot and Tots-arrh Mountains.

Dugway: Town at entrance to Dugway Proving Ground, initiated in 1942.

Elko County: Nevada county; possibly named for elk, with an *o* added to the end; or may be the Shoshone word for "white woman" and was the location where the Indians first saw a white woman (Carlson 1974, 101).

EskDale: Community in northern Snake Valley about 5 miles north of US Highway 6/50; named for the family lands of the founder, Dr. Glendenning, along the River Esk in Scotland (Van Cott 1990, 131).

Ferguson Desert: Large expanse at south end of Snake Valley; named for Bob Ferguson, a settler in the late 1870s (Quate 1993, 125).

Fish Springs: Mountain range, springs, and wildlife refuge named for numerous springs that contain Utah chub.

Foote Reservoir: Reservoir around Bishop Spring east of Gandy; named for Chester and Elnora Foote, who moved here about 1920 to take over the homestead of Elnora's uncles Tom and Joe Carter (M. Bates 1994, 49).

Gandy: Community in northern Snake Valley originally called Smithville. When the post office was established and a new name was needed because Smithville was already taken, the community was renamed Gandy in honor of its oldest citizen, Isaac Gandy (Quate 1993, 213).

Garrison: Community in southern Snake Valley; named for its first postmaster and schoolteacher, Emma Garrison. The community was previously known as Snake Creek (Quate 1993, 176).

George II. Hansen Peak: Highest peak in the Fish Springs Range; named after a geology professor at Brigham Young University (http://www.summitpost.org).

Gold Hill: Mining area and town at the north end of Snake Valley; named after gold-bearing hills nearby (Van Cott 1990, 156).

Hampton Creek: Perennial creek in the North Snake Range; named after early settler Ben Hampton, who had a sawmill in the drainage (Day and Ekins 1951, 535).

Haystack Peak: Second-highest peak in the Deep Creek Range; possibly named because its peak resembles a haystack.

Hendrys Creek: Perennial creek in the North Snake Range; named after early settler William Hendrie, who had a sawmill along the creek. He also had a house in Osceola and was justice of the peace there.

Hogum: Mining area south of Osceola; name derived from miners arriving and seeing that the claims had all been staked, and only a few had "hogged them" (Read 1965, 160).

Horse Canyon: Drainage in the North Snake Range; presumably named for numerous horses seen there.

Horse Heaven: High-elevation meadow near Snake Creek; possibly wild horses once roamed there (Carlson 1974, 137).

Ibapah Peak: Highest peak in the Deep Creek Range; Ibapah means "the place of deep down water" (Bateman 1984, 442). Originally called Haystack Peak; that name is now assigned to the second-highest peak in the range.

Indian Farm Canyon: Canyon in the Deep Creek Range; named after a Goshute farming settlement there.

Indian George Wash: Located northwest of Gandy; probably named after an Indian called Indian George, who was born in 1885 on the Swallow Ranch in Spring Valley (Robison 2006a).

Jeff Davis Peak: High peak in the South Snake Range; originally the name was applied to the higher peak to the west, which is now called Wheeler Peak. In 1854 Colonel Steptoe christened it Jefferson Davis Peak in honor of the US secretary of war. After Lieutenant Wheeler's name was reassigned to the higher peak, the name Jeff Davis was given to its neighbor (Waite 1974, 542–44).

Johnson Lake: Lake at the headwaters of the middle fork of Snake Creek in the South Snake Range; named for Alfred Johnson, who mined tungsten near the lake (Quate 1993, 175).

Juab County: Utah county; named by the local Uab, Yuab, or Yoab Indians of the Paiute Tribe. The name means flat or level plain (Van Cott 1990, 208).

Kern Mountains: Mountains between the Deep Creek and North Snake Ranges; named after a group of miners who came from Kern County, California, and staked claims there (Smith 1976).

King Top: Highest peak of the Confusion Range.

Kious Basin: Drainage in the South Snake Range that includes Kious Spring, a perennial spring often used by wildlife and stock; named for Bill Kious, who came to Snake Valley in the late 1860s with the Hockmans (Sam Smith, personal communication, 2007).

Knoll Springs: Springs north of EskDale that were an early stopping point for freighters and travelers due to their dependable water supply; descriptive name.

Lehman Caves, Lehman Creek: Located in the South Snake Range; named after Absalom Lehman, who many credit with finding the cave and who did much of the early development to allow visitors to enter.

Lexington Arch, Lexington Creek: Located in the South Snake Range; possibly named by miners who remembered places so denoted in Massachusetts and Kentucky (Carlson 1974, 155).

Lincoln Peak: Peak in the South Snake Range; named after President Abraham Lincoln (Carlson 1974, 155).

Mahogany Spring: Spring in southern Snake Valley surrounded by mahogany trees; descriptive name.

Millard County: Utah county; named for President Millard Fillmore (Van Cott 1990, 251).

Mill Creek: Located in the South Snake Range; creek was one of many housing a sawmill. At one time it was known as Water Canyon.

Miller Wash: Located at the south end of the North Snake Range.

Mormon Gap: Utah Highway 21 goes through this gap at the south end of the Burbank Hills and the north end of the Mountain Home Range; named for early Mormon settlers.

Mount Moriah: Highest peak in the North Snake Range; named after George W. Baker's wife, Maria, who settled in Snake Valley in the late 1800s. The 1890 White Pine County assessment book refers to Mount Maria (Shaputis 1999).

Nevada: State; in 1857, the original name for the territory was to be Sierra Nevada Territory, but it was shortened. *Nevada* is a Spanish word meaning "snow-covered" (Carlson 1974, 176).

Old Man Canyon: Canyon in the North Snake Range.

Osceola: Mining community in the South Snake Range; named after a Seminole chief (Carlson 1974, 183).

Partoun: Community in northern Snake Valley; named by Dr. Maurice Glendenning for Partoun, Scotland. *Partoun* means "hilltop."

Pleasant Valley: Valley in the Kern Mountains; named when a Mr. Doolittle and a Mr. White rediscovered the valley while driving cattle to California and one of the men remarked what a pleasant valley it was (M. Bates 1994, 71).

Pruess Lake: Reservoir in southern Snake Valley; originally a shallow lake noted by the Simpson Expedition and named in honor of John C. Frémont's cartographer, George Karl Ludwig Preuss. A typographical error changed the spelling.

Rowland Ranch: Ranch in southern Snake Valley where Ab Lehman of Lehman Caves fame lived for many years; later named for the Rowland family, who lived there from 1891 to 1911 (Quate 1993, 150).

Rudolph Canyon: Canyon in the South Snake Range near Young Canyon; named for Rudolph Mercham, who farmed hay there (Sam Smith, personal communication, 2007).

Sacramento Pass: Located on US Highway 6/50 between the North and South Snake Ranges; may have been named by early prospectors (Carlson 1974, 207).

Salt Marsh Lake: Lake next to Gandy Salt Marsh in northern Snake Valley; descriptive name.

Sand Pass: Pass at the south end of the Fish Springs Range; descriptive name.

Shoshone: Mining district and post office in Spring Valley, Nevada; named for Shoshone Indians (Carlson 1974, 214).

Silver Creek: Creek in the North Snake Range that flows into a reservoir by the same name; the water has a silver tint to it.

Smith Creek, Smith Canyon: Located in the North Snake Range; named for early settler Mr. Smith, who was the first to haul timber out (Day and Ekins 1951, 535).

Smithville: Original name for the community of Gandy in northern Snake Valley, for Smith Creek Ranch, and for a community next to Gandy Salt Marsh. Josiah Smith was the largest cattle owner in Gandy in the early days (M. Bates 1994, 9).

Snake Creek: Creek in the South Snake Range; named due to the serpentine road that crossed and recrossed the creek many times to reach the sawmill (Quate 1993, 121).

Snake Range: Mountain range that forms the western border of Snake Valley; may have been named for their sinuous form or for the Snake Indians (Carlson 1974, 219).

Snake Valley: Valley in eastern Nevada and western Utah; possibly named for the Snake Indians that were said to once inhabit the valley (Day and Ekins 1951, 180), or because the Snake Range curved like a snake (Carlson 1974, 219), or for the many snakes that were once present (D. Taylor 1954, 3).

Stella Lake: Subalpine lake in the South Snake Range; named after early settler Stella Lake (Quate 1993).

Strawberry Creek: Creek at the north end of the South Snake Range; presumably named after strawberries found there (Carlson 1974, 225).

Table: High-elevation plateau in the North Snake Range; its flatness led to this descriptive name.

Teresa Lake: Subalpine lake in the South Snake Range; probably named after Teresa, an early settler in Baker (Waite 1974, 157).

Tooele County: Utah county originally known as Tuilla County, after a Goshute Indian chief, or a reference to bulrushes, known as tules, in the swampy areas in the valley (Van Cott 1990, 372).

Toms Canyon: Canyon in the Deep Creek Range; named after Indian Tom. Spelled Thoms on some maps.

Trout Creek: Perennial creek in the North Snake Range; named for native Bonneville cutthroat trout. Community named after the creek.

Utah: State; named after the Ute Indians (Van Cott 1980, 382).

Uvada: Alternate name for Pleasant Valley school and post office location; contraction for Utah-Nevada; named by Mrs. Henriod, who lived there (Schoppmann 1953, 1).

Warm Springs Creek: Creek that flows from near Gandy Mountain; descriptive name.

Weaver Creek: Intermittent creek in the South Snake Range; named after early settler Dave Weaver.

Wheeler Peak: Highest peak in the South Snake Range; named after Lieutenant George Wheeler, who climbed it in 1869. Originally called Pe-up by Native Americans, meaning "big mountain." In 1854, Colonel Steptoe called it Jefferson Davis Peak in honor of the president of the confederacy. The next year it was named Williams Peak for the first white man to summit it, Mr. Williams of the Mormon White Mountain Mission. The earlier name was more favored and shortened to Jeff Davis Peak. In 1869, Captain James H. Simpson crossed Sacramento Pass and had an outstanding view of the mountain. Due to its connected form, he christened it Union Peak. Nevertheless, the name Wheeler Peak stuck, and the name Jeff Davis was applied to the slightly lower peak to the east of the highest peak (Waite 1974, 542–44).

White Pine County: Nevada county; named for a large stand of pines thought to be white pines; later it was found that there are no white pines in the pines (Carlson 1974, 245);

Willow Springs: First name for the community now called Callao; descriptive name.

Yelland Dry Lake: Dry lake bed in Spring Valley; named for John Yelland, who came from England and settled nearby (Carlson 1974, 249).

Young Canyon: Located in the South Snake Range; named for Brigham and Can Young, early ranchers in Baker (Read 1965, 140).

Mammal Species of Snake Valley

Adapted from "Mammals of Great Basin National Park" (Rickart et al. 2008) and USFWS Fish Springs National Wildlife Refuge Comprehensive Conservation Plan (2004). Species are alphabetized within Orders. Starred entries (*) indicate an introduced species.

Rabbits And Hares—Order Lagomorpha

Black-tailed Jackrabbit	*Lepus californicus*
Desert Cottontail	*Sylvilagus audubonii*
Mountain Cottontail	*Sylvilagus nuttallii*
Pygmy Rabbit	*Brachylagus idahoensis*

Shrews—Order Socorimorpha

American Water Shrew	*Sorex palustris*
Inyo Shrew	*Sorex tenellus*
Merriam's Shrew	*Sorex merriami*
Vagrant Shrew	*Sorex vagrans*

Bats—Order Chiroptera

Big Brown Bat	*Eptesicus fuscus*
California Myotis	*Myotis californicus*
Fringed Myotis	*Myotis thysanodes*

Hoary Bat	*Lasiurus cinereus*
Long-eared Myotis	*Myotis evotis*
Long-legged Myotis	*Myotis volans*
Mexican Free-tailed Bat	*Tadarida brasiliensis*
Pallid Bat	*Antrozous pallidus*
Silver-haired Bat	*Lasionycteris noctivagans*
Spotted Bat	*Euderma maculatum*
Townsend's Big-eared Bat	*Corynorhinus townsendii*
Western Pipistrelle	*Pipistrellus hesperus*
Western Small-footed Myotis	*Myotis ciliolabrum*
Yuma Myotis	*Myotis yumanensis*

Carnivores—Order Carnivora

Badger	*Taxidea taxus*
Bobcat	*Felis rufus*
Cougar (Mountain Lion)	*Puma concolor*
Coyote	*Canis latrans*
Ermine (Short-tailed Weasel)	*Mustela erminea*
Gray Fox	*Urocyon cinereoargenteus*
Kit Fox	*Vulpes macrotis*
Long-tailed Weasel	*Mustela frenata*
Raccoon	*Procyon lotor*
Red Fox*	*Vulpes vulpes*
Ringtail Cat	*Bassariscus astutus*
Striped Skunk	*Mephitis mephitis*
Western Spotted Skunk	*Spilogale gracilis*

Rodents—Order Rodentia

American Beaver	*Castor canadensis*
Antelope Ground Squirrel	*Ammospermophilus leucurus*
Botta's Pocket Gopher	*Thomomys bottae*
Bushy-tailed Woodrat (Packrat)	*Neotoma cinerea*
Canyon Mouse	*Peromyscus crinitus*
Chisel-toothed Kangaroo Rat	*Dipodomys microps*
Cliff Chipmunk	*Tamias dorsalis*
Dark Kangaroo Mouse	*Microdipodops megacephalus*
Deer Mouse	*Peromyscus maniculatus*
Desert Woodrat (Packrat)	*Neotoma lepida*
Golden-mantled Ground Squirrel	*Spermophilus lateralis*
Great Basin Pocket Mouse	*Perognathus parvus*
House Mouse*	*Mus musculus*
Least Chipmunk	*Tamias minimus*
Little Pocket Mouse	*Perognathus longimembris*
Long-tailed Pocket Mouse	*Chaetodipus formosus*

Long-tailed Vole	*Microtus longicaudus*
Montane Vole	*Microtus montanus*
Muskrat	*Ondatra zibethicus*
North American Porcupine	*Erethizon dorsatum*
Northern Grasshopper Mouse	*Onychomys leucogaster*
Ord's Kangaroo Rat	*Dipodomys ordii*
Pinyon Mouse	*Peromyscus truei*
Piute Ground Squirrel	*Spermophilus mollis*
Townsend's Ground Squirrel	*Spermophilus townsendii*
Rock Squirrel	*Spermophilus variegatus*
Sagebrush Vole	*Lemmiscus curtatus*
Uinta Chipmunk	*Tamias umbrinus*
Western Harvest Mouse	*Reithrodontomys megalotis*
Yellow-bellied Marmot	*Marmota flaviventris*

Even-Toed Ungulates—Order Artiodactyla

Bighorn Sheep	*Ovis canadensis*
Cow*	*Bos taurus*
Elk (Wapiti)	*Cervus elaphus*
Mule Deer	*Odocoileus hemionus*
Pronghorn	*Antilocapra americana*

Odd-Toed Ungulates—Order Perissodactyla

Horse*	*Equus caballus*

Fish, Amphibian, and Reptile Species of Snake Valley

Within each section of fish, amphibians, and reptiles, species are organized by Order and then alphabetized. Starred entries (*) indicate an introduced species.

Fish

Trout—Order Salmoniformes

Bonneville Cutthroat Trout	*Oncorhynchus clarki utah*
Brook Trout*	*Salvelinus fontinalis*
Brown Trout*	*Salmo trutta*
Lahontan Cutthroat Trout*	*Oncorhynchus clarki henshawi*
Rainbow Trout*	*Oncorhynchus mykiss*

Minnows and Suckers—Order Cypriniformes

Carp*	*Cyprinus carpio*
Least Chub	*Iotichthys phlegethontis*
Redside Shiner	*Richardsonius balteatus*
Speckled Dace	*Rhinichthys osculus*
Utah Chub	*Gila atraria*
Utah Sucker	*Catostomus ardens*

Catfish—Order Siluriformes

Channel Catfish*   *Ictalurus punctatus*

Killifishes—Order Cyprinodontiformes

Mosquito Fish*   *Gambusia affinis*

Perchlike Fishes—Order Perciformes

Bluegill*   *Lepomis macrochirus*
Largemouth Bass*   *Micropterus salmoides*
Sacramento Perch*   *Archoplites interruptus*
Smallmouth Bass*   *Micropterus dolomieu*

Sculpins—Order Scorpaeniformes

Mottled Sculpin   *Cottus bairdi*

Amphibians—Order Anura

Bullfrog*   *Rana catesbeiana*
Columbia Spotted Frog   *Rana luteiventris*
Great Basin Spadefoot   *Spea intermontana*
Northern Leopard Frog   *Rana pipiens*
Woodhouse's Toad   *Bufo woodhousei*

Lizards and Snakes—Order Squamata

Desert Horned Lizard   *Phrynosoma platyrhinos*
Gopher Snake (Blowsnake)   *Pituophis catenifer*
Great Basin Collard Lizard   *Crotaphytus bicinctores*
Great Basin Rattlesnake   *Crotalus oreganus lutosus*
Great Basin Whiptail Lizard   *Aspidoscelis tigris*
Long-nosed Leopard Lizard   *Gambelia wislizenii*
Long-nosed Snake   *Rhinocheilus lecontei*
Night Snake   *Hypsiglena torquata*
Northern Side-blotched Lizard   *Uta stansburiana*
Ringneck Snake   *Diadophis punctatus*
Sagebrush Lizard   *Sceloporus graciosus*
Sonoran Mountain Kingsnake   *Lampropeltis pyromelana*
Striped Whipsnake   *Coluber taeniatus*
Western Fence Lizard   *Sceloporus occidentalis*
Western Skink   *Eumeces skiltonianus*
Wandering Garter Snake   *Thamnophis elegans vagrans*

BIRD LIST

This list consists of a compilation of Great Basin National Park and Fish Springs National Wildlife Refuge bird lists, excluding birds that were classified as accidentals. The taxonomic order and nomenclature are according to the American Ornithological Union Checklist of North American Birds, 7th edition, 52nd supplement (Chesser et al. 2011). Order names end in –iformes and family names end in –idae. Starred entries (*) indicate an introduced species.

Geese, Swans, & Ducks ANSERIFORMES
ANATIDAE

Snow Goose	*Chen caerulescens*
Canada Goose	*Branta canadensis*
Trumpeter Swan	*Cygnus buccinator*
Tundra Swan	*Cygnus columbianus*
Wood Duck	*Aix sponsa*
Gadwall	*Anas strepera*
American Wigeon	*Anas americana*
Mallard	*Anas platyrhynchos*
Blue-winged Teal	*Anas discors*
Cinnamon Teal	*Anas cyanoptera*

Northern Shoveler	*Anas clypeata*
Northern Pintail	*Anas acuta*
Green-winged Teal	*Anas crecca*
Canvasback	*Aythya valisineria*
Redhead	*Aythya americana*
Ring-necked Duck	*Aythya collaris*
Lesser Scaup	*Aythya affinis*
Bufflehead	*Bucephala albeola*
Common Goldeneye	*Bucephala clangula*
Hooded Merganser	*Lophodytes cucullatus*
Common Merganser	*Mergus merganser*
Red-breasted Merganser	*Mergus serrator*
Ruddy Duck	*Oxyura jamaicensis*

Quail, Pheasants, & Grouse GALLIFORMES
ODONTOPHORIDAE

California Quail	*Callipepla californica*
Gambel's Quail	*Callipepla gambelii*

PHASIANIDAE

Chukar*	*Alectoris chukar*
Ring-necked Pheasant*	*Phasianus colchicus*
Ruffed Grouse	*Bonasa umbellus*
Greater Sage-Grouse	*Centrocercus urophasianus*
Dusky Grouse	*Dendragapus obscurus*
Sharp-tailed Grouse	*Tympanuchus phasianellus*
Wild Turkey*	*Meleagris gallopavo*

Loons GAVIIFORMES
GAVIIDAE

Common Loon	*Gavia immer*

Grebes PODICIPEDIFORMES
PODICIPEDIDAE

Pied-billed Grebe	*Podilymbus podiceps*
Horned Grebe	*Podicpes auritus*
Eared Grebe	*Podicpes nigricollis*
Western Grebe	*Aechmophorus occidentalis*
Clark's Grebe	*Aechmophorus clarkii*

Cormorants SULIIFORMES
PHALACROCORACIDAE

Double-crested Cormorant	*Phalocrocorax auritus*

Pelicans, Bitterns, Egrets, & Ibises PELECANIFORMES
PELECANIDAE
American White Pelican   *Pelecanus erythrorhynchos*

ARDEIDAE
American Bittern	*Botaurus lentiginosus*
Great Blue Heron	*Ardea herodias*
Great Egret	*Ardea alba*
Snowy Egret	*Egretta thula*
Cattle Egret	*Bubulcus ibis*
Black-crowned Night-Heron	*Nycticorax nycticorax*

THRESKIORNITHIDAE
White-faced Ibis   *Plegadis chihi*

Vultures, Hawks, & Eagles ACCIPITRIFORMES
CATHARTIDAE
Turkey Vulture   *Cathartes aura*

PANDIONIDAE
Osprey   *Pandion haliaetus*

ACCIPITRIDAE
Bald Eagle	*Haliaeetus leucocephalus*
Northern Harrier	*Circus cyaneus*
Sharp-shinned Hawk	*Accipiter striatus*
Cooper's Hawk	*Accipiter cooperii*
Northern Goshawk	*Accipiter gentilis*
Red-shouldered Hawk	*Buteo lineatus*
Swainson's Hawk	*Buteo swainsoni*
Red-tailed Hawk	*Buteo jamaicensis*
Ferruginous Hawk	*Buteo regalis*
Rough-legged Hawk	*Buteo lagopus*
Golden Eagle	*Aquila chrysaetos*

Falcons FALCONIFORMES
FALCONIDAE
American Kestrel	*Falco sparverius*
Merlin	*Falco columbarius*
Peregrine Falcon	*Falco peregrinus*
Prairie Falcon	*Falco mexicanus*

Rails & Cranes GRUIFORMES
RALLIDAE

Virginia Rail	*Rallus limicola*
Sora	*Porzana carolina*
American Coot	*Fulica americana*

GRUIDAE

Sandhill Crane	*Grus canadensis*

Plovers, Sandpipers, & Gulls CHARADRIIFORMES
CHARADRIIDAE

Black-bellied Plover	*Pluvialis squatarola*
Snowy Plover	*Charadrius nivosus*
Semipalmated Plover	*Charadrius semipalmatus*
Killdeer	*Charadrius vociferus*

RECURVIROSTRIDAE

Black-necked Stilt	*Himantopus mexicanus*
American Avocet	*Recurvirostra americana*

SCOLOPACIDAE

Spotted Sandpiper	*Actitis macularius*
Solitary Sandpiper	*Tringa solitaria*
Greater Yellowlegs	*Tringa melanoleuca*
Willet	*Tringa semipalmata*
Lesser Yellowlegs	*Tringa flavipes*
Long-billed Curlew	*Numenius americanus*
Marbled Godwit	*Limosa fedoa*
Western Sandpiper	*Calidris mauri*
Least Sandpiper	*Calidris minutilla*
Baird's Sandpiper	*Calidris bairdii*
Pectoral Sandpiper	*Calidris melanotos*
Long-billed Dowitcher	*Limnodromus scolopaceus*
Wilson's Snipe	*Gallinago delicata*
Wilson's Phalarope	*Phalaropus tricolor*
Red-necked Phalarope	*Phalaropus lobatus*

Gulls & Terns LARIDAE

Bonaparte's Gull	*Chroicocephalus philadelphia*
Franklin's Gull	*Leucophaeus pipixcan*
Ring-billed Gull	*Larus delawarensis*
California Gull	*Larus californicus*
Caspian Tern	*Hydroprogne caspia*

Black Tern	*Chlidonias niger*
Forster's Tern	*Sterna forsteri*

Doves & Pigeons COLUMBIFORMES
COLUMBIDAE

Rock Dove (Pigeon)*	*Columba livia*
Eurasian Collared-Dove	*Streptopelia decaocto*
White-winged Dove	*Zenaida asiatica*
Mourning Dove	*Zenaida macroura*

Owls STRIGIFORMES
TYTONIDAE

Barn Owl	*Tyto alba*

STRIGIDAE

Flammulated Owl	*Otus flammeolus*
Western Screech Owl	*Megascops kennicottii*
Great Horned Owl	*Bubo virginianus*
Northern Pygmy Owl	*Glaucidium gnoma*
Burrowing Owl	*Athene cunicularia*
Long-eared Owl	*Asio otus*
Short-eared Owl	*Asio flammeus*
Northern Saw-whet Owl	*Aegolium acadicus*

Goatsuckers CAPRIMIMULGIFORMES
CAPRIMULGIDAE

Lesser Nighthawk	*Chordeiles acutipennis*
Common Nighthawk	*Chordeiles minor*
Common Poorwill	*Phalaenoptilus nuttallii*

Swifts & Hummingbirds APODIFORMES
Swifts APODIDAE

White-throated Swift	*Aeronautes saxatalis*

Hummingbirds TROCHILIDAE

Black-chinned Hummingbird	*Archilochus alexandri*
Calliope Hummingbird	*Stellula calliope*
Broad-tailed Hummingbird	*Selasphorus platycercus*
Rufous Hummingbird	*Selasphorus rufus*

Kingfishers CORACIIFORMES
ALCEDINIDAE
Belted Kingfisher — *Megaceryle alcyon*

Woodpeckers PICIFORMES
PICIDAE
Lewis's Woodpecker — *Melanerpes lewis*
Williamson's Sapsucker — *Sphyrapicus thyroideus*
Yellow-bellied Sapsucker — *Sphyrapicus varius*
Red-naped Sapsucker — *Sphyrapicus nuchalis*
Downy Woodpecker — *Picoides pubescens*
Hairy Woodpecker — *Picoides villosus*
American Three-toed Woodpecker — *Picoides dorsalis*
Northern Flicker — *Colaptes auratus*

Flycatchers PASSERIFORMES
TYRANNIDAE
Olive-sided Flycatcher — *Contopus cooperi*
Western Wood-Pewee — *Contopus sordidulus*
Willow Flycatcher — *Empidonax traillii*
Hammond's Flycatcher — *Empidonax hammondii*
Gray Flycatcher — *Empidonax wrightii*
Dusky Flycatcher — *Empidonax oberholseri*
Cordilleran Flycatcher — *Empidonax occidentalis*
Say's Phoebe — *Sayornis saya*
Ash-throated Flycatcher — *Myiarchus cinerascens*
Cassin's Kingbird — *Tyrannus vociferans*
Western Kingbird — *Tyrannus verticalis*
Eastern Kingbird — *Tyrannus tyrannus*

Shrikes LANIIDAE
Loggerhead Shrike — *Lanius ludovicianus*
Northern Shrike — *Lanius excubitor*

Vireos VEREONIDAE
Plumbeous Vireo — *Vireo plumbeus*
Warbling Vireo — *Vireo gilvus*

Jays & Crows CORVIDAE
Pinyon Jay — *Gymnorhinus cyanocephalus*
Steller's Jay — *Cyanocitta stelleri*
Western Scrub-Jay — *Aphelocoma californica*
Clark's Nutcracker — *Nucifraga columbiana*

Black-billed Magpie	*Pica hudsonia*
American Crow	*Corvus brachyrhynchos*
Common Raven	*Corvus corax*

Larks ALAUDIDAE

Horned Lark	*Eremophila alpestris*

Swallows HIRUNDINIDAE

Tree Swallow	*Tachycineta bicolor*
Violet-green Swallow	*Tachycineta thalassina*
Northern Rough-winged Swallow	*Stelgidopteryx serripennis*
Bank Swallow	*Riparia riparia*
Cliff Swallow	*Petrochelidon pyrrhonota*
Barn Swallow	*Hirundo rustica*

Titmice PARIDAE

Black-capped Chickadee	*Poecile atricapillus*
Mountain Chickadee	*Poecile gambeli*
Juniper Titmouse	*Baeolophus ridgwayi*

Bushtits AEGITHALIDAE

Bushtit	*Psaltriparus minimus*

Nuthatches SITTIDAE

Red-breasted Nuthatch	*Sitta canadensis*
White-breasted Nuthatch	*Sitta carolinensis*
Pygmy Nuthatch	*Sitta pygmaea*

Treecreepers CERTHIIDAE

Brown Creeper	*Certhia americana*

Wrens TROGLODYTIDAE

Rock Wren	*Salpinctes obsoletus*
Canyon Wren	*Catherpes mexicanus*
Bewick's Wren	*Thryomanes bewickii*
House Wren	*Troglodytes aedon*
Winter Wren	
Marsh Wren	*Cistothorus palustris*

Gnatcatchers POLIOPTILIDAE

Blue-gray Gnatcatcher	*Polioptila caerulea*

Dippers CINCLIDAE
American Dipper — *Cinclus mexicanus*

Kinglets REGULIDAE
Golden-crowned Kinglet — *Regulus satrapa*
Ruby-crowned Kinglet — *Regulus calendula*

Thrushes TURDIDAE
Western Bluebird — *Sialia mexicana*
Mountain Bluebird — *Sialia currucoides*
Townsend's Solitaire — *Myadestes townsendi*
Swainson's Thrush — *Catharus ustulatus*
Hermit Thrush — *Catharus guttatus*
American Robin — *Turdus migratorius*

Thrashers MIMIDAE
Gray Catbird — *Dumetella carolinensis*
Northern Mockingbird — *Mimus polyglottos*
Sage Thrasher — *Oreoscoptes montanus*
Brown Thrasher — *Toxostoma rufum*

Starlings STURNIDAE
European Starling — *Sturnus vulgaris*

Pipits MOTACILLIDAE
American Pipit — *Anthus rubescens*

Waxwings BOMBYCILLIDAE
Bohemian Waxwing — *Bombycilla garrulus*
Cedar Waxwing — *Bombycilla cedrorum*

Warblers PARULIDAE
Orange-crowned Warbler — *Oreothlypis celata*
Virginia's Warbler — *Oreothlypis virginiae*
MacGillivray's Warbler — *Geothlypis tolmiei*
Common Yellowthroat — *Geothlypis trichas*
Yellow Warbler — *Setophaga petechia*
Yellow-rumped Warbler — *Setophaga coronata*
Black-throated Gray Warbler — *Setophaga nigrescens*
Townsend's Warbler — *Setophaga townsendi*
Hermit Warbler — *Setophaga occidentalis*
Wilson's Warbler — *Cardellina pusilla*
Yellow-breasted Chat — *Icteria virens*

Sparrows EMBERIZIDAE

Green-tailed Towhee	*Pipilo chlorurus*
Spotted Towhee	*Pipilo maculatus*
Rufous-crowned Sparrow	*Aimophila ruficeps*
American Tree Sparrow	*Spizella arborea*
Chipping Sparrow	*Spizella passerina*
Brewer's Sparrow	*Spizella breweri*
Vesper Sparrow	*Pooecetes gramineus*
Lark Sparrow	*Chondestes grammacus*
Black-throated Sparrow	*Amphispiza bilineata*
Sage Sparrow	*Amphispiza belli*
Savannah Sparrow	*Passerculus sandwichensis*
Fox Sparrow	*Passerella iliaca*
Song Sparrow	*Melospiza melodia*
Lincoln's Sparrow	*Melospiza lincolnii*
White-throated Sparrow	*Zonotrichia albicollis*
Harris's Sparrow	*Zonotrichia querula*
White-crowned Sparrow	*Zonotrichia leucophrys*
Dark-eyed Junco	*Junco hyemalis*

Tanagers, Grosbeaks, & Buntings CARDINALIDAE

Western Tanager	*Piranga ludoviciana*
Rose-breasted Grosbeak	*Pheucticus ludovicianus*
Black-headed Grosbeak	*Pheucticus melanocephalus*
Blue Grosbeak	*Passerina caerulea*
Lazuli Bunting	*Passerina amoena*
Indigo Bunting	*Passerina cyanea*

Blackbirds & Orioles ICTERIDAE

Bobolink	*Dolichonyx oryzivorus*
Red-winged Blackbird	*Agelaius phoeniceus*
Western Meadowlark	*Sturnella neglecta*
Yellow-headed Blackbird	*Xanthocephalus xanthocephalus*
Brewer's Blackbird	*Euphagus cyanocephalus*
Great-tailed Grackle	*Quiscalus mexicanus*
Brown-headed Cowbird	*Molothrus ater*
Hooded Oriole	*Icterus cucullatus*
Bullock's Oriole	*Icterus bullockii*
Scott's Oriole	*Icterus parisorum*

Finches FRINGILLIDAE

Gray-crowned Rosy-Finch	*Leucosticte tephrocotis*
Black Rosy-Finch	*Leucosticte atrata*
Cassin's Finch	*Carpodacus cassinii*

House Finch	*Carpodacus mexicanus*
Red Crossbill	*Loxia curvirostra*
Pine Siskin	*Spinus pinus*
Lesser Goldfinch	*Spinus psaltria*
American Goldfinch	*Spinus tristis*
Evening Grosbeak	*Coccothraustes vespertinus*

Weaver Finches PASSERIDAE

House Sparrow*	*Passer domesticus*

Most Common Plants Listed by Habitat

Some of the most common plants in Snake Valley are listed below based on their habitat(s). This list is adapted from the Nevada Department of Wildlife's Comprehensive Wildlife Conservation Strategy (2005). Common names are from the USDA Plants Database (http://plants.usda.gov). Within each habitat type, the vegetation is organized by trees, shrubs, and herbs/forbs/grasses/other and alphabetized. Starred entries (*) indicate an introduced species.

Intermountain Cold Desert Scrub
(generally below 5,000 feet)

Shrubs

Bud sagebrush	*Artemisia spinescens*
Fourwing saltbush	*Atriplex canescens*
Greasewood	*Sarcobatus vermiculatus*
Quailbush	*Atriplex lentiformis*
Shadscale saltbush	*Atriplex confertifolia*
Spiny hopsage	*Grayia spinosa*
Winterfat	*Krascheninnikovia lanata*

Herbs/Forbs/Grasses/Other

Cheatgrass*	*Bromus tectorum*
Common reed*	*Phragmites australis*
Indian ricegrass	*Achnatherum hymenoides*
Needle-and-thread	*Hesperostipa comata*
Rocky Mountain beeplant	*Cleome serrulata*
Russian thistle*	*Salsola kali*
Saltgrass	*Distichlis spicata*
Saltlover (Halogeton) *	*Halogeton glomeratus*
Sand dropseed	*Sporobolus cryptandrus*
Virginia glasswort (Pickleweed)	*Salicornia virginica*

Sagebrush/Grasslands
(5,000–7,000 feet)

Shrubs

Antelope bitterbrush	*Purshia tridentata*
Basin big sagebrush	*Artemisia tridentata tridentata*
Black sagebrush	*Artemisia nova*
Low sagebrush	*Artemisia arbuscula*
Mormon tea	*Ephedra* spp.
Mountain big sagebrush	*Artemisia tridentata vaseyana*
Mountain snowberry	*Symphoricarpos oreophilus*
Rubber rabbitbrush	*Ericameria nauseosus*
Winterfat	*Krascheninnikovia lanata*
Wyoming big sagebrush	*Artemisia tridentata wyomingensis*
Yellow rabbitbrush	*Chrysothamnus viscidiflorus*

Herbs/Forbs/Grasses/Other

Basin wildrye	*Leymus cinereus*
Bluebunch wheatgrass	*Pseudoroegneria spicata*
Bluegrass	*Poa* spp.
Cheatgrass*	*Bromus tectorum*
Hairspine pricklypear	*Opuntia polyacantha*
Indian paintbrush	*Castilleja* spp.
Indian ricegrass	*Achnatherum hymenoides*
Medusahead*	*Taeniatherum caput-medusae*
Needle-and-thread	*Hesperostipa comata*
Penstemon	*Penstemon* spp.
Redroot buckwheat	*Eriogonum racemosum*
Redstem stork's bill*	*Erodium cicutarium*
Scarlet globemallow	*Sphaeralcea coccinea*
Sheep fescue	*Festuca ovina*

Pinyon-Juniper Woodlands
(6,000–8,000 feet)

Trees
Curl-leaf mountain-mahogany   *Cercocarpus ledifolius*
Singleleaf pinyon   *Pinus monophylla*
Littleleaf mountain mahogany   *Cercocarpus intricatus*
Utah juniper   *Juniperus osteosperma*

Shrubs
Antelope bitterbrush   *Purshia tridentata*
Black sagebrush   *Artemisia nova*
Greenleaf manzanita   *Arctostaphylos patula*
Saskatoon serviceberry   *Amelanchier alnifolia*
Stansbury cliffrose   *Purshia stansburiana*

Herbs/Forbs/Grasses/Other
Arrowleaf balsamroot   *Balsamorhiza sagittata*
Basin wildrye   *Leymus cinereus*
Indian paintbrush   *Castilleja* spp.
Palmer's penstemon   *Penstemon palmeri*
Sandberg bluegrass   *Poa secunda*
Sego lily   *Calochortus nuttallii*
Squirreltail   *Elymus elymoides*

Mixed Conifer Forest
(7,000–10,000 feet)

Trees
Curl-leaf mountain mahogany   *Cercocarpus ledifolius*
Douglas fir   *Pseudotsuga menziesii*
Ponderosa pine   *Pinus ponderosa*
Quaking aspen   *Populus tremuloides*
White fir   *Abies concolor*

Shrubs
Common juniper   *Juniperus communis*
Greenleaf manzanita   *Arctostaphylos patula*
Mountain big sagebrush   *Artemisia tridentata vaseyana*
Mountain snowberry   *Symphoricarpos oreophilus*

Herbs/Forbs/Grasses/Other
Anderson's larkspur   *Delphinium andersonii*

Bluebunch wheatgrass	*Pseudoroegneria spicata*
Creeping barberry	*Mahonia repens*
Common yarrow	*Achillea millefolium*
Fendler's meadow-rue	*Thalictrum fendleri*
Jones' fleabane	*Erigeron jonesii*
Mule's ear	*Wyethia amplexicaulis*
Sticky purple geranium	*Geranium viscosissimum*
Silvery lupine	*Lupinus argenteus*
Western valerian	*Valeriana occidentalis*

Subalpine
(9,500–11,800 feet)

Trees

Great Basin Bristlecone pine	*Pinus longaeva*
Engelmann spruce	*Picea engelmannii*
Limber pine	*Pinus flexilis*

Shrubs

Common juniper	*Juniperus communis*
Currant	*Ribes* spp.

Herbs/Forbs/Grasses/Other

Fendler's meadow-rue	*Thalictrum fendleri*
Ross' sedge	*Carex rossii*

Alpine
(above 10,500 feet)

Shrubs

Shrubby cinquefoil	*Dasiphora fruticosa*
Singlehead goldenbush	*Ericameria suffruticosa*

Herbs/Forbs/Grasses/Other

Alpine timothy	*Phleum alpinum*

Biological crusts

Blackroot sedge	*Carex elynoides*
Cushion phlox	*Phlox pulvinata*
Dunhead sedge	*Carex phaeocephala*
Ross' avens	*Geum rossii*
Tufted hairgrass	*Deschampsia caespitosa*

Riparian

Trees
Narrowleaf cottonwood	*Populus angustifolia*
Quaking aspen	*Populus tremuloides*
Water birch	*Betula occidentalis*
Redosier dogwood	*Cornus sericea*
Russian olive*	*Elaeagnus angustifolia*
Saltcedar (Tamarisk)*	*Tamarix ramosissima*
Willow	*Salix* spp.

Shrubs
Woods' rose	*Rosa woodsii*

Herbs/Forbs/Grasses/Other
Colorado blue columbine	*Aquilegia coerulea*
Rush	*Juncus* spp.
Sedge	*Carex* spp.
Western columbine	*Aquilegia formosa*
Columbian monkshood	*Aconitum columbianum*
Parry's primrose	*Primula parryi*
Seep monkeyflower	*Mimulus guttatus*
Western sweetroot	*Osmorhiza occidentalis*

REFERENCES

Angel, Myron. (1881) 1958. *History of the State of Nevada.* Oakland, CA: Thompson and West. Reprint, Berkeley, CA: Howell-North.

Armstrong, W. P. 2007. "Watermelon Snow." Accessed April 12. http://waynesword.palomar.edu/plaug98.htm.

Baker, Craig. 2007. Interview and notes by Gretchen M. Baker.

Baker, Dean. 1999. Videotaped interview by Boyd Quate.

Baker, G., N. Darby, T. Williams, and J. Wullschleger. 2008. *Bonneville Cutthroat Trout Restoration Project—Great Basin National Park.* Natural Resource Report NPS/NRPC/NRR 2008/055. Fort Collins, CO: National Park Service.

Ballenger, Liz. 2002. "*Marmota flaviventris.*" Animal Diversity Web. Accessed April 12, 2007. http://animaldiversity.ummz.umich.edu/site/accounts/information/Marmota_flaviventris.html.

Bateman, Ronald R. 1984. *Deep Creek Reflections: 125 Years of Settlement at Ibapah, Utah, 1859–1984.* Salt Lake City: Self-published.

Bates, Jerald. 2007. Videotaped interview and notes by Gretchen M. Baker.

Bates, Marlene. 1994. *North Snake Valley,* Part 1. Snake Valley, UT: Self-published.

———. 2007. Videotaped interview and notes by Gretchen M. Baker.

Belnap, J., J. H. Kaltenecker, R. Rosentreter, J. Williams, S. Leonard, and D. Eldridge. 2001. *Biological Soil Crusts: Ecology and Management.* Technical reference 1730-2. Denver: US Department of the Interior.

Bensen, Joe. 1995. *The Traveler's Guide to the Pony Express Trail.* Helena, MT: Falcon Press.

Benson, A. J. 2007. "*Melanoides tuberculatus.*" USGS Nonindigenous Aquatic Species Database, Gainesville, FL. Accessed February 15. http://nas.er.usgs.gov/queries/FactSheet.asp?speciesID=1037.

Berger, Reita. 2006. Videotaped interview and notes by Gretchen M. Baker.

Bluth, John Frederick. 1978. "Confrontation with an Arid Land: The incursion of Gosiutes and Whites into Utah's Central West Desert, 1800–1978." PhD diss., Brigham Young University.

Bradley, Martha Sonntag. 2007. "The MX Missile project." Utah History to Go, State of Utah. Accessed April 18. http://historytogo.utah.gov/utah_chapters/utah_today/themxmissileproject.html.

Brown, J. H. 1978. "The Theory of Insular Biogeography and the Distribution of Boreal Birds and Mammals." *Great Basin Naturalist Memoirs* 2:209–27.

Bryan, Alan L. 1977. "Smith Creek Cave." In *The Archaeology of Smith Creek Canyon, Eastern Nevada*, 162–252. Edited by Donald R. Tuohy and Doris L. Rendall. Nevada State Museum Anthropological Papers, no. 17, 1979. Carson City, NV.

BWG (Biological Work Group). 2009. *Biological Monitoring Plan for the Spring Valley Stipulation*. Las Vegas, NV: US Department of the Interior and Southern Nevada Water Authority.

Carlson, Helen S. 1974. *Nevada Place Names: A Geographical Dictionary*. Reno: University of Nevada Press.

Carr, Stephen L. 1972. *The Historical Guide to Utah Ghost Towns*. Salt Lake City: Western Epics.

Charleston, Mrs. William, and Mrs. Paul Pascuzzo. 1992. Letter to Mr. Al Hendricks, director, Great Basin National Park, October 19. Great Basin National Park files, Baker, NV.

Chesser, R. T., R. C. Banks, F. K. Barker, C. Cicero, J. L. Dunn, A. W. Kratter, I. J. Lovette, P. C. Rasmussen, J. V. Remsen, Jr., J. D. Rising, D. F. Stotz, and K. Winker. 2011. "Fifty-second Supplement to the American Ornithologists' Union Check-list of North American Birds." *The Auk* 128:600–613.

Childs, Doug. 2007. Videotaped interview and notes by Gretchen M. Baker.

Coffman, Marjorie. 2006. Videotaped interview and notes by Gretchen M. Baker.

Cole Jr., A. C. 1942. "The Ants of Utah." *American Midland Naturalist* 28:358–88.

Conrad, Bob. 1996. Videotaped presentation at the tenth anniversary of Great Basin National Park, Baker, NV.

Crum, Steven J. 1994. *The Road on Which We Came: A History of the Western Shoshone*. Salt Lake City: University of Utah Press.

Dalton, W. S. 1922. *Report of Cases Decided in the Supreme Court of the State of Utah*. Vol. 58, *April 1921–November 1921*. Chicago: Callaghan.

Darton, N. H. 1908. "Marble of White Pine County, Nev., near Gandy, Utah." In *Contributions to Economic Geology 1907*, Part 1. *Metals and Nonmetals, Except Fuels*, edited by C. W. Hayes and Waldemar Lindgren, 377–80. USGS Bulletin 340. Washington DC: Department of the Interior.

Davies, Ladd. 1999. Videotaped interview by Boyd Quate.

Day, Stella H., and Sebrina Ekins. 1951. *Milestones of Millard: 100 Years of History of Millard County*. Daughters of Utah Pioneers of Millard County, Art City Publishing.

Dearden, Bill. 2007. Videotaped interview and notes by Gretchen M. Baker.

DeCourten, Frank L. 2003. *The Broken Land: Adventures in Great Basin Geology*. Salt Lake City: University of Utah Press.

Denton, Craig. 1999. *People of the West Desert: Finding Common Ground*. Logan: Utah State University Press.

Ege, Carl L. 2005. *Selected Mining Districts of Utah*. Salt Lake City: Utah Geological Survey.

Elliott, P. E., D. A. Beck, and D. E. Prudic. 2006. *Characterization of Surface-Water Resources in the Great Basin National Park Area and Their Susceptibility to Ground-Water Withdrawals in Adjacent Valleys, White Pine County, Nevada.* USGS Scientific Investigations Report 2006–5099, US Department of the Interior.

Elliott, Russell R. 1987. *History of Nevada.* Lincoln: University of Nebraska Press.

Fiero, Bill. 1986. *Geology of the Great Basin.* Reno: University of Nevada Press.

Garland, Annette. 2007. Interview and notes by Gretchen M. Baker.

Garrett, James. 2001. *Ibex and Selected Climbs of Utah's West Desert.* Self-published.

Georgetta, Clel. 1972. *Golden Fleece in Nevada.* Reno, NV: Venture Publishing.

Gonder, Daisy Eldridge. 2002. Videotaped presentation at Great Basin National Park.

Greeley, Horace. 1860. *An Overland Journey from New York to San Francisco in the Summer of 1859.* New York: Saxton, Barker.

Griggs, Jeannette S. 1974. *Let There Be Light.* Forest Grove, OR: Times Litho.

Griswold, Terry. 2006. *Bee Inventory and Selection of Potential Indicator Species at U.S. Army Dugway Proving Grounds.* 2006 annual report, USDA Agricultural Research Service. Accessed February 1, 2007. http://www.ars.usda.gov/research/projects/projects.htm?ACCN_NO=408577

Hall, Shawn. 1994. *Romancing Nevada's Past.* Reno: University of Nevada Press.

Hanks, Arlene. 2007. Videotaped interview and notes by Gretchen M. Baker.

Healy, Lenora. 2006. *Cleveland Ranch History.* Available from http://www.lulu.com/fussell40.

Heaton, Timothy H. 1985. "The Quaternary Paleontology and Paleoecology of Crystal Ball Cave, Millard County, Utah: With Emphasis on the Mammals and the Description of a New Species of Fossil Skunk." *Great Basin Naturalist* 45:337–90.

Hill, Kathy. 2007. Videotaped interview and notes by Gretchen M. Baker.

Hintze, Lehi F. 1997. *Utah Geologic Highway Map.* Brigham Young University Geology Studies Special Publication 3. Provo, UT.

Hintze, Lehi F., and Fitzhugh D. Davis. 2003. *Geology of Millard County, Utah.* Utah Geological Survey, Bulletin 133. Salt Lake City, UT.

Hose, Richard K., and M. C. Blake Jr. 1976. "Geology." In *Geology and Mineral Resources of White Pine County, Nevada.* Bulletin 85. Reno: MacKay School of Mines, University of Nevada.

Howard, H. 1952. "The prehistoric avifauna of Smith Creek Cave, Nevada, with a description of a new gigantic raptor." *Southern California Acad. Sci. Bull.* 51(2):50–54.

Howard, Janet L. 2004. "*Pinus longaeva.*" Fire Effects Information System. USDA Forest Service, Rocky Mountain Research Station, Fire Sciences Laboratory. Accessed March 20, 2007. http://www.fs.fed.us/database/feis.

IPCC (Intergovernmental Panel on Climate Change). 2007. Climate Change 2007: Synthesis Report; Contribution of Working Groups I, II and III to the Fourth Assessment Report of the Intergovernmental Panel on Climate Change. Geneva, Switzerland: IPCC.

Kelsey, Michael R. 1997. *Hiking, Climbing and Exploring Western Utah's Jack Watson's Ibex Country.* Provo, UT: Kelsey Publishing.

King, Richard B. 2003. "Mendelian Inheritance of Melanism in the Garter Snake *Thamnophis sirtalis.*" *Herpetologica* 59:486–91.

Kitchen, Stanley G., and Gary L. Jorgenson. 1999. "Annualization of Rodent Burrow Clusters and Winterfat Decline in a Salt-Desert Community." USDA Forest Service Proceedings, RMRS-P-11.

Kitchen, Stanley G., and E. Durant McArthur. n.d. *Desert Experimental Range.* Leaflet from US Forest Service Shrub Sciences Laboratory. Provo, UT.

Koyle, Denys. 2002. Videotaped presentation at Great Basin National Park for Women's History Month.

Krejca, Jean K., and Steve J. Taylor. 2003. *A Biological Inventory of Eight Caves in Great Basin National Park.* Illinois Natural History Survey, Center for Biodiversity Technical Report 27:1–72.

Lambert, Darwin. 1991. *Great Basin Drama.* Niwot, CO: Roberts Rinehart Publishers.

Lange, Arthur L. 1958. "Stream Piracy and Cave Development along Baker Creek, Nevada." Western Speleological Institute Bulletin Number 1.

Layland, RaeJean. 2007. Videotaped interview and notes by Gretchen M. Baker.

Lewis, Wesley. 2007. Videotaped interview and notes by Gretchen M. Baker.

Lincoln Highway Association. 2007. Accessed March 12. http://www.lincolnhighwayassoc.org/.

Lyman, Edward Leo. 2007. "Struggle for Statehood." Utah History to Go. State of Utah. Accessed July 4. http://historytogo.utah.gov/utah_chapters/statehood_and_the_progressive_era/struggleforstatehood.html.

McDonald, Dan M. 1913. "White Pine County." Chap. 64 in *The History of Nevada,* vol. 2. Edited by Sam P. Davis. Los Angeles: Elms Publishing.

McKee, Maggie. 2004. "Genesis Crash Linked to Upside-Down Design." *New Scientist.* Accessed March 16, 2007. http://www.newscientist.com/article.ns?id=dn6541.

McPhee, John. 1982. *Basin and Range.* New York: Farrar, Straus, and Giroux.

———. 1997. *Irons in the Fire.* New York: Noonday Press.

Mead, E. M., and J. I. Mead. 1989. "Snake Creek Burial Cave and a Review of the Quarternary Mustelids of the Great Basin." *Great Basin Naturalist* 49:143–54.

Menzies, Richard. 1981. *The Last Days of Trapper Jim: Conversations with James P. Harrison, Last of the Old-Time Fur Trappers.* Salt Lake City: Notebook.

Miller, B. F. 1924. "Nevada in the Making, Being Pioneer Stories of White Pine County and Elsewhere." *Nevada State Historical Society Papers,* vol. 4, 225–474. Carson City.

Mock, K. E., J. C. Brim-Box, M. P. Miller, M. E. Downing, and W. R. Hoeh. 2004. "Genetic Diversity and Divergence among Freshwater Mussel (*Anodonta*) Populations in the Bonneville Basin of Utah." *Molecular Ecology* 13:1085–98.

Muchmore, W. B. 1962. "A New Cavernicolous Pseudoscorpion Belonging to the Genus *Microcreagris.*" *Postilla* 70:1–6.

NASA (National Aeronautics and Space Administration). 2007. "Genesis: Search for Origins." NASA Jet Propulsion Laboratory, California Institute of Technology. Accessed March 16. http://genesismission.jpl.nasa.gov/.

NDOW (Nevada Department of Wildlife). 2004. "Field Trip Report, Shoshone Ponds." Accessed November 28, 2010. http://water.nv.gov/hearings/past/spring/exhibits/USFWS/FWS-2078.pdf.

———. 2005. *Comprehensive Wildlife Conservation Strategy.* Reno, NV. http://www.wildlifeactionplans.org/pdfs/action_plans/nv_action_plan.pdf.

Nielsen, Carl.1947. "Home on the Range." In *Hiking, Climbing, and Exploring Western Utah's Jack Watson's Ibex Country*, 163–65. Michael Kelsey, 1997. Provo, UT: Kelsey Publishing.

NPS (National Park Service). 2005. "Night Sky Quality Monitoring Report: Great Basin NP, Nevada, Mt. Washington, October 7, 2005" Accessed October 31, 2010. http://www.nature.nps.gov/air/lightscapes/monitorData/grba/MW20051007.cfm.

Nutt, Constance J., David R. Zimbleman, David L. Campbell, Joseph S. Duval, and Brian J. Hannigan. 1990. *Mineral Resources of the Deep Creek Mountains Wilderness Study Area, Juab and Tooele Counties, Utah*. USGS Bulletin 1745. Washington, DC: US Government Printing Office.

Olson, Donald W. 2002. "Garnet." USGS Publication SP-14-95. Accessed March 21, 2007. http://minerals.usgs.gov/minerals/pubs/commodity/gemstones/sp14-95/garnet.html.

Orndorff, Richard L., Robert W. Wieder, and Harry F. Filkorn. 2001. *Geology Underfoot in Central Nevada*. Missoula, MT: Mountain Press Publishing.

Osborn, G., and K. Bevis. 2001. "Glaciation in the Great Basin of the Western United States." *Quaternary Science Reviews* 20:1377–1410.

Peck, Joseph H. 1959. *What Next, Doctor Peck?* Englewood Cliffs, NJ: Prentice-Hall.

Quate, Boyd E. 1993. *Pioneers of Snake Valley 1865–1935 as Remembered by Their Descendents*. Norfolk, VA: Self-published.

Read, Effie O. 1965. *White Pine Lang Syne: A True History of White Pine County, Nevada*. Denver: Big Mountain Press.

Reinemann, S. A., D. F. Porinchu, A. M. Bloom, B. G. Mark, and J. E. Box. 2009. "A Multi-Proxy Paleolimnological Reconstruction of Holocene Climate Conditions in the Great Basin, United States." *Quaternary Research* 72, no.3:347–58.

Richardson, Genevieve "Gen." 2006. Videotaped interview and notes by Gretchen M. Baker, February 20.

Rickart, E. A., S. L. Robson, and L. R. Heaney. 2008. "Mammals of Great Basin National Park, Nevada: Comparative Field Surveys and Assessment of Faunal Change." *Monographs of the Western North American Naturalist* 4:77–114.

Robison, Russell. 2006a. *Our Swallow Heritage*. Vol. 2, *History of George Swallow and His Sons*. Self-published at Lulu.com.

———. 2006b. *Our Swallow Heritage*. Vol. 1, *History of the Thomas Swallow Family*. Self-published at Lulu.com.

Rosenberg, Donald J. 2007. "Utah and the Jessie James Gang." Northwest Heritage. Accessed March 11. http://sc.supchapters.org/files/2011/02/Goodin-Albert-Ross-1.pdf.

Schlabsz, Patsy Baker. 2007. Videotaped interview and notes by Gretchen M. Baker.

Schoppmann, Lola Henriod. 1953. *Proud Grandma Nurse Lola*. Cedar City, UT: Self-published.

Schultz, W., P. T. Tueller, and R. J. Tausch. 1990. "Ecology of Curlleaf Mahogany in Western and Central Nevada: Community and Population Structure." *Journal of Range Management* 43, no. 1:13–20.

Shaputis, June. 1999. "1887 and 1890 Assessment Roll Book, White Pine County." Accesssed February 19, 2007. http://www.webpanda.com/white_pine_county/Goverment/.

Shear, W. A. 2007. "Cave Millipeds of the United States. V. The genus *Idagona* Buckett & Gardner (Chordeumatida, Conotylidae, Idagoninae)." *Zootaxa* 1463:1–12.

Shear, W. A., S. J. Taylor, J. J. Wynne, and J. K. Krejca. 2009. "Cave Millipeds of the United States. VIII. New Genera and Species of Polydesmid Millipeds from Caves in the Southwestern United States." *Zootaxa* 2151:47–65.

Sherwin, R. E. 2009. "A Study on the Use of Rose Guano Cave, Nevada, by Mexican Free-Tailed Bats (*Tadarida brasiliensis*)." Report to the BLM, Ely District Office.

Sigler, William F., and John W. Sigler. 1987. *Fishes of the Great Basin: A Natural History.* Reno: University of Nevada Press.

Sims, Tom. 2006. Videotaped interview and notes by Gretchen M. Baker.

———. 2007. Interview and notes by Gretchen M. Baker.

Smith, Roscoe M. 1976. "Mineral Resources." In *Geology and Mineral Resources of White Pine County, Nevada.* Bulletin 85. Reno: MacKay School of Mines. University of Nevada.

Spendlove, Earl. 1967. "Joy and No-Nose Maggie." *Real West* (May):10–13, 57–58.

———. 1968. "Bad Blood in Snake Valley." *The West* (June): 11–13, 41–44.

Stein, Bruce A. 2002. *States of the Union: Ranking America's Biodiversity.* Arlington, VA: NatureServe.

Stock, C. 1936. "A New Mountain Goat from the Quaternary of Smith Creek Cave, Nevada." *Southern California Acad. Sci. Bull.* 35(3):149–53.

Summers, Paul. 2001. "Hydrogeologic Analysis of Needle Point Spring, Fillmore Field Office, Utah." Bureau of Land Management report.

Taylor, Dee Calderwood. 1954. "The Garrison Site." University of Utah Anthropological Papers no. 16. Salt Lake City, UT.

Taylor, S. J. and J. R. Holsinger. 2011. "A new species of the subterranean amphipod crustacean genus *Stygobromus* (Crangonyctidae) from a cave in Nevada, USA." *Subterranean Biology* 8: 39-47. doi: 10.3897/subtbiol.8.1130

Taylor, S. J., J. K. Krejca, and M. E. Slay. 2008. *Cave Biota of Great Basin National Park, White Pine County, Nevada.* Illinois Natural History Survey, Technical Report 2008(25).

Taylor, Val. 1996. Videotaped presentation at Great Basin National Park.

———. 2006. Videotaped interview and notes by Gretchen M. Baker.

Time. 1980. "Taking Aim at the MX Missile." April 7.

Trexler, Keith A. 1966. *Lehman Caves . . . Its Human Story.* Baker, NV: Lehman Caves National Monument.

Trimble, Stephen. 1989. *The Sagebrush Ocean.* Reno: University of Nevada Press.

Tuohy, Donald R. 1979. "Kachina Cave." In *The Archaeology of Smith Creek Canyon, Eastern Nevada,* 1–89. Edited by Donald R. Tuohy and Doris L. Rendall. Nevada State Museum Anthropological Papers, no. 17. Carson City, NV.

Twain, Mark. 1872. *Roughing It.* Pleasantville, NY: Reader's Digest Association.

UDWR (Utah Division of Wildlife Resources). 2004. "Life cycle of *Centrocestus formosanus.*" *The Ichthyogram* 15, no. 4:6.

Unrau, Harlan D. 1990. *A History of Great Basin National Park, Nevada.* Historic resource study. Denver: US Department of the Interior, National Park Service.

USC&GS (US Coast and Geodetic Survey). 1885. *Annual Report of the Superintendent of the U.S. Coast and Geodetic Survey Showing the Progress of the Work for the Fiscal Year Ending with June 1884*. Washington DC: Government Printing Office.

USFS (US Forest Service). 2007. "The Table, Mt. Moriah Wilderness." Accessed April 16. http://www.fs.fed.us/r4/resources/geology/geo_points_interest/activities/mountains_ranges_basins.shtml#ht.

USFWS (US Fish and Wildlife Service). 2004. "Fish Springs National Wildlife Refuge Comprehensive Conservation Plan." US Department of the Interior.

Van Cott, John W. 1990. *Utah Place Names*. Salt Lake City: University of Utah Press.

Waite, Robert Starr. 1974. "The Proposed Great Basin National Park: A Geographical Interpretation of the Southern Snake Range, Nevada." PhD diss., University of California, Los Angeles.

Warner, Angie Dearden. "History of Garrison." 1951. In *Milestones of Millard: A Century of History of Millard County, 1851–1951*, 530–31. Edited by Stella H. Day and Sebrina C. Ekins. Springville, UT: Art City Publishing.

Wasley, Tony. 2004. *Nevada's Mule Deer: Population Dynamics; Issues and Influences*. Biology Bulletin no. 14. http://www.ndow.org/about/pubs/reports/muledeer.pdf (accessed 17 March 2007).

Welch, A. H., D. J. Bright, and L. A. Knochenmus, eds. 2007. *Water Resources of the Basin and Range Carbonate-Rock Aquifer System, White Pine County, Nevada, and Adjacent Areas in Nevada and Utah*. USGS Scientific Investigations Report 2007–5261. Reston, VA: US Geological Survey.

Wells, Susan J. 1993. *Archeological Investigations at Great Basin National Park: Testing and Site Recording in Support of the General Management Plan*. Publications in Anthropology 64. Tucson, AZ: Western Archeological Center, National Park Service, Department of the Interior.

Wheeler, George C., and Jeanette N. Wheeler. 1986. *The Ants of Nevada*. Los Angeles: Natural History Museum of Los Angeles County.

Wheeler, Lorene. 2007. Videotaped interview and notes by Gretchen M. Baker.

Wilde, James D., and Reed A. Soper. 1993. *Baker Village: A Preliminary Report on the 1991 and 1992 Archaeological Field Seasons at 26WP63, White Pine County, Nevada*. Technical Series no. 93–10. Provo, UT: Brigham Young University, Museum of Peoples and Cultures.

Wilson, Elijah Nicholas, and Howard R. Driggs. 1991. *The White Indian Boy: The Story of Uncle Nick among the Shoshones*. Salt Lake City: Paragon Press.

Wilson, James R. 1995. *A Collector's Guide to Rock, Mineral, and Fossil Localities of Utah*. Miscellaneous Publication 95-4. Salt Lake City: Utah Geological Survey.

Wilson, Pearl D. 1999. *A History of Juab County*. With June McNulty and David Hampshire. Salt Lake City: Utah State Historical Society, Juab County Commission.

Wright, Bart. 2006. Videotaped interview and notes by Gretchen M. Baker.

Zeppelini, D., S. J. Taylor, and M. E. Slay. 2009. "Cave *Pygmarrhopalites* Vargovitsch, 2009 (Collembola, Symphypleona, Arrhopalitidae) in United States." *Zootaxa* 2204:1–18.

INDEX